with best wishes

ONE LAND
ONE BILLION MINDS

Insights on Branding in India

ONE LAND
ONE BILLION MINDS

Insights on Branding in India

Ramanujam Sridhar

Productivity and Quality Publishing Private Limited
Madras

One Land One Billion Minds
Insights on Branding in India

ISBN 81-85984-17-4

Published by:
Productivity and Quality Publishing Private Limited
38 Thanikachalam Road, T Nagar
Madras - 600 017, India.
Phone: (044) 24344519 Fax: (044)24342009
E-mail: service@kkbooks.com
website: http://www.productivityquality.co.in

Printed in India at:
Sudarsan Graphics
27 Neelakanta Mehta Street
T Nagar, Madras - 600 017.
Phone: (044) 24342947 Fax: (044) 24312281
E-mail: print@sudarsan.com
website: http://www.sudarsan.com

CONTENTS

11. PR

BUT FOR THEM...

The hint of a desire to someday write a book, was fanned into a flame the day I made my foray into journalism as a columnist, for the 'Third Umpire' column in the Hindu Business Line, the 'Ad speak' column in Deccan Herald and various other newspapers and magazines that have published my writings in India. Many of these articles have been reproduced here. This probably explains the repetition of a couple of brands and quotes. The other way to view this is that these brands and writers have made a profound impression on me! So too, has cricket and I do hope you, dear reader, will forgive the constant references to the game within the books' covers !

I would like to acknowledge Balki, India's creative genius, my friend of 18 years for writing the 'Foreword' in his usual ebullient and forthright style. I would like to thank Prof. Apte my teacher, Mr. N.R. Narayana Murthy, India's most respected business leader, Mr. A.G. Krishnamurthy, my one time boss and all time mentor, Mr. Sam Balsara my former colleague, and an acknowledged expert in advertising and media, Mr. Bhaskar Bhat my friend and one of the most astute marketing minds in India, Dr. Bob Hoekstra my client and India lover, Mr. Santosh Desai, my former colleague who is arguably India's best account planner. These distinguished gentlemen have honoured me by writing words of 'advance praise' for my book.

I remember reading an acknowledgement once, which went like this, "I would like to thank my children without whose co-operation the book might have been finished in half the time". I can't say the same about my family. My wife Saroj, and children Kaushik and Deepak, have always been very supportive of whatever I undertook to do. So have my parents, my brothers and sister, my nieces and my solitary nephew! Not to forget my colleagues particularly Patricia, Pavan and the entire creative, servicing and PR teams of brand-comm.

I would also like to place on record my thanks to Esther Yates who was my colleague when I entered advertising. She has edited the book with great care and spent many days refining it to bring it into the shape it is currently in.

And it would be remiss of me not to mention my clients to whom I owe everything – my experiences, my learning, my limited recognition and my loss of hair, if you will!

Ramanujam Sridhar

FOREWORD

Once upon a time, there was a man who read the first ad I ever wrote and said *'fantastic, fantastic'*. But his eyes had a faint *' I know you're going to rewrite this'* glint behind the thick spectacles. I went back and rewrote the ad. In an instant, Sridhar had taught me the art of communicating.

That was 17 years ago. Mudra was the most threatening agency around. Sridhar joined as the head of the newly opened Bangalore branch and I joined as his first copy trainee. I worked with him for 7 years. I was fortunate to start and grow in the most ideal environment for advertising creation. An environment created and nurtured by Sridhar.

Sridhar to me is a synonym for simplicity. I once asked him how he manages advertising people so well. He replied, self effacingly (the South Indian's way of being arrogant), *'When you like advertising and you like people, people in advertising would like you to manage them'*. There are no two sides to the man. The professional and the person are the same. The incredible natural strength this simplicity gives a human being is what has made Sridhar what he is today.

When he finally told me he was writing a book, I was happy for the advertising world. At last we could have a book written with a natural born-in-Madras-cricket-lover's sarcasm, with a complete disdain for advertising jargon. And I have to confess, Sridhar does write better than most copywriters.

But that's not why I believe this book is important.

The author is a man with a deep understanding of the need for India to have its own voices in the world of advertising. I mean 'voices' because India is not one voice. The saturated world of advertising is fortunate to have, in India, genres and forms that could breathe new life into advertising creation. Sridhar has always believed that Indian communication has to have faith in its voices not only for its own sake, to sell better to Indians, but for a larger cause. To create a new genre, a new language in advertising. To rewrite rules. To make the world aware of what over a billion people find creative. And think of as great communication.

I believe this book is important because its written by a man who has believed in the power of intuition & commonsense over all theory, all through his life. It's the obvious idea staring at you all the time which when picked up seems like a stroke of genius.

Read this book to remember what we should never forget.

Balki
R. Balakrishnan
National Creative Director
Lowe India

"Any damn fool can put on a deal,
but it takes genius, faith and
perseverance to create a brand"

- David Ogilvy

BANKING ON ADVERTISING

"Branding is a journey, not a destination"

- Andrew Welch

Banking on Advertising

10th December, 1973. It was another warm day in Madras, now renamed Chennai. December is not really hot in South India, even in Madras, strange though that may seem. I walked into the air-conditioned office of the Lloyds branch of National and Grindlay's Bank to begin a career in banking.

> 'My parents, (like most), wanted their children to be more successful than them'

I belonged to an ordinary Tamil family from South India. My parents, (like most), wanted their children to be more successful than them and sent me to Don Bosco Matriculation School and then to Loyola College where I completed a Masters degree in Economics and, more significantly, played for the college cricket team.

I was given the royal title of 'clerk' and was going to be paid a princely salary of Rs. 382 per month. Like the famous Wodehouse characters, Psmith and Mike Wrykyn, I started my banking career in the despatch department. My job description was simple: write the names of account holders on envelopes, which their bank statements would later be put into. I am sure it may seem bizarre today but people actually wrote with pens in those days! (I still do, but that is another story).

This banking career, which began in a despatch room in Madras, continued for another 6½ years. It took me to Manek Chowk market in Ahmedabad, Nariman Point in Bombay, Manipal in Karnataka and Kodambakkam in Madras, which anyone will tell you, is the home of the Tamil film industry. Sadly, rather thankfully, my association with the film industry has been more from the outside, as a contributor to the box office.

My life in banking was like any bank employee's. I spent a lot of time counting other people's money and writing out other people's fixed deposit receipts. The counting took on different dimensions in Gujarat as the cheques were written in Gujarati, numbers et al! I used to surreptitiously check the numbers with the bus ticket (which had the numerals printed in Gujarati), faithfully preserved by me for such noble uses! My salary reached an all time high of Rs. 1600 per month and my sense of boredom - now saturating every part of my intellect - reached the skies. I trained myself to count 4 columns deep in Syndicate Bank where unconfirmed reports suggested, that "Every Pai counts!" (Syndicate Bank is headquartered in Manipal in South Kanara, which at that time, had its fair share of people with the surname 'Pai').

As my boredom grew, so did my interest in a completely unrelated profession - advertising. I really don't know how or when the interest took root but it certainly multiplied over time. I read David Ogilvy (see chapter titled 'Open Letter to a Legend') and George Lois in the reference section of the USIS library in Madras. It was in George Lois' book that I found the Cutty Sark campaign with the most riveting headline I had ever seen. I was spellbound by the campaign, which carried the compelling headline "Don't give up the ship." I am still loyal to the ship, but that is another story. Advertising had me hooked. It filled my every waking moment. It gave even cricket, which was my passion, a run for its money in my life! I created a scrapbook of ads of existing brands of those days. These were not ads that were published. These were ads created by me for these brands. The creative spark within me was just waiting to leap into a flame. And it did.

> 'As my boredom grew, so did my interest in a completely unrelated profession - advertising'

I desperately wanted to be a copywriter and so I hastened to the only agency I knew of and thence to my first encounter with its corporate denizens, which I still recall with faint humour.

HTA as it used to be called then, had one of its copy supervisors check me out. The gentleman's demeanour all but proclaimed that he was either a direct descendant of J. Walter Thompson or God. I could take my pick! After giving my precious scrapbook a cursory once over he patronizingly suggested that I could start as a trainee. That meant no salary! Obviously! Here I was earning Rs1,600 and this dude asks me if I can write for free. We 'Tambrahms' (Tamil Brahmins) may know our onions but we are pretty conservative too. We don't take decisions involving money lightly. We have a discussion with the whole joint family, which for me, at that point in time numbered a mere 23. To cut a long story short, the final question from the family was, "Are you out of your mind?" So, that, as they say, was that. Well, almost.

I decided to stay on with the bank, for the time being at least. But then I decided that if the advertising industry wouldn't hire me as a trainee I would see to it that it would hire me as a manager. I decided to do my MBA and joined the Indian Institute of Management in Bangalore which, in those years was the best city in the country. It was only later that IIM Bangalore became the best management institute in the country. (I am sure alumni of IIM Ahmedabad just love me for this!)

The two years at IIMB transformed me as an individual and as a professional. While I theoretically specialized in marketing and finance, I spent every spare moment reading books on advertising and was sure that I would work only in that profession. I devoured Bill Bernbach. Till today, I quote him and a few other giants of the advertising industry. My first job in advertising materialized in 1983 when I joined R. K. Swamy Advertising Associates in Bangalore. Ironically, I was supposed to handle the computer account of BPL. Obviously someone thought I knew something about computers, which I didn't. Fortunately, it was never found out that I was computer illiterate - as ultimately we did not get the business - but I did get to handle the BPL consumer electronics business and that meant I was in business! I was a hands-on Sr. Account Executive. I wish I could say the rest is history but that would be an advertising claim, or 'mere puffery'.

In 1998, on the 18th of December to be precise, things changed, for the better. I launched brand-comm. The reason for this was quite simple: I realized that there is far more to life than a 30-second TV commercial. I got hooked onto 'total branding'. I now understood the 'power of insight' in its totality and decided to offer the subject at various management institutes. I started to understand, appreciate and advocate public relations too, to my clients. Today, some of the biggest brands in India are our clients in brand consulting, advertising and public relations.

Over these years, everyday I have been reminded of what Bob Dylan said.

> *"If you get up in the morning*
> *and go to sleep at night*
> *and in between do what you like*
> *consider yourself a successful man"*

In that respect, I have been successful. What I have attempted to do on these pages is to share my observations, insights and learning in the last 22 years, about consumers, advertising, communication, brands and life. And, I am still learning.

'I got hooked onto 'total branding'.
I now understood the
'power of insight' in its totality'

CONSUMERS FIRST

"I am irresistible, I say,

as I put on my designer fragrance.

I am a merchant banker,

I say, as I climb out of my BMW.

I am a juvenile lout, I say,

as I down a glass of extra strong lager.

I am handsome, I say,

as I don my Levi's jeans"

- *John Kay*, *Economist*

CHAPTER

One Land, a Billion Minds

"Come to India. A billion people can't be wrong" was the cheeky line on my son's T-shirt. **A billion people!** Mind boggling to even think of, especially to people in the West who often live in areas where it is common not to see anyone on the road for several miles at a stretch. It is easy to refer to this colossal country that is India in clichés. We have seen, heard and read enough of those; but cliché or not, the Indian market represents a tremendous opportunity not just

'Yet many foreign and Indian brands have lost their way in their quest for the "vast Indian middle class"'

to Indian marketers but to the world at large. Yet many foreign and Indian brands have lost their way in their quest for the 'vast Indian middle class'. Someone once asked Sir Hugh Rigby, Sergeant Surgeon to King George V, what went into the making of a great surgeon. His response was direct and to the point. *"There isn't much to choose between surgeons in manual dexterity.* What distinguishes the great surgeon is that he **knows more."**

The marketing and advertising fraternities need to ask an honest, if somewhat embarrassing question of themselves. How much do we know about the Indian consumer? And how are we leveraging the knowledge we possess? Is it to commercial advantage? What new effort is being made

by commercial organisations
including market research
companies and educational
institutions such as the
IIMs, to further the existing
(perhaps, limited) body of
knowledge? I hope and
sincerely trust that there
is a lot of genuine
enterprise on this
front and I, true to
my nature, am
ignorant of this.

Below, is a modest
collection of obser-
vations of the Indian
consumer that re-
present my exposure
and my understanding
of this 'entity'. While not being the last word on the subject,
I submit that these remarks are born out of real and practical
experience and thus perhaps worthy of some consideration.

We all know that people buy into new concepts slowly and
reluctantly, sometimes, never. Let me give you two illustrations of
this behaviour within the Indian context. Dalmia Cements, the
second example, is my client and thus my comments on this client
carry more weight and greater clarity.

Breakfast Fit for a King?

What do Indians have for breakfast? If you are a traditional,
conservative and die-hard South Indian like me, you would say
"Idli Vada" with a cup of hot "Kaapi" (coffee). (Often this lands
me in a soup as I insist on ordering "idli" wherever I am in India,
and have often had the mortification of being served 'idlis' that

rival hard white cricket balls used in one-day internationals). People in India who have a western orientation (which is a fraternity that is growing by leaps and bounds) may ask for "Omelette on Toast". Folks from the Western parts of India, for instance Maharashtra, might say "Vada Paav" - the 'Paav' being the Indian or native version of bread. The North Indians might order "Alu Paratha". And a few might even ask for breakfast cereals.

Enter Kellogg's, a hugely successful global brand launched in the mid-nineties in India with great fanfare and a major marketing and promotional bonanza. Breakfast cereals, they blazoned, were healthier, more nourishing, fat-free and significantly, this was the way the world 'breakfasted'.

The initial response to the Kellogg's blast was lukewarm, at best. Middle-class India did not take to it as a duck does to water. Breakfast cereal was a concept way ahead of its time, at that time, in India, and selling a new concept is far from simple and easy.

It requires time, effort and investment, as Kellogg's discovered. India would not be just another pin stuck on its global marketing map. To further its marketing woes, Mohun's cornflakes, an Indian brand, which had been around for some time, increased its sales and market share.

What happened? People bought the concept of breakfast cereals from Kellogg's - after a few years - but went out and bought the actual bag of cheaper cereal from the Indian company. Sometimes, we underestimate the power of customs and belief systems. People don't change. Nor, do traditions, habits and customs die, easily.

The strategy that accomplishes this paradigm shift has to be razor-sharp, skilfully thought through and with a thorough understanding of the target audience's preferences.

From Numbers to Applications

Cement is another interesting category. A recent visitor from Singapore was quite amazed at the magnitude of advertising for cement in this country, which was in startling contrast to his own, where cement was treated fundamentally, as a commodity. Cement is essentially a 'low involvement' product. To India and Indians 'building a house' is building a roof over their heads and therefore a 'high involvement' activity. It is the ambition of every Indian to build a house for himself and his family in his own lifetime. But he delegates many portions of the decision-making to the contractor or the mason. In the case of more affluent individuals, the choice is given to the architect who designs the house. In other words, the average house owner, despite his deep emotional involvement in the building of his house, might not even know the brand of cement that is being used. I keep stressing on 'him' which even if not politically correct, is perhaps correct in a marketing sense, as our research

Creative: brand-comm

suggests the importance of males in decision-making in this category.

Enter Dalmia Cements, a highly successful niche player in Tamil Nadu and Kerala, two of the largest southern states in India. This company acted on a tremendous strategic insight. They asked themselves, why not segment the market based on application? Why not create a separate brand for the roof and another one for the foundation? These were traditionally strong application areas in the house. The market, which always bought cement according to numbers (33 grade, 43 grade and 53 grade), was not ready for this unique marketing strategy. Additionally, cement buyers displayed a greater propensity to accept a separate brand of cement for the roof of the house. We also found that advertising was not necessarily the best solution. Dissemination of information through dealer meets, mason meets and product literature was found to be far more effective. Oh yes, we keep learning, all the time and very often to our great cost!

The Gift of Time

Certain concepts have left their indelible marks over time. Gifting for instance, a concept as old as the hills has taken on the dimensions of another industry. Ranging from chocolates, to biscuits to clothes to furniture to jewellery, people have been presenting gifts and will continue to engage in this immensely satisfying activity. Then along came Titan, India's pre-eminent watch brand. Titan tossed out a challenge to the gift buyer: "Hey, why don't you gift watches?" The wave caught on and slowly but surely, the market lapped up the concept, for birthdays, weddings, anniversaries. Today, gifting accounts for over 50% of Titan's sales and since then people have moved up to 'Anytime Gifting'. There is more of Titan in this book in a later chapter. Right now the point I wish to establish is that a

concept when clearly articulated, cleverly communicated and properly executed can and will deliver in India. But be willing to wait and, more importantly, to persevere.

The Influence of the Family

Another feature of Indian life is the influence of the family in decision-making.

"The consumer is not a moron. She is your wife" said David Ogilvy. In India, savvy marketers are realizing, that beyond the wife, there is the involvement of the family as well, in the purchase of goods and services. Business Today, a prominent business magazine has this to say, "For many a brand, the statement it makes on behalf of its user must first pass the test of the other members of the family". I realized the increasing influence of the family in my own buying behaviour a few years ago. We were in the market for a second car. This car was for my working wife who had grown tired of her Maruti Zen. We were considering four cars: the Santro, the Matiz, the Indica and the Fiat Uno. Traditional wisdom would suggest that buying a car in a two-income family would be a decision involving husband and wife – very logical given the fact that all assets are in the wife's name and all loans in the husband's name. A lifetime of delegation (or is it abdication?) made me sit on the fence. My wife was undecided on the brand (if I had been a courageous male, I might have said

"dithering") and my second son who was all of 11 years of age then, got into the act. He read Auto India, watched the BBC show and everything else kids of his age saw, heard, and surfed ... and said, "Let's buy the Santro".

Now the Santro is a fine car, but its looks hardly make it the Preity Zinta of cars! Not even if she was its current endorser at that time. Our objections were generally swept under the floor mats - eleven-year olds can get their way! A brand new Santro

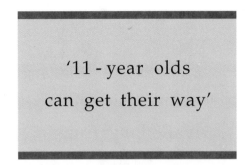

'11 - year olds can get their way'

bought by car finance made its way home soon after that. So now, whenever I see another Santro pass me on the road, I quickly take a look to see if there is an eleven-year old in the back seat giving (buying) instructions!

India is perhaps different from the West in a few other ways, too. It is a young country (59% of the Indian population is below the age of 24) and whilst the youth of the world, thanks to the influence of the Net, Cable TV and music, might have similar tastes in television serials, films and the current noise that passes for music, it is also necessary to record differences that that are evident. I have seen seventeen-year old teenagers in India shop for a pair of jeans accompanied by their mother! They are also largely influenced by her preferences. And, she actually pays for it! I am sure a seventeen-year old Western youth would not be caught dead with his mother in the jeans' store. It is important for marketers to realize the differences that India presents from the rest of the world.

India Watches Cricket and Movies

India is a diverse country – ah! a woefully inadequate description! The languages are different, the customs are different, the eating habits are different, the castes are different and even the sub-sects are different. So what holds India together, then? A few common interests, perhaps? At the top of the heap is Cricket, the game that Bernard Shaw described so inaccurately saying, "Cricket is a game played by 22 fools and followed by

> 'Cricket in this country, is only rivalled by films'

22,000 fools". I daresay he would not have ventured to make that statement in India. Indians are prepared to queue for hours to enter a stadium and then subject themselves to sitting together, packed like a can of sardines to watch the game. They paint their faces and drape themselves with the national flag, the tricolor and shout themselves hoarse. They watch the 'highlights' the following day, read all the media reports, discuss the game at work and preen themselves on being 'masters of the game'. When Sachin Tendulkar bats like a man possessed and leads India to victory, the whole of India celebrates. Cricket in this country, is only rivalled by films. Amitabh Bachchan is God. If he tells India to buy a Parker, you can bet your last rupee that it will. Celebrities from cricket and films are used in India for just about everything. A question pops up here: Are the celebrities being overused and abused? Another section of the book addresses this issue.

Value for Money

The average middle-class Indian is a value shopper discovering the factory outlet for almost any category – clothes, shoes, watches even durables – patronizing brands that provide value.

Bajaj has been one of the most successful two-wheeler brands, for several years now, though recently TVS and other two-wheeler brands are giving it a run for its money. Hero Honda in fact, has actually overtaken it.

Two of the most successful launches in the Indian context have been Sonata watches from Titan and Peter England branded apparel from Madura Garments. Both these brands (which you will read more about, later in the book) offered 'acceptable quality at affordable prices'.

Brands have Value

Indians in general and youth in particular know the value of brand names. Several years ago, I was sitting in a group discussion and there was this pretty young

thing, who must have been all of 17 years of age who put it bluntly: "When I wear Levis (jeans) I tuck my shirt in as I want the world to know that I am wearing Levis. When I wear Newport, I wear my shirt out as I don't want Rs.399 breathing down my hip."

Well that's certainly great news for strong brands, isn't it? There is an element of aspiration about certain brands (read foreign), which marketers can capitalize on. Indian brands - in my view at least - are just getting there.

You are what you know

And yet, we are merely scratching the surface. It's worth noting that success will come to those who truly get to know the Indian consumer. Chief Executives of big FMCG companies are getting further away from their corporate offices and closer to their consumers. Nariman Point is realizing the value of understanding the cross - cultural difference of consumers from Mylapore, Muzzafarpur and Mandya. A word of caution here: it's not only the Chief Executives, but, everyone in marketing and communication, who must realize that the knowledge of the consumer leads to creation of value and subsequent economic power. Let us invest in the

> "Indians in general and youth in particular know the value of brand names"

knowledge of the consumer, understand the drives, aspirations and the metamorphosis that the consumer is going through. Knowledge will be the key to success in the market place. The well-known fable says it well - the speed of the hare and the perseverance of the tortoise, win the race. Add to that potent combination, a keen desire to know, and you have what India needs most in the 21st century. And more than anything else, she needs a sense of urgency to do it *NOW*. For every one of our billion people, especially our marketers, the mantra might well be summed up in Tom Peter's statement:

"Y-O-U CAN MAKE A DIFFERENCE!
TAKE CHARGE OF YOUR LIFE!
BE DISTINCT...OR EXTINCT!
IT'S A NEW MILLENNIUM:
IF NOT NOW...W-H-E-N?"

CHAPTER

Do You Know Your Customer?

"Tell me something I don't already know." These words are heard often enough in the hallowed portals of clients as they sit in for brand reviews and presentations on market research. There is an ever-increasing need for the professionals in brand management to find new and undiscovered characteristics of consumers and their behaviour patterns. There is an even greater need for people who are in the

> 'The hard reality however is that key insights which build exceptionally effective communication are relatively hard to come by'

business of creating ads and TV commercials to acquire key insights into consumers' behaviour patterns.

All of us are different. We are different consumers using different products and different services and we respond better to different stimuli and different messages, which we are comfortable with. The savvy communicators are those who recognize this characteristic and then create advertising to strike a chord with the consumer who then sees the ad, looks up and says, *"Hey, that's me"*.

These vectors of learning often determine the direction of the advertising plan. The hard reality however, is that key insights which build exceptionally effective communication are relatively hard to come by.

We Live in a "Me - Too" World

A 'key insight' is an extremely valuable input for planners and creative folk and it's something they aggressively pursue. The key insight can be either from the product, the manufacturer, the consumer or the media, all of which comprise the complete manufacturing - sales - buying structure.

In short, this is where we have a 'key insight' into the consumer and her behaviour, which enables us to beat the clutter, stand out from the crowd, get noticed and most importantly, push the consumer into doing what we want her to do - buy our products and services.

Let me illustrate this with a few examples.

Oh Brother!

There is divided opinion on the advantage of being born as a younger brother or sister. If the older one is hardworking, sincere, organized, does his homework, combs his hair and is his teacher's pet, then you have the misfortune (!) of being his younger brother – and boy, are you in trouble! The trouble is compounded if you go to the same school. Comparisons flow thick and fast, and usually unfavourably. It's not only your parents who make the comparisons; teachers can be worse and generally are. I was one such 'younger brother' who not only got handed down books and clothes, but also odious comparisons as well. Shades of the 'Juicy Fruit' chewing gum commercial which I was involved in producing.

There is divided opinion on the advantage of being born as a younger brother or sister'

The story goes like this. Older kids are playing cricket and they shoo away the younger one who sits on the sidelines. No sooner does he open his 'Juicy Fruit' gum packet, he suddenly becomes the centre of attention, a part of the game and the subsequent hero of the game. The simple basic communication struck a chord in kids' minds. Any kid can empathize with being kept out of a game being played by older people. All of us have experienced this. Just try breaking into your elder brother's gang!

The Apple of Your Eyes

Just ask any parent about his kids and if they think there is anything wrong with them. You won't get too many surprises. *"He watches too much TV." "She keeps playing on the computer"* and there may be a slight variant if the parent had been active with games and sports in his own youth. *"I wish he'd go out and play."* Post-independence India has spawned a generation who surf channels faster than Shoaib Akhtar bowls and who have more screens open on their computer terminals than the strokes Sachin has for each delivery he faces. Given this laidback, lethargic and indoorsy nature of the audience, LG Golden Eye TV shows an anguished mother searching frantically for her bespectacled son who is peacefully watching a cricket match in a dealer outlet. The reason? He is not allowed to watch TV at home. The mother fears for her son's eyesight. And the brand comes with a solution, a technology that means 'no strain' on the eyes. Wouldn't most parents relate to and empathize with the characters and storyline? Wouldn't they end up buying the brand if and when they had a chance? I suspect they would. Although one hopes that it is not a mere advertising claim and the product actually delivers on what it promises to achieve.

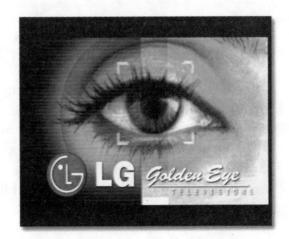

> 'The onus is on the advertising agency to discover new preferences of the consumer and more value-factors'

When Hero Honda first launched a 100cc motorcycle, which delivered 80 kms to the litre, it left the competition far behind. The superior product performance made the advertising agency's task easy. The user had to fill it, shut it and then, everyone could forget the competition. A Gillette Mach III razor with its superior technology does not need exceptional creative, but a mere statement of the product's superior attributes.

The world is full of 'me-too' products similar in performance and attributes to their competition and without a single superior or distinctive attribute. So, the onus is on the advertising agency to discover new preferences of the consumer and more value-factors in the context of the product that is being advertised and its benefits to the consumer. Altogether, they enable a better understanding of the consumer's behaviour, which in turn helps in the creation of advertising that strikes a chord in the consumer's mind and compels her to behave just the way we would like her to.

Does she or Doesn't she Care about Pimples?

Pimples are a part of growing up. And if you were to ask any sixteen year old, it is the most excruciating part of growing up. I guess sixteen year olds can handle bombs, revolutions, and earthquakes, at times even their parents, but not pimples. **Lifebuoy Gold** with its bunch of teenagers and the catchphrase **"I don't care"** captures the insecurities of a normally confident (or is it arrogant) generation and immediately strikes a chord with the target audience. This is an excellent example of a key insight into the consumer mindset and the application of that knowledge to create striking advertising.

All around us are little nuggets of information, that are indicators of what people are...they are the pointers that can give us creative direction.

'How many of us can program the VCR to record the England - Brazil match which will be played while you are at work?'

'How many of us love to cook but hate to clean?'

'How many of us find anything in the refrigerator to eat even if it is 350 litres?'

'How many of us want to marry a truly dark girl?'

And the list goes on.

So my advice to agencies is that if you are stuck for an idea with a 'me - too' product and can't find anything worthwhile to say, just look elsewhere. Look at the consumer. And you will find what you need to make her tick.

Tough Days – Pleasant Evenings

Another problem which we normally face, is that we let our own experiences and prejudices colour our judgement. People in Bangalore have their own experiences and views about people's drinking habits – exposed as they are to pubs with their hip décor, pulsating music and under - aged kids that swarm to them. This notion was washed down the drain when we discovered, while attempting to launch a strong beer in Mumbai, that the strong beer drinker was a blue - collar worker, whose day and job was monotonous, boring and physically taxing. He commuted three hours to and fro from work. He stayed in a small apartment with his wife, children and parents and could not drink at home. He would hit the Irani restaurant near the train station, drink 2 bottles of strong beer every evening and head home to his family for dinner. The beer was the high point of his otherwise predictable day, enabling him to handle the next boring day. Clearly this was not a social drinker. He didn't care for darts or wish to have wafer - thin models clinging to his arms. In fact, he hardly considered himself to be a macho man.

"Clearly this was not a social drinker"

We rejected the traditional advertising archetypes since we had enough data points on the target audience to prove the opposite. We came up with a concept which was less glamorous but exceedingly effective, which said, **"There's always the evening to look forward to"**. Intensive research, a clear understanding of the consumer, quality time with the prospect, observations of people who consume our brand or shop for it are invaluable windows for providing key insights into consumer behaviour.

Does the Average Family Exist?

The popular belief that the average American family is husband, wife, 2.4 kids and a dog makes interesting reading. GE trashed this theory in its commercial declaring that each family was different and yet each had several things in common, which all families could relate to.

"Kids never come home from college empty handed"
(they come with loads of dirty clothes).
"Those who bring home the bacon shouldn't have to eat it cold".

Significantly, all of these observations are extremely relevant in the context of the appliances that GE makes and sells in large numbers. What great insights do we have about the Indian consumer and her family? I was greatly impressed to hear that creative people at Leo Burnett India spend time with housewives to understand how they use detergents, their experiences and expectations from it – all of which must help in planning their future communication. Let's think, sleep and dream the brands that we create advertising for.

> 'Each family was different and yet each had several things in common, which all families could relate to'

Attitude says it all

Youth is most often bewildering and almost always challenging to communicate with. Just ask any parent! A few years ago, when we sat in on a couple of focus groups, it seemed pretty clear that today's eighteen year old wants to belong to the group. That's crucial. He wants to be an informal leader. Leadership is not to be flaunted or sought after, but to be achieved. He wouldn't be part of the herd - the differentiator being attitude here, which is youth's principal armoury to take on the world. The Weekender commercials with the tag line 'Wear your Attitude' struck a chord with the target audience and made a huge difference to the brand's ranking and market value.

And yet, this was nothing compared to the Lowe Lintas Worldwide's commercial for 'The Independent'. The key insight being that youth hates to be told what 'to do' and even more what 'not to do'. The commercial for 'The Independent' hits the nail on the head and looks at the world from the target audience's eyes: A world full of adults who simply 'don't' understand them. The entire script is an example of a wonderful understanding of youth and the way a largely non - understanding world talks to them, used to great effect to sell 'The Independent'.

Newspaper of the Year

THE INDEPENDENT

"Don't talk. Don't jog. Don't walk. Don't walk in the night. Don't walk on the right. Don't drink. Don't think.

Don't smoke. Don't do drugs. Don't envy. Don't eat junk.

Don't be fat. Don't be thin. Don't chew. Don't spit.

Don't swim. Don't breathe. Don't cry. Don't bleed. Don't kill.

Don't experiment. Don't live. Don't exist. Don't do anything.

Don't fry your food. Don't fry your brain.

Don't sit close to the tele. Don't walk on the grass.

Don't put your elbows on the table. Don't put your feet on the seats. Don't roam with scissors and don't play with fire. Don't rebel. Don't smack. Don't masturbate.

Don't be childish. Don't be old. Don't be ordinary.

Don't be different. Don't stand out. Don't drop out.

Don't buy. Don't read. THE INDEPENDENT.

Do you or don't you know your customer?

CHAPTER 3

Can You Read My Lips?

There is this story (actually it is a real-life anecdote) that I heard in a management seminar. A gentleman was trading in his old car for a new one. (Don't we live in a world of trade-ins? I know of people who would cheerfully trade-in their boss and children given half a chance!) Be that as it may, as this gentleman drove out proudly, in his new car, to his delight when he switched on the radio in his new traded-in car, the order of radio stations was identical to the one in his old car. The first was news, the second the weather, the third rock, the fourth country and so on. To say that you could have knocked him down with a feather would be an understatement. In hindsight, it was all very simple. Someone had merely observed the customer's preferences and acted upon it. The result was sheer magic for the customer. There are two learnings that can be acquired from this incident. One, that it's not rocket science to know what your

consumer needs. You merely have to be observant. The second being, that it is not merely the top man in the service provider's organisation who must be passionate about customer service but everyone who has an opportunity to serve a customer. And this leads me to an important question: Who in your organisation knows your customer?

I remember Toyota Qualis running an ad campaign with the line "We know Mrs. Malini Sharma likes a dash of lemon juice in her Russian salad." While the ad is interesting, I am more impressed and intrigued by the business philosophy behind this. Many organizations could benefit from such a philosophy and a similar passion for customers.

I Am an Individual. Do You recognize Me?

Each one of us is an individual and would like to be treated as one. Each one of us wears multiple hats as well and here I am going to speak as a customer who is in the market for goods and services. I bank with Corporation Bank, which is arguably the best nationalized bank, at least in my opinion and experience. I believe I am a valued customer of the bank not because they have given me the title but because I am treated like one. I am always greeted with a smile and often collect my cash even before my cheque comes to the cash counter. I have another outstanding example of recognition from the unlikeliest of sources. The temple near my house! The purohit knows my name, my star and my gothram! So we don't go through this process every time he performs an archana for me. I can probably hear you saying, "Big deal!" But in reality, knowing your customer, her preferences and gearing yourself to serve her is, really, a big deal. It's what Tom Peters would call "the blinding flash of the obvious". Just review your customer database, your records and evaluate your relationship with customers. It's easy for people who run small businesses to take the easy way out and say that it is only for big businesses. It is not. It is for anyone who has customers.

What's in a Name? Everything, if it's Yours

All of us may not love our own names. Remember we didn't have a say in its choice. And yet, it is a standard principle in direct response that personalising the communication improves the hit rate. A letter addressed 'Dear Mr. Ramesh' is certainly better than 'Dear cardholder'. Yes, personalizing has its advantages and today, we have the technology to individualise and digitally print, one copy at a time. (But that's another story). I have spoken at seminars and panel discussions, written about it and will continue to protest till I receive a remedy. Let me quickly cut to the chase.

I belong to the First Citizen's Club (FCC) of 'Shoppers Stop', which, according to them is a privileged set of customers. These customers are given bonus points when they shop, privileges like extended hours shopping at crowded times like Diwali and various other offers. These offers are normally communicated by letters, which are addressed by name. These pieces of communication have saved me on numerous occasions when they have reminded me of my wedding anniversary, (after all, an anniversary is a date that one spouse never seems to remember and the other never seems to forget!). And yet, whilst I have probably got sixty such mailers from this retail chain, the sad reality is that every single one has been addressed to 'Sridhar Raitanujam'. I know that Ramanujam is not the easiest of names to spell or pronounce. But the

July, 1999

Mr. Sridhar Raitanujam
653, Akshaya,
6th C Main 3rd Phase,
J P Nagar,
Bangalore - 560078

Dear Mr. Raitanujam,

As I write this letter, I'm pleased to inform you been completed and you will find the minor the past.

During the last 3 month change-over to our new of the trouble caused to you. Many of you may being available.

We are deeply indebted to you for your patien we would not have been able to upgrade so quic

Now, the store is ready to receive you as before And, what's more, the benefits just seem to mul satisfy your choice.

> 'Success is in the details. And getting your customer's name right is an important detail'

fact of the matter is that Ramanujam is my name and like most individuals, I feel strongly about it being spelt correctly. And this was reflected in my rather animated response to their CEO asking for 3 suggestions to improve their service and I was prompted to write in as follows:

Suggestion No. 1, spell my name right, Suggestion No. 2, spell my name right, Suggestion No. 3, spell my name right!

Needless to say, I got no response from the retail chain. I do not wish to labour the point, but this is not about a small organisation. We are talking about a large, successful retail chain, which is known for its marketing skills. This leads me to believe that companies know what is to be done to keep their customer happy. It is just that they don't seem to be doing what they know they should be doing. Success is in the details. And getting your customer's name right is an important detail.

Consolidation Vs Specialization

Today, many of us are customers for a range of products and services and yet, it is the smart companies that can see the interlinkages between them and us and the consequent high net worth of customers. Let me give you an example. I am a borrower with HDFC, the housing finance company and the letters EMI are etched in my brain! I trade in shares through Investsmart, a former group company of theirs.

I have a savings account with HDFC bank and a loan against shares account with the same bank. (Remember the momentum stocks that were supposed to make us rich?) My organisation has a current account with HDFC bank too. And yet, I am not sure that the HDFC group has seen my value.

I have chosen to deal with their group companies on my own accord and not because they have seen my collective value. Today, the technology is available for companies to gather data on their customers and yet HDFC bank still keeps calling me and asks me to open an account with their bank! And yet, HDFC as we all know, is an enormously successful organisation with an enlightened management team. I wonder about smaller companies. I am sure that many of you who own credit cards must be receiving calls from the same credit card company offering you more cards! Wouldn't our life be easier without direct selling agents!

Consumers are going to become more demanding, if they are not so already, and high net-worth individuals are going to be increasingly hard to come by. To say that we live in challenging times is obviously a cliché. Customers will expect more and want to pay less. The starting point and the ending point for business is the customer. Let's start by knowing more about our customer. The customer is talking. Let's listen to her.

"Don't expect the work to speak for itself.
Even the most ingenious solutions must be sold."

- *Suzanne Young*

CHAPTER

The Customer is King. Sez Who?

"I am a cricket lover." That's a convenient euphemism or a gross understatement. It's a bit like calling the Taj Mahal a pretty nifty tomb as one of P.G. Wodehouse's characters did. For I live, sleep, think and dream cricket. In between live telecasts, highlights, cricket golds, Hitz, cricket classics, newspaper reports, blogs, animated conservations, I do the other things that normal human beings do – work, spend time with family, yoga – if there is any time left. I do plan my life around cricket, but despite my best-laid plans, I cannot be in front of a TV set on some match days. And this happened a few months ago in Hyderabad, on the day of a NatWest match between Australia and England. Follow the scenario described below.

I check into a hotel, anxiously flip channels to see if ESPN is on. It is. I attend the scheduled meeting with my client, with my mind on the ensuing match. I return to the room in the evening only to find ESPN not on. I lose my cool (you can almost hear my family say "so what's new?"). The manager of the hotel is very polite but firm saying that he is prohibited from showing the channel lest Hathway Cable take him to court. And I silently fume because I do understand something (though not a great deal) about media and I do know that media planners sell ESPN or Star Sports in the country based on the estimated number of viewers of cable and satellite TV in the country. Rarely, if ever, are all programmes of these two great channels shown in every cable and

> 'How are TRPs
> worked out?
> Do they have any
> relevance in this
> sort of set-up?'

satellite home in the country; though it is every one of these homes that form the selling-price basis for media planners. Thanks to this on-going tussle between TV channels and cable operators, I hate going to Delhi and Mumbai because I am certain that I will miss an important moment in my life like Glenn McGrath's 500th wicket.

It may seem slightly ludicrous (even) to someone who does not follow the game. But my question is pretty basic. As a consumer, am I not eligible to ask for the telecast of cricket? And as media buying companies is it not the bounden duty of Mind Share and Mediaedge:cia to ensure that their client's commercials are telecast everywhere and not only in the monitoring agency's TV set? How are TRPs worked out? Do they have any relevance in this sort of set-up? The scenario keeps happening all the time – and each time under a different pretext. Tamil channels get blocked out in Karnataka whenever there is a problem with its neighbouring state, which seems to be all too frequent. Although some of these, I do agree are non-controllable, I sometimes feel much inclined to ask God to permit me to commit homicide just once. And the victim would be...you guessed it - my cable operator.

And the travails continue

But let's get back to me in my hotel room in Hyderabad. I am defeated but not yet out for the count. After all, I have my mobile phones: Two of them! I go to Reliance to check out the cricket score. Not surprisingly RWorld is not ready. I go to Airtel, which incidentally is a pretty good mobile service provider notwithstanding its propensity to share my mobile number with every credit card, hotel, bank and car salesman in the country. But I am unable to access it. Now, I am on the verge of panic. I SMS my brother in England who is in the stands at Leeds who messages me every wicket fall. But I go to the Assistance Operator who as my luck would have it, is a trainee. "Roaming subscribers don't have access to 646" says he. I am foxed. I must be the largest single user of 646 in this country and I am usually on 'Roaming' and I have used this facility, not once, but several times. I ask to speak to the supervisor. I crib to her. She apologizes for her colleague's ignorance. She promises to sort it out and actually does. Lo and behold, I get connected. But what follows is simply mind-blowing. Everybody wants me to enlist for KBC. That's 'Kaun Banega Crorepati'. But I am not tempted. I am focused; single-minded, if you will. I will not be distracted. I wait patiently. Cricket is 14th in the queue. Do I believe it?! I can and am still there.

Finally the voice says, "For live coverage of cricket, say cricket". And I repeat the magic word anxious to know the score and anxious to be in touch. And the Anglo-Saxon voice says, "Sorry I didn't get that". I repeat the word 'cricket' in every possible accent – Tamilian, Malayali, Hyderabadi, even with an Aussie accent, all of which are met with the same lyrical, "Sorry I didn't get that." What must a cricket lover do then? Well he goes to a TV dealership under the pretext of buying a plasma TV and sees Hussey's histrionics in the dying minutes of the game. At least someone is serving his prospective customer, even if buying a 3rd TV set, in a different city, seems a bit far-fetched, even for me.

> 'Let me ask you a simple question. Aren't you more demanding than you were five years ago?'

You could view these as the rantings and ravings of a rabid cricket fan or the anguish of a distraught customer missing a 'value added service' that the brand prides itself on. However years ago, Mike Clasper, President, Procter and Gamble made this prediction: "I would label the consumer of 2025 in three ways: more demanding, wiser and more worried." Let me ask you a simple question. Aren't you more demanding than you were five years ago? I for one most certainly am (if you ask my family I am also more of a pain). But my question is simple – am I not entitled to watch the TV channels that include me as their target audience when they sell their channels to their customers? And just because the cable operator plays truant, should I miss out on what I am due? Should I not get the value added services that are the reason for my patronizing a particular mobile service provider?

And on to the Airtel brand

Today a mobile phone is a product for just about everybody. After all Dhirubhai Ambani had the philosophy 'Roti, Kapada aur Mobile' in his quest for reach and acceptance. This is a far cry from those early days of mobile phones in India. I think the year was 1995 and I remember AT&T charging Rs.16.80 per minute. And people used to complain about being charged for incoming calls! Mobile services have come a long way since, permeating every socio-economic class in the country. Today, a mobile instrument may be something to flaunt, but the image associations with the service provider that you use do not register immediately. And yet, Airtel is a

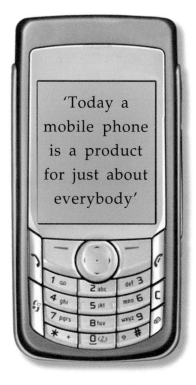

'Today a mobile phone is a product for just about everybody'

dominant brand that has not only acquired customers but other competitors, aggressively. It is growing significantly and has a pretty good technology back-up for service. The supervisor usually checks after your interaction with the service representative to enquire if the transaction was satisfactory. I am appalled though, at the setting for the 2 new Airtel commercials. One set in a hairdresser's shop and the other in the 'paan' shop. The message being with the Rs. 200 tariff, just about anyone can own an Airtel connection. I say, I am appalled because of this: Airtel wants numbers, fine. But in its quest for new subscribers, is it putting off the loyalists who have stayed with the brand for years. Besides, why is there a need to strongly profile the user? I have no problems with 'chai wallahs' and assistants in 'paan' shops. Theoretically, anyone can be your customer. But there are enough and plenty of mass brands that have got it right. Airtel, has got many things right over the years, but not their two most recent commercials.

At the End of the Day

The learning for all marketers and service providers is simple. If you promise something to the consumer, deliver it. None of it is rocket science. Execution is key and God is in the details.

Jan Carlzon speaks of five Moments of Truth in the airlines industry.

- Making a reservation
- Getting tickets
- Boarding
- Flying
- Retrieving Baggage

It is important that each one of us identifies the 'Moment of Truth' in our respective industries.

Customers will be fickle, demanding and unreasonable like me. In fact today's consumer's mission statement is the (at times), annoying word, 'more'. We cannot wish it away. Because the difficult customer is also of 'high net worth', if my mobile bills are any indication. But I do know that as a customer, when I do get outstanding service, I talk about it and on occasion write about it. As Regis McKenna says, "Customer loyalty begins with an experience". I am ready to be loyal. But I want experiences that satisfy, time after time. And the time for companies to get their service act together is now. Or it just may be never.

CHAPTER

Every Little Bit Counts...

Have you taken a flight out of Bangalore airport of late? If you have, you would understand what I have experienced and maybe even empathise with me. Every recent trip of mine to the airport in the last three months has been in pouring rain. And you know as well as I do that every city in India has had a problem with either too little or too much rain. Bangalore has had a problem of plenty. And the associated problems are plentiful too. Huge jams, bumper-to-bumper traffic, vehicles which start and stop on Airport Road for hours on end, as they crawl

> 'The airport authorities ensure that people are constantly reminded that air travel is a privilege that you must earn'

past the flyover which is being built for as far back as I can remember. This flyover, I am tempted to believe, has been awarded the status of a heritage building – work on it is never ending and continues at a lengthy pace; with much trepidation and painstaking care. My ride, which in happier days and climes would have taken thirty five minutes, now takes a mere ninety. I enter the airport – harassed, wet and ready to explode. I snap at my driver and jump out of the car, only to be met by a man in red who asks me if I am travelling by Kingfisher Airlines. I am surprised but recover my poise sufficiently, to say "Yes". He promptly picks up my bags and escorts me to the check-in counter and checks me in. He carries my bags to the security. I am floored. I still have to continue to experience the largesse of Bangalore's airport that easily gives you the impression of being at Madras Central station or Hubli bus station, so chaotic is it. The airport authorities ensure that people are constantly reminded that air travel is a privilege that you must earn. The queue is a mile long and passengers file slowly past the solitary X-ray machine at each terminal. So the little snatch of 'customer delight' that one had with one's baggage thanks to Kingfisher Airlines quickly becomes a distant memory. After all, this is India and you know that we are **"like that only"**!

Up, Up and Away

Amidst pelting rain and smiling stewardesses, I board the flight. Service, as any self-styled expert will tell you, is all about meeting customer expectations. Not having paid the earth for my ticket, and having experienced the service of other 'no-frills' airlines in the recent past, I found that my expectations, albeit limited, were exceeded.

The aircraft was new, smelling good and the airhostess was good-looking and Vijay Mallya was speaking. He welcomed us aboard the flight and said he had instructed his crew to treat us as guests and we should contact him if we had a problem. I didn't have occasion to take up his offer this time and hope I don't ever have to, but at least he was putting his money where his mouth was.

There was a small TV terminal in front of me, which had a range of entertainment options of my sort. The TV had sports and other enjoyable channels; and there were audio channels that offered a wide choice of music also available. I was given a pouch in which the headphones were housed, as a take-away. Like any and every Indian, I love anything and everything that is free. I carried the headphone home and along with it, a few good memories about the airline. The good times continued on flight with a hot meal and solicitous airhostesses. Used as I am, to buying a tiny bottle of water at Rs.10 in similarly priced flights, I was thrilled to say the least.

Breakfast in London, Lunch in New York

Nearly two decades ago, Saatchi & Saatchi had done a brilliant poster for the Concorde being run by British Airways with the line 'Breakfast in London, Lunch in New York' and below that someone had scribbled 'And baggage in Bermuda'. Baggage handling continues to be a nightmare in India as normal Indian (or is it normal Airports Authority) behaviour takes over. I am not sure if the baggage arrived earlier on the flight but I felt good after my flight. It vindicated my belief in Indian service. After all, we have a legacy of service, having served the British for generations, Mangal Pandey notwithstanding.

Miles to Fly

Today, if we were to talk about any category it becomes clear that we live in a world of parity. Why do people choose an airline service in preference over another? Is it because it arrives at the destination at an ideal time, so that you can squeeze the maximum number of hours there? Is it because it has the best rates going? Is it because you get mileage points on that airline? Is it because you get a free trip if you collect six boarding cards? Or is it because of the little things that the airline has institutionalised as service offerings that set it apart from the competition? My suspicion is that the 'little things' will make a big difference to brand choice. Kingfisher Airlines has discovered a few little things that matter, at least to me; I suspect that it matters to other harassed and hassled passengers too. The key to service excellence is in having employees who care and who can be trained. I was recently reading a book called 'A spirit of greatness'. It is an amazing book of stories about the employees of American Airlines. Some of the anecdotes of service brought tears to my eyes. Kingfisher would do well to institutionalise these 'little things that count' to every single employee. Then it will truly make a difference to airline travel in India. Every company has a few outstanding individuals that go the 'extra mile' for service. The challenge is to institutionalise that 'spirit of service'. Kingfisher Airlines must do this and one suspects it will.

Brands are Long Term

Kingfisher is a brand that has made a difference and here I am speaking about the beer. It embodies the vision and the spirit of its charismatic leader. This extension even if not logical seems to provide a great opportunity to move from product to service, building on an existing equity. And yet building an airline brand is neither easy nor cheap. One remembers Richard Branson, (I must remember to say "Sir Richard Branson") being asked in an interview as to how to become a Millionaire and his answer was typically cheeky, typically Branson. He said, *"You start out by being a*

> 'The key to service excellence is in having employees who care and who can be trained'

billionaire and then you start an airline". Mr. Vijay Mallya is a billionaire. And he has started an airline. But one is reasonably sure that his airline will not go the way of Damania or East West, even if he gets his way of serving Kingfisher beer to thirsty passengers! But success will be his, as long as he remembers that a service brand is built not only by the big bucks, but also by the little things that make a difference to passengers like you and me. Consumers like you and me will make demands, at times unreasonably. We will make unfair comparisons, across categories. And yet we will be loyal to service providers who care. For it is every little bit that counts and means a lot to us.

> 'A service brand is built not only by the big bucks, but also by the little things that make a difference'

"Just give me one good **reason why**
I should buy your brand
instead of someone else's"

- Your next new consumer

BRANDING
-AN OVERVIEW

"Really strong brands are the ones that have done all my thinking for me"

- Marieke van der Werf
Founder, New Moon communications agency

CHAPTER

A Question of Brands

Remember the Tamil film Thiruvilayadal? If it was before your time, let me quickly jog your memory and draw your attention to an oft-shown, oft-talked about scene between Nagesh and Sivaji Ganesan where Nagesh, resolute about testing the thespian, questions him. Yes, like Nagesh I realize that it is easier to ask questions than to find answers to problems in branding. I have read too,

> 'It is easier to ask questions than to find answers to problems in branding'

that "It is better to know some of the questions than all of the answers". Here, I have attempted to look at a variety of brands both international and national. They belong to widely - differing categories, consumers and countries. And yet, I believe they have an important lesson for us in India, faced as we are with a host of complex issues that threaten our brands. I have always been a great admirer of the management guru Gary Hamel and perhaps it is time to recall once again what he said, *"If a company is interested in finding the future, most of what it needs to learn, it must learn outside its own industry"*. It is that time of year when it is appropriate to look ahead with anticipation and also think outside the box like some of these brands have done.

Mind or Heart?

A brand is a blend of rational and emotional benefits. One wonders though, whether, we as marketers are too obsessed with the rational and the functional. Yes, positioning as per Al Ries and Jack Trout is the 'battle for the mind'; but how about the heart of the consumer? Let's take a quick look at a brand that has captured just that: Harley Davidson, the original cult brand.

Aimed at individuals who love the freedom one feels on two wheels, Harley's 'Weekend Fun' positioning, is extremely interesting and inclusive. Whilst the typical Harley user might be a blue-collar worker with limited resources, the inclusive positioning makes it aspirational and hence Harley customers include engineers, lawyers and doctors. Yes, Harley has widened its customer base. And Harley has captured and fired its customer's imagination. Another cult brand, which appeals to the heart, is Apple. Many of us lead buttoned-down and regimented lives. Can your brand provide a breath of fresh air? Does it give customers a break from the monotony of life? Does it appeal to the heart?

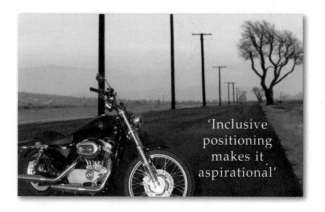
'Inclusive positioning makes it aspirational'

Customer? Or lover? Or both?

Everyone wants their customer to love their brands. They want to delight their customers too. And yet there is the interesting and intriguing example of Ferrari. There are millions of Ferrari lovers across the world, and yet many of them could never realistically become customers of the brand. The love and admiration, which this brand inspires is at once a challenge as well; because the more people admire a brand, the more they expect and demand from it. Just ask Sachin Tendulkar. Millions of people have linked their dreams and hopes to this diminutive genius and boy is he under pressure!

The love and affection that people hold for a brand can spawn line extensions and an expansion of your customer base. Who is your brand's consumer? Can you widen the base and make more people love your brand?

> 'The love and affection that people hold for a brand can spawn line extensions and an expansion of your customer base'

What Business without Philosophy?

Businesses are built around brands. At times, however, we tend to forget that what holds a company together is a strong guiding philosophy. A philosophy anchored in a strong, consumer-benefit proposition. Britannia's tagline of "Eat Healthy. Think Better" represents an attempt to inform consumers about the importance of the brand and its relevance to customers. The philosophy anchors a vast and diverse product line. LG, another multi-product company has anchored its philosophy in health, and extended it to Ravi Shastri's exhortation to the captains of the competing World Cup cricket teams to indulge in healthy competition. One is reminded of the successful GE campaign that said 'We bring good

things to life'. It was generic, almost, and provided a much wider canvas. It permitted the company to hang its multi-product peg on this customer benefit statement. Is your philosophy reflected in your communication?

Time for Excitement?

Titan is a solid successful Indian brand. It has been a brand that has been innovative in more ways than one. Remember gifting? Well, Titan not only changed the way the Indian consumer looked at time but changed the way we looked at gifting. I can tell you that from my own experience. For my 5th wedding anniversary I got a Titan watch as a gift. And for my 10th wedding anniversary, yes another Titan. And for the 15th, hold your breath, yet another Titan. Hardly surprising that gifting accounts for over 50% of Titan's sales. And yet, the last few years have seen a slowdown in the durable market. Titan too saw sluggish sales, an offspring of the fact that the multiple ownership of watches didn't happen at the pace that Titan hoped for and the value-conscious watch buyer was buying Sonata. Yes, things were slow at India's premier watchmaker's end.

'Now tell me, what is the new exciting thing that has happened to your brand or company in recent times?'

It is in this context that the launch of Titan Edge and Titan Steel become relevant. They were electrifying. The slimmest watch in the world caused more than a ripple. I think it was a technologically-inspired wave that has not only benefitted the brand but the company as well. Yes, brands and companies need excitement, particularly when the economy is slow and the mood is downbeat. Now tell me, what is the new exciting thing that has happened to your brand or company in recent times? The answer to that question might well determine your brand's future.

Can Personal Branding give you an Edge?

From a brand that changed the face of time, let's move on to a face that is a brand. We are not talking of Aishwarya Rai here. In a recent study conducted by brand-comm, students across leading management institutes overwhelmingly chose N. R. Narayana Murthy of Infosys as the business leader they admired most, for the fourth consecutive year in a row. And guess why? No surprises here, 'Leadership style, vision, entrepreneurial spirit and ethics'. Undoubtedly, the other corporate leaders in India have some catching up to do in image terms at least. Branding is all about consistency, coherence and long-term thinking. Corporate leaders can and will become brands in their own right. There have been people before Narayana Murthy like Jack Welch, Richard Branson and Anita Roddick who have been the face of the organisation they headed, making the later 'Company of choice' to customers, employees and investors.

> 'Who is the "face" of your organisation to the external world? Or is it a well-kept secret?'

Who is the 'face' of your organisation to the external world? Or is it a well-kept secret?

Speed. The Name of the Game?

Earlier brand building was slow and steady. Brands took time, a long time to be built. Take Dalda, Colgate, Coke or Lux. All these brands are great brands. Built, carefully and consistently, over a period of time - a long period of time. And yet, consider some of the technology brands that have been built in recent times – Amazon, Yahoo, America Online, MSN, Rediff.com... they didn't take too long did they? And that throws up an interesting question. At what speed is your own brand cruising? Why not pitch your speed of growth or visibility higher?

Speaking of speed, I would be anxious to see when Reliance Infocomm stirs up the market. Will the company that believes that growth is a way of life show that WLL is the way to go? The only thing that I am sure of is that whatever Reliance does, they will do it fast. They will not aim low. They won't be satisfied too easily and will keep raising the bar even as they keep lowering the prices. Yes, better, bigger and quicker may just happen. Can it happen for your brand too?

So here's that pesky list of questions again:

Q. **Does your brand appeal to the heart?**

Q. **Do you have mere customers or do you have brand lovers?**

Q. **Is your philosophy reflected in your communication?**

Q. **What exciting thing has happened to your brand in recent times?**

Q. **Who is the face of your company to the external world?**

Q. **How fast is your brand cruising?**

And as a final thought, let me quote Rainer Maria Rilke, *"Live your questions now and perhaps even without knowing it you will live along some distant day into your answers"*.

CHAPTER 2

Imagine a Life Without Brands !

It's 5.25 a.m., on a wintry January morning at Bangalore. I am up, if not about. My hand eagerly reaches for the remote control in anticipation of a great day's test cricket. As I furiously punch the buttons in my remote control, I find that every channel is on, except ESPN, which also means that I cannot watch the first ball being bowled. A consequence, of an on-going battle of rates between ESPN and my local cable operator as briefly touched upon earlier in this book. I am hopping mad to put it mildly and, if one were given the freedom to murder one person in one's lifetime, as I've mentioned earlier too, I guess my cable operator would win the contest hands down. My love for cable operators is well-documented by now!

It's 6.30 p.m., one evening, again at Bangalore, and I get a frantic call from my mother on my mobile phone. It's one of the early days of the Rajkumar – Veerappan imbroglio (the first named being a hugely popular South Indian film star ; the second being the much wanted and hunted brigand of South India, since then captured and shot dead).

The Tamil channels in Bangalore are blocked. The cable operators of Bangalore are the culprits. My mother says, quite agitatedly, that she would like to move back to Chennai, which she left 14 years ago as she feels her life is very incomplete without Sun TV and her serials. (Thankfully, the channels have since been put back on the air). Interestingly enough, a generation like mine, which was told not to live in a place without a temple is being exposed to the travails of living in a place without satellite TV!

This experience should be more than familiar for tipplers. They go to the club and ask for Royal Challenge or Director's Special, only to be told that it is Election Day and hence a dry day. (In India liquor is not sold on election days as a precautionary measure). You look for your Nike shoes and discover that they're in the washing machine. Your news agent fails to deliver Sportstar on Wednesday along with the newspaper... and so ...the tale of woe continues.

Brands are important and an integral, vital part of people's lives. Our lives would be incomplete without brands and that's a gross under-statement. Equally important perhaps, is the fact that we have two sets of people in the world: the people who make products and services available; and the larger, more significant set of people who use these products and services - the millions of consumers all over the world. Consumers matter to companies and brands matter to consumers. Often, companies and marketers tend to forget this critical piece of the puzzle. Whilst, it is they who create and build brands, ultimately, the brands belong to the consumer. The consumer decides what to buy, how important it is and whether one can do without the brand or not. Fortunate are the brands that mean so much to consumers and their lifestyles.

> 'Fortunate are the brands that mean so much to consumers and their lifestyles'

I'd like to Buy the World a Coke

When Coca-Cola replaced its flagship Cola with a new formula to beat the Pepsi challenge in 1985, a 'classic' (pun intended) case of the importance of a brand to the consumer, was amply demonstrated. The new formula scored well over Pepsi in taste tests run with 1,90,000 consumers. (That's right, 1,90,000!) The change was announced with a huge media and marketing splash. What followed was incredible. Angry consumer responses rejected the new formula instantly, violently. Thousands of angry calls and letters followed. Coke represented an American icon and not a bottle of Cola. The 'vintage' Coke Classic in the meanwhile, was sold at a premium.

As Al Ries asks, *"How can you have a 'new' presumably 'better' Coke? How can the real thing have been bad? Why on earth would you ever change it? It's like introducing a new god"*. It was a bit like asking for a new, improved Sachin! The company had learnt a lesson which it wouldn't forget in a hurry and the American consumer realised how significantly important the brand Coke was and always will be to his life. How woefully true that companies tend to look

> 'Only those companies, that understand the emotional bonding between brands and consumers can, and will, continue to grow'

inwards far too often and forget that the action is out there in the stores and cafés and not in their own boardrooms. Only those companies, that understand the emotional bonding between brands and consumers can, and will, continue to grow.

Engineering an Image Change

Closer home, is a similar story, perhaps less dramatic and without any major headlines though it impacted the heads of several men. I refer to Brylcreem, a brand that was around when I was a kid. You don't have to be a mathematician to figure out that it belonged to a generation previous to mine.

The celebrity endorsing the brand in the sixties was India's dashing wicket keeper and batsman – Farookh Engineer. Get the picture and the vintage? And then, a few years later, Brylcreem said, 'Let's target and talk to the Channel `V' generation which is a third of the age of the original Brylcreem customer and psychographically and demographically, a completely different animal least ways from a grooming perspective'.

The packaging, the product offering and the advertising were radically different. Some of the people born in pre-independent India - the original Brylcreem users - felt the new perfume gave them a headache. The more affluent ones asked their sons to get the original Brylcreem from Singapore or London.

It is quite likely that the company's attempt to make its brand's image in India more contemporary was hugely successful. It is important to remember that we do not have access to success parameters like market share, so our comment is not on the strategy but merely to make a point on consumer reaction to the familiar becoming the unfamiliar. The consumer has a preference, which, if not allowed to be voiced will cause him to drift away, quietly, from our fold.

'The consumer has a preference, which, if not allowed to be voiced will cause him to drift away, quietly, from our fold'

Marketers beware! Understand your consumer. Know what makes your consumer tick. Know the brand preferences of your consumer. And try not to throw the baby out with the bath water.

True, the only permanent thing in life is change. However, change though exciting, need not necessarily be for the better. Before we rush to change something, it is worthwhile to ask this question. To whom does the brand belong? The manufacturer who produces it? The marketer who brands it? The dealer who stocks it and decides its fate?

Or, the consumer who buys it? To me, it is clear that the brand belongs to the consumer.

All through life, we will encounter brands of some sort or the other. Sometimes we will experience them as consumers and sometimes as marketers. The trick is to make your brand intrinsic to your consumer's life, like a brisk walk on a misty morning, a hot cup of tea on a cold evening, a morning newspaper in a desolate hill station or a glass of chilled beer after an intense cricket match played at 40°C. It's a sign of reassurance that all is well with the world. It's an emotional bonding with the moment, and the brand.

As Howard Schultz, Chairman and CEO of Starbucks Coffee Company says, *"A brand has to feel like a friend"*. A brand is a friend. Let's try to make our brand an important and integral part of the consumer's life. If the consumer's life is incomplete without your brand, your success is complete - a blinding flash of the obvious.

Imagine a life without a friend. I can't. Can you?

> 'If the consumer's life is incomplete without your brand, your success is complete - a blinding flash of the obvious'

"In the average half-hour trip to the supermarket, 30,000 products vie for the shopper's attention"

- *Thomas Hine*

CHAPTER

The Relevance of Being Different

Brands (and if one may add branding) are creating a buzz not only in the market place but in the media as well. That's a far cry from the days when people had difficulty in pronouncing the word, leave alone understanding the concept. The 21st century student of branding has a wide, affordable choice of knowledge banks on the subject: there are seminars on branding, columns in the business press on the subject, and television programmes airing the views of experts, not to forget 3 credit courses on branding in every management institute in the country. A variety of definitions of branding are doing the rounds – from the exotic to the functional.

> "In the twenty-first century, branding will ultimately be the only differentiator between companies. Brand equity is now a key asset"
>
> **- Fortune Magazine**

So, Where lies the Importance of a Brand?

According to Fortune Magazine *"In the twenty-first century, branding will ultimately be the only differentiator between companies. Brand equity is now a key asset"*. This prediction has considerable merit and highlights 'equity' which is really what everyone who is concerned with brand management is attempting to maximize all the time. While on the subject, it would be valuable to understand what makes brands successful.

The Relevance of Being Different

Brands live in a world of extreme and unprincipled competition. Every category is crowded. Every channel and newspaper is cluttered. The only brands that survive are of the successful kind. These are the brands, which are relevant and different. They are relevant to consumers and different from the competition. The question is how does one differentiate one from the other? Sadly, it appears easier to inscribe it in lofty (and similar-sounding) mission statements than to actually practice it.

> 'The only brands that survive are of the successful kind. These are the brands which, are relevant and different'

Think about it. How different is your brand? If you try and answer the question honestly enough you are bound to find that unless you are one of the fortunate few it is well-nigh impossible to be different from the welter of competing brands in your category.

Think Different

Apple, the original Silicon Valley company is a wonderful example of a company that *'Think(s) Different'*. The tag line was not a mere, advertising slogan but a guiding philosophy that is worth remembering and is worthy of mention in The Hall of Fame.

Brands must have a raison d'etre. The essence of the brand has to permeate every thought, strategy and action concerning its identity and existence. Apple's guiding principle of *'Thinking*

Different' has resulted in products that *are* different – whether they are coloured monitors or I-pods. Starbucks makes a difference to the average American's life. And the difference comes from the philosophy. Howard Schultz the founder wanted his retail chain to fill a gap in consumer's lives. He realized that the average American had two important places in his life – his home and his place of work. He was confident that his retail outlets could be

'The essence of the brand has to permeate every thought, strategy and action concerning its identity and existence.'

'the third place' in the average American's life. The rest, as they say, is history. So, the inference is simple for aspiring brand managers and owners. Start right. Get the brand's essence right. And you will see and make a difference, to the one person who really matters - the consumer.

Be Different

There are several elements to any brand – the name, the packaging, the identity, the shape, the touch and feel of it, the colours associated with the brand, its positioning and so on. At the risk of sounding obvious one must still say that crucial to brand success is a strong product or service. Though, a very significant element of the brand is clearly the name.

'One would like to believe that it is an investment that we are talking about'

Does the brand name stand out? Clearly an Apple in computers or an orange in mobile services will stand out. But it is important to bear one fact in mind. If the name cues the category (e.g. Airtel) that's fine, but if it doesn't, there must be a clue as to what the name stands for. There is a cost to this, yet, let's view it as an investment - a long term one.

Packaging can be another point of difference. Sadly, packaging does not get the attention that it deserves. Advertising can be glamorous, creative and fun. So it gets senior management attention and involvement. Packaging in real life is often enough relegated to junior management. This is probably why packaging revolutions like the sachet, which brands like Velvette (initially) and Chik (later) exploited are relatively few and far between. The packaging of brands like Absolut Vodka or Harpic come to mind here. Speaking of Absolut one must speak of its advertising appeal, but that would merit an entire chapter and not a mere passing mention. Related perhaps to the packaging is the product form. Take Toblerone for example. I should be the last person to speak about chocolates (people my age are better off ignoring the entire category) and yet Toblerone's shape makes it different enough to capture my interest and even be a temptation.

Look! It's Different

Symbols engage intelligence, imagination, emotion in a way that nothing else does. The logos of a few brands clearly beat the clutter, because they are different, in styling, look, feel and colours.

While no two people seem to agree on their favourite colour, most people are in agreement with the need to have a distinctive identity for their brand. Brands like Pizza Hut, Citibank, Shell, Chase and IBM can be easily recalled for this virtue. Whether it is 'Big Blue's' Venetian blinds or Citibank's distinctive colours or Coke's vibrant red.... they have one thing in common: they are distinctly different.

> 'Symbols engage intelligence, imagination, emotion in a way that nothing else does'

Brands try to own colours. Coke tries to own the colour red, Pepsi the colour blue. As the wag said, "Just whisper the word blue and the Coke guy will see red.... And if you whisper the word red the Pepsi guy will go blue in the face." The Nike swoosh is so distinctive that you don't even need the brand name.

The question therefore is how distinctive is your brand's identity?

Think Small

Brands are built by advertising. And what better example is there than Volkswagen – the original small car. A German car in post-war America! A midget in a land of giants! Fundamental to brand success is advertising that stands out. Not for nothing was the Volkswagen ad voted as the best ad of the last century. Not far behind is the campaign for Avis, the car rental company that '...tried harder because it was No.2'. Very often, brands suffer because their positioning is fuzzy, resulting in hazy advertising that leaves consumers cold. Lazy strategies will not deliver. Focus on differences. Be the coolest one if you must, but for heaven's sake, be something.

So what is your difference? Can you create one if you don't have it naturally? But very often the fault lies not in our brand but in us. We are too easily satisfied with things being in status quo. We don't rock the boat. We accept mediocrity. We breed more of the same. The future is in creating successful brands.

Quickly. And while we have many successful examples behind us they are nothing compared to what lies ahead of us.

The time to be different is now.

'Very often brands suffer because their positioning is fuzzy, resulting in hazy advertising that leaves consumers cold'

CHAPTER

Be First or Be Different

"In the future", said the head of an international telecom major, *"there will be only two sorts of companies. Those that are quick and those that are dead"*. The logic applies equally to television serials (and game shows) as well. 'Kaun Banega Crorepati' was the first and is still, on top of the charts. 'Sawaal Dus Crore Ka' came later and died a quick death. The Tamil version of popular game show 'Kaun Banega Crorepati (KBC)' was launched in August 2005 with engineering student Abhishek Gaurav in the hot seat, qizzed by a 'Tamil-speaking' Bachchan. Yes indeed, KBC is already starting to make waves in Tamil Nadu after sweeping the rest of India off its feet. Whereas, Sawaal Dus Crore Ka has met the fate of so many 'me-too-products' that fell victim to the curse of being 'also rans' in several supermarkets in the world and in 'kirana' shops all over this country. Though, in all fairness, TV audiences of this country have been a lot less patient than they have been as consumers of fast-moving consumer goods.

> 'There will be only two sorts of companies. Those that are quick and those that are dead'

Be First to be Top of Mind

Initially, I was no raving fan of 'Kaun Benega Crorepati' (I am not, even now). The programme hadn't started to be called

'KBC' yet (today people refer to the acronym as endearingly and affectionately as some of my friends refer to 'RC' and DSP'* after sunset). The 'Big B' by his own admission, was still coming to terms with the small screen. The 'Computerji', was a scream. The questions were inane. ("How many teeth does a human being have?"). Cocktail parties had superior people like me silently (and not so silently) preening themselves on their intelligence. After all, didn't we know how many teeth we had or at least should have?

"Lowest common denominator" said one superciliously. (After all, its difficult not to feel superior under the influence of a couple of stiff ones). "What's wrong with Siddarth Basu". "You mean guys are desperate to get into **this**?"

You could hear similar 'intellectual' statements being echoed across several metros. But, I realised the truth fairly quickly, although I didn't advertise it all that much. I was not the target audience! But a lot of Indians were, and they loved India's first big money game show, that had struck a chord within them and became the favourite of several media plans. like old wine mellowed. The program improved. The pubs lost their charm and customers.

Quiz books printed at Chandni Chowk gave Arundati Roy a run for her money. And then, 'Nawate' happened. The manifest greed of the audience given respectability by as every second participant and his brother-in-law spoke about donating to social causes. Yes, KBC came (on air); (People) saw; and it conquered (the ratings)!

More of The Same?

The time Zee TV took to launch its own programme was spent well by Star Plus!

* *Royal Challenge and Director's Special are popular brands of Indian whisky.*

Star augmented its ratings and the audience improved its vocabulary. Expressions like "Sure?", "Lock kiya jaye" and "Phone-a-friend", invaded living rooms, cafeterias and smoking corridors. The Internet and the media spawned their own slew of jokes on the programme: "Can I phone a friend?" asks an optimistic husband when his wife complains of a 'headache'.

Life in India wasn't the same. Life wasn't the same at Zee telefilms either, as the stock markets unlocked the stock from their portfolio, with their fastest fingers, first. Zee came out with their version of the programme, which at first blush seemed all too similar. More of the same. Prize money of 10 crores instead of 1 crore. Two comperes instead of one. 21 short-listed participants instead of 10. More of everything, except audience viewership and television rating points.  Comparisons one knows are odious. People compared with Anupam, the questions, the sets, the costumes, and the accent. To sum up... the ambience, the choice of expressions and the whole show was perceived to be 'me-too', undifferentiated. Retribution has been swift and, ruthless.

Differentiate or Die

Programmes and brands must be unique and differentiated if, they have to survive first and then, thrive. I have seen enough biscuit packets designed to look like Britannia packs. I have seen enough tooth pastes designed to look like Colgate. And yet, it's fairly obvious that you don't beat the market leader by aping it but by standing out and apart from him. The Tide pack for instance, is designed to stand out from the clutter of detergent packs and the competition. The distinctive packaging for Dalmia Vajram Cement broke the clutter in the crowded cement markets of Tamilnadu and Kerala. Savvy marketers ensure that their products and commercials do not cue the competition (in the consumer's mind) in any way. They appropriate colours, situations and music tracks, which are theirs and theirs alone. In fact, even whilst using comparative advertising, some brands refer to their competition as brand 'X' (even when they can name the competing brand) as they don't wish to confuse the consumer who already has difficulty in remembering the number of teeth he has. Zee erred, in that, its changes seemed like changes for the sake of change. Its offering, wasn't clearly better or sufficiently different.

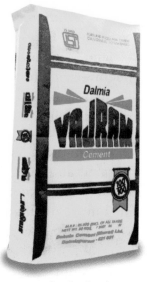

Creative: brand-comm

Perfection has a Price

I spent 6 ½ years of my life working in a bank counting other people's cash and writing out other people's fixed deposit receipts. My co-pen pusher was a perfectionist. He wrote out a fixed deposit receipt painstakingly and meticulously, and this took him 45 minutes, almost as if it was being carved in stone. The customer took this work of art from him almost reverently. He still cashed the FD after 12 months. I, on my part, took 1 ½ minutes to write a similar receipt. The customer might have wondered about my speed but he had no complaints about my quickly written FD. He still en-cashed it after 12 months. But I had 43 ½ minutes spare to spend on other things like smiling at disinterested female customers. But there's a moral here. Perfection has a price. A cost if you will. In perfecting a product, idea or a programme, are you

> 'Is our anxiety to create the perfect four-wheel drive causing us to miss the bus?'

losing valuable time? Yes, as my one-time boss and all-time mentor, A.G. Krishnamurthy of Mudra, would say, *"People want a Picasso. But they can't wait 10 years for it".* The question each one of us needs to ask ourselves is this, "Is our anxiety to create the perfect four-wheel drive causing us to miss the bus?"

One of Manisha Koirala's first questions in 'Sawaal' was the number of 'a's in the word January. The questions in the real world of marketing tend to be a lot more difficult. But straight 'A's are got by the marketers who are

a) First

b) Different

c) Consistently upgrading themselves (even if it means wooing Rajnikant)

d) Unsettling the competition (just ask Glenn Mcgrath what he would do to Brian Lara – although Lara unlike "Sawaal", has certainly bounced back to become the leading run-scorer in tests).

Kaun Banega Crorepati (even without trying) has felled Sawaal Dus Crore Ka. The follower has shot himself in the foot. But this is a lesson which companies seem increasingly reluctant to learn. They somehow believe that they are not destined to fail or come up with excuses like Zee, who blame their stars Anupam Kher and Manisha Koirala for their current ills. Imagine Shakespeare's foresight when he said, *"The fault dear Brutus lies not in our stars".* True. It lies in being late.

"A Brand becomes stronger
when you narrow the focus."

- *Al Ries & Laura Ries*

LAUNCHING BRANDS

"A brand is what people say about
you when you are not there"

CHAPTER

New Venture ? Start Up Right !

Planning a start up? Good luck to you. But make no mistake. It will be your baby, in every which way (even when a few come to say 'cheese' and claim the credit when the lad graduates). No parent will trade the happiness he gets when he watches his baby grow. The first turn, the first smile, the first halting step, are sources of great pride to any parent and sources of great revenue to the photography industry.

A start up's growth can be equally satisfying to the promoter. The sense of

'Yet there is one question, which often enough does not get the importance it deserves. And that's the relevance of branding the start up'

achievement in building an organisation (maybe an empire, even) from scratch is a tremendous feeling that only a few get to experience and savour. But let that not deter you from taking the plunge. As someone who has 'been there', (even if I haven't exactly 'done that') I have just one suggestion: Start young and don't wait, (like I did), for your 46th birthday.

Having decided to take the plunge, a budding entrepreneur has several things to worry about, each perhaps more critical than the other. Will venture capitalists fund the project? Will talent buy into your vision and join you? What is the revenue model? When will you break even? How big is the market? Who will be the competition? Is your product / service / technology unique? How right are the projections of the market size? These questions are weighty enough. And yet there is one question, which often enough does not get the importance it deserves. And that's the relevance of branding the start up. As a promoter, have you thought of your company's brand name and what your brand should stand for? The last few years have seen a slew of companies that have 'started up', more so in the technology space. Technologists often enough get preoccupied with their technology to the exclusion of all else. And that could be dangerous. As Floathe Johnson warns, *"The road to hell is paved with companies who developed their technology but neglected their brand"*. And yet the road ahead for the start up could be very satisfying if the principles of branding are taken care of, in the early stages of a 'start up's' life.

> "The road to hell is paved with companies who developed their technology but neglected their brand"
>
> - **Floathe Johnson**

A good Beginning

In cricket and in business there is nothing greater than a good beginning. One of the biggest letdowns in cricket was the 1999-2000 Australia, South Africa Series which Australia won by a mile. What was billed as the 'World Championship of Cricket' turned out to be among the most one-sided contests. The difference? Quite simple, really: the tremendous beginnings provided by Mathew Hayden and Justin Langer. The advantage, which a powerful brand name can provide, can be equally dramatic in the context of a start up. So, has enough thought and research gone into this all-important choice? The brand name could well be the trump card. Remember the name Pentium was one of 3300 alternatives. How many have you considered?

Matters of Identity

Companies with large advertising budgets can announce their birth with a bang. Remember Home Trade? But how many of you can use Shahrukh, Sachin and Hrithik to launch your brand. There are other ways of launching a product, less dramatic perhaps, but definitely not as expensive. Developing an identity that encompasses lettering, logo, and colour scheme (all of them count) is essential. Companies like MindTree have realised the power of a distinctively designed logo. Even a retail financial services company like Way2Wealth has a very striking logo

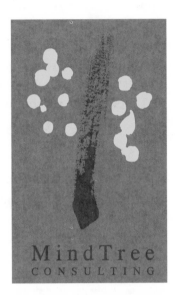

that cuts through the clutter. Sometimes 'start ups' don't realise the value of appropriating certain colours as their own. As I have mentioned earlier, cola companies for instance have capitalized on this. Can start-ups learn from these consumer giants even if they aren't going to compete on advertising spends with these big spenders?

The Battle for the Mind

And yet there's something more important: What do you want your 'start up' to be? What do you want it to stand for? Remember you have an advantage in starting late – strange though it may seem. It's quite simple really. You are starting up late and you know what your competition is standing for (or trying to stand for), so you should strive to position yourself uniquely in a manner that will make your company stand out.

It is important though, that companies recognize the risk they run of becoming inward focussed.

Every company has three primary targets: customers who buy from it, employees who join it and investors who fund it. Is your positioning relevant to these people? The other risk is that the positioning you so carefully choose, often enough is not communicated to the people concerned. Mass media advertising is all very fine, but internal communication is equally important, and that takes me to the next important point.

Total Branding

David D'Alessandro says in his book Brand Warfare, *"Brand is everything, the stuff you want to communicate to consumers and the stuff you communicate despite yourself. By definition "Brand" is whatever the consumer thinks of when he or she hears the company's name".*

> "Brand is everything, the stuff you want to communicate to consumers and the stuff you communicate despite yourself"
>
> **- David D'Alessandro**

This has an important bearing on people who work for any organisation. Clearly, a CEO must be passionate about his brand. But, what about other employees? They can't afford to be ill informed about the brand and its core values. Have they been told? Very often companies are caught up with visible stuff like identity, which is important, but branding goes beyond this; it is all-encompassing.

Cheaper and Not Necessarily less Effective

Some of the best-known companies as brands have been launched by public relations and not by advertising. The flip side to the opportunity is the question you need to ask yourself. How newsworthy is your product or project? Many of us are trained to think conventionally. We are all a product of our upbringing,

> 'How newsworthy
> is your product
> or project?'

education and environment. Opportunities exist for companies that defy tradition. Have you considered every opportunity to build brand recognition? Let me quickly clarify one issue too. I am from the advertising business and realise and appreciate its value. Advertising works. Make no mistake about that. And yet when you happen to be one of those less fortunate ones who cannot afford to spend money, leave alone burn it, then that is the time, to look for the best returns at the least cost.

Branditude

Branding is not rocket science. It's a clear articulation of a strategy and a painstaking execution of the detail. It's not an event, but a process. It's a quest for a holy grail, which always seem just a little beyond your reach. But the starting point is with the entrepreneur, who recognises its importance, amongst the million things he has to do, to start his enterprise. He must be passionate about his brand and communicate that passion to the relevant publics.

"Your attitude determines your altitude" is an oft-quoted statement. Just have the right attitude to your brand and watch your start up take off.

"If you don't know where you are going,
any road will take you there"

- *Yogi Berra*

CHAPTER

Jumpstart Your Venture. Brand it Right.

We have no control over our names. Our names largely represent the pet preferences of doting parents and/or religious dispositions of well-meaning grand parents – not to forget experts in numerology. And yet, I have met enough Aravinds, Amitabhs and Abhisheks cursing their stars as they find it almost impossible to give proxies for attendance in college or are almost invariably first for vivas and practicals. My

> 'And yet, how many of us apply the same principles of having a unique and differentiated brand name'

schoolmate from Chennai (or Madras as it was then) had a few more attendant problems. His father (or so the story went) was an unabashed admirer of the Supreme Commander of the Allied Expeditionary Forces during World War II, and named his son after the President of the United States of America! Yes, EISENHOWER! Imagine the travails of a kid with a name like that, in a class full of Sridhars, Sureshes, Srinivasans and Prabhakars. Children can be insensitive and sometimes even cruel. In retrospect, I guess the sixties generation was no different from today's kids and would do anything to raise a laugh. Our man with the given name (or is it given baggage) of an American, was the butt of jokes, wisecracks and merciless ribbing. And now 4 decades later (I must confess that I am not very quick on the uptake), I realize the value of his name. The name was different, noticeable and unforgettable even after 40 years. 'Eisenhower' was a brand whilst all the rest of us were just a bunch of nondescript kids. And yet, how many of us apply the same principles of having a unique and differentiated brand name, when we start our own venture, particularly when we consider that the new venture represents our life-long ambition to make a mark in the corporate world.

What's in a Name? Everything

Who hasn't heard of William Shakespeare? We have all read him, (mis) quoted him and even acted his lines out in school plays. He was a genius whose creative achievement has not been surpassed in any age. Shakespeare was a brand. In every possible way you choose to look at it, yet, here is what Shakespeare had to say about brand names.

"What's in a name?
That which we call a rose
by any other name
would smell as sweet"

The choice of a company's name is an important strategic decision. Resist the impulse to name it after yourself and there must be better ways of pleasing your wife than putting her name on your company's letterhead. Avoid too, the temptation to do a permutation and combination of letters from the names of your entire family aided and abetted by numerologists. Every one of us begins small and it's perhaps easy to fall into the trap of thinking small. We would like

'We would like our 'start-up' to become an organisation and eventually an institution. Not a 'Mom & Pop' store'

our 'start-up' to become an organisation and eventually an institution. Not a 'Mom & Pop' store. Whilst there may be enough examples of personal giants like J. Walter Thompson, David Ogilvy, Bill Bernbach or Arthur Andersen, still having their names adorn the doors of their hugely successful corporations, I guess organisations today need more than the promoters' personal equity to get them up and

> 'They need a team, a value proposition, a clear vision and a good brand name to begin with'

running. They need a team, a value proposition, a clear vision and a good brand name to begin with.

I remember Psmith, the celebrated Wodehouse character, requesting Mike, another Wodehouse protagonist, to spell his name with a 'P' to stand out from the myriads of 'Smiths' that were blots on the English landscape. The first principle in this whole brand name maze is to be unique and different.

And yet in today's day and age, where 97% of the words in the Webster's dictionary are already registered as brand names, what chance do we have of finding something unique or different? Unless you are one of the fortunate few who can dish out $7.5 million for a business.com or $1.03 million for Wallstreet.com. Because the reality is, that today's brand name must be relevant and available in the virtual world too.

If you look at some of the successful brands of the past, they have some interesting origins.

- Coca Cola reflected the ingredients in the product.

- The Christian name of Daimler's daughter was Mercedes.

- Taurus – originally a code name given to the car during its design stage as both the Chief Engineer's and Product Manager's wives were born with the same star sign. The code name stayed.

- Adidas is a contraction of Adolph Dassler and Harpic of Harry Picman.

All of these are big brands today, commanding tremendous equity and value, making one believe that what one does with a brand is perhaps more critical than the name first given to it.

It's not easy finding the right name. It's hard work. It involves research, brainstorming and a list of numerous alternatives to choose from. And yes, there is a method to choosing your product's name. The word "Pent" means 5 in Greek and the brand represented the fifth generation of the X86 family. Pentium was selected from 3300 alternatives. Hardly chance is it? And this leads me to ask another question, which could possibly be embarrassing to some brand managers. "How much work do you put in on an important project like the choice of a brand name?" Let me add that its not hard work, which is as critical as 'smart work'.

> 'How much work do you put in on an important project like the choice of a brand name?'

There are several rules that successful brand marketers follow in the choice of names. How short is it? Does it sound well? Is it easy to pronounce? (Imagine someone asking for 'Ultra Doux' (French word where the last consonant is silent) in Mayiladutharai, deep down in Tamil Nadu! And yet some companies have veered away from the premise that the brand name has to sound good (Kodak and Exxon truly sound good) or evoke pleasant memories. Smuckers Jelly, recognizing that its name was a mixed bag probably veering more toward 'dislikeable' than 'likeable', challenges the customer with a line like this" "With a name like Smuckers, it has to be good". Another dotcom brand that one kept seeing on TV in the heydays of the dotcom boom, was Zatang.com. All the commercials feature guys with shocked expressions, perhaps asking,

'A brand name can be exotic. As long as the target audience can understand it and relate to it'

"How can anyone have such a bizarre name?" One has no idea whether this strategy of registering the brand name has worked – but this is another Smuckers, if you ask me.

If the brand name can represent the business we are in – it will definitely help. 'Toys-R-Us', the largest toy store in the world, clearly states what its business is in the brand name itself. So does Kleenex and Oral-B. The Mach III razor from Gillette is an example of a different kind. If you have a technologically superior product, then that may be a far more significant advantage than a nifty brand name. Speaking of nifty brand names, a young name like 'Yahoo' helps good creative and a cheeky voice asks, "Do you Yahoo?" Yes, man, I do. Would it have gotten through research? The possible scenario in a rundown garage is described by Daryl Travis: "Somebody says, "Hey, dudes, we gotta have a name, so like, let's call it Yahoo!" And the others give their assent with a diffident, "Cool, man". The dot com world threw up a whole range of different and at times, irreverent brand names. Names like Amazon, which have created history. So the question we need to ask ourselves is this: "Whom are we talking to?' So will the brand name be relevant to our target audience? A brand name can be exotic. As long as the target audience can understand it and relate to it. Consider 'Hedonism' as the name of a resort in the Western part of Jamaica. When you are addressing affluent people who have been everywhere and seen everything, then maybe you can intrigue them. Yes, you can be adventurous and you have the support of branding experts like Al Ries who say that a generic brand name does not work. The example of Amazon is given which is vastly superior to say, a 'books.com'.

A brand name that is really catchy is the name 'Jump Start Up', a venture capital fund that was one of our earliest clients. This name, which they had come up with on their own, was different, had a nice ring to it, conveyed the business they were in and gave us plenty of creative scope in the execution of the company's identity, look and feel. All around us are example of tremendously successful international techno-brands with powerful brand names. Names like Intel, Nokia, Yahoo, Amazon... the list goes on. You too have an opportunity to add to the list of success stories.

Get it Right. First time Around

Technology companies would do well to do a quick checklist before they rush to the Registrar of Companies to check the availability of a brand name. How big is your original list before you narrow it down and arrive at a winner? And...

- Is the proposed name unique?
- Is it short and crisp?
- Is it different?
- Does it intrigue?
- Does it reflect the company's core competencies?
- Does it represent the company's current technological thrusts?
- Is the same URL available?

Today, we are part of a global economy. The name must have equal neutrality (if not relevance) in Bangalore as well as in Boston. Many of us are familiar with Chevrolet. Nova was a non-starter (pun intended) in Mexico as 'No va' means 'It doesn't go' in Spanish. Let's ensure that our new venture has the steam of a memorable brand name to take it places.

And what about Identity?

Remember, you don't start a new company every day. Remember too that you don't get a second opportunity to make a first impression. Make a great start to your new venture. Get the brand name right. And that's not enough. Not by a long shot. It's important to get a long-term view on what the company's vision is. What does the company stand for? How is it going to be positioned? Is it going to be a 'knowledge company', a company that is `serious' in outlook and tone of voice or an 'aggressive', 'on-the-ball' company with an attitude? These questions are fairly strategic in nature and need to be addressed sooner than later. The other graphic elements of the identity like the choice of colours and the typeface to be used are also important. IBM has its 'Venetian blinds'. Nike has its celebrated 'Swoosh'. Coke and Pepsi cans are instantly recognisable by their prominent `red' and `blue' (respectively) colours. Whilst legend has it that the Coca-Cola lettering style was done by the accountant, we no longer need to leave such important decisions to chance. There are experts who can portray the identity uniquely, differently and strikingly. But it's also important to remember

> 'The promoter and/or CEO and the senior management must clearly articulate their vision and position'

that ultimately it's your company and not the advertising agency's. The promoter and or CEO and the senior management must clearly articulate the vision and position. Then, creating a design becomes manageable.

We live in "New", "improved" Times

Consumer product companies keep making improvements in their products, their packaging and their advertising. Technology companies in India seem to have a greater reliance on projects rather than products. Their company (very often) is their No. 1 brand. Does the company's identity reflect its current position and standing? Is it comparable with that of the newer kids on- the-block? Or is it 'fuddy-duddy' and dated?

PSI Data Systems, a 25-year old company desired to alter its identity to appeal to young software engineers. It also wished to represent its current vibrancy and sense of aggression. It also had an association with 'Bull' which could change. The new logo represented dynamism, vigour and aggression. The revised identity has been very well-received by the target publics. However, most unfortunately, this company did not have the opportunity to use its new logo extensively as it was taken over by a large group of companies and was merged into its corporate identity.

So Think before you put Mouse to Screen

Corporate identity is more than colours, typefaces and visuals, although all these are important. The more important thing is the 'soul' of the corporation. Just as an individual cannot project himself to be something he isn't, a corporation cannot project itself to be something it isn't. Do research. Soul-search. Be objective. Determine what you can possibly become. Then, to create a unique, differentiated 'look and feel' for your company isn't so difficult.

Give your new venture a jumpstart. Give it the right name. Brand it right. And be prepared to create history.

CHAPTER

Launching Your Product Victoriously

The year: 2001. The air: filled with tension. The cause: The uneasy relationship between TVS and Suzuki. The final straw on the camel's back: the planned launch of the indigenously designed TVS Victor. The result: the parting of ways between TVS

and Suzuki. The new entity: TVS Motor Company. The learning: how to get into a joint venture, and how to get out of it (relatively) unscathed. The future of TVS: glorious.

The relationship of 19 years, which at best could be described as uneasy, had come to its predictable end.

Some viewed the break as a 'desperate pull-out' on the part of Suzuki Motor Company who wanted to enter the Indian market - although they were only allowed to do so in 2004. Some others have highlighted the risks (and if one may add, the heartburn) associated with joint ventures.

But to me, as an Indian and a well-wisher of the TVS group, the more important questions are as follows. Will the stand-alone TVS brand survive? More importantly, will it thrive and be the dominant player that it wishes so desperately to be? And what is the key learning here for other Indian companies who are probably chafing a little at the bit as a result of their own, less-than hunky-dory relationships with foreign partners.

Launching a new product can be exciting, even heady. And yet, it can be hazardous. The odds are stacked against success. According to conventional wisdom, 8 out of 10 new products are failures. Some (optimistic!) pundits claim that failure runs as high as 94%.

Another analyst report suggests that only **ONE** out of 671 new products ideas ever make it to the market and achieves its sale or profit targets. That's a sobering thought. And yet why do companies rush headlong into this minefield? That's because a successful new product can launch a company into a 'different orbit' (to borrow a phrase from the late Dhirubhai Ambani). In the case of TVS Motor Company, it was a real necessity.

The company needed this new product to succeed, to prove a point that Indian design capabilities can hold their own and, to also shore up the bottom line. From an initial off take of 10,000 units a month, TVS Victor in 2002 sold over 40,000 units a month. The rest as they say is history.

How Did it All Begin?

Shakespeare might well have asked, "What's in a name?" but savvy marketers know the value of a brand name and its power in the market place. Microsoft has a brand value of $70.2 billion trailing closely behind a top-ranked Coca-Cola, which has a brand value of $72.2 billion according to a study conducted by the international branding consultancy Interbrand. However, the study found that Coca-Cola, which held the top spot for a second straight year, saw its brand value slip by 13 percent from the previous year.

> 'The consumer looks for constancy and consistency in branding'

The consumer looks for constancy and consistency in branding – that's the ideal scenario. TVS however has been through its own journey of chopping and changing. The brand was initially launched as 'Ind-Suzuki' in 1984. Later, it was changed to 'TVS-Suzuki' in 1987, and the brand continued a trifle uneasily for 14 years.

Name Change or Change the Rules of the Game?

There was also the exclusive use of the Suzuki brand name for motorcycles like Fiero, Samurai and other products. All of these are now promoted as the brand 'TVS', the name being no stranger to this country, least of all to South Indians who used to set their watches by the company's prompt bus service, which began way back in 1911.

The question uppermost in everybody's minds at the time of the parting of ways of Suzuki and TVS was, "Will TVS, which is a household name in Southern India, manage to hold its own with the Hondas, Kawasakis and, the Suzukis of the world? Will it be able to substantially build equity for TVS in the northern and western markets in the absence of Suzuki?"

TVS bought itself time till 2004 before Suzuki entered the market. And Suzuki delayed its own launch in the Indian market and is still to be launched. In those 30 months (a lot in the life of a brand, if used intelligently and strategically,) TVS created its own logo, a new look and feel for its brand and a well-defined strategy with a clear blueprint for its execution. Whilst this is a decision that will have far-reaching implications, it's patently a decision that wasn't taken a moment too soon. As Anthony Robbins said, "It is in your moment of decision that your destiny is shaped". Clearly, the intention was to focus on shaping the TVS brand as a 'victor' in more ways than one. And TVS had to look ahead into the future and create its own destiny without looking over its shoulder at the past.

TVS has had a fair share of product successes in the past. Notable amongst them was the Scooty, whose monthly volume has been as high as 18,000. The significant fact about the Scooty is that it created a new market. The TVS Victor however had a different challenge in front of it. It had to grab share from existing players such as Hero Honda, CBZ and Splendor who were already doing well. And TVS Victor was able to succeed in a crowded market where well-entrenched, well-established players with resources, were active.

Customers or Respondents?

The customer is the source of all business. TVS has historically relied on market research, which involved marketing, but it made a significant departure from the traditional, in this scenario. The Company realized the value of treating people who were being researched as 'users' and not merely as 'respondents'.

What are the practical implications of such a mind set? Discussions with users are unstructured, free-flowing and open. Interviews that are normally 20-30 minutes extend to 3 - 4 hours. In addition, to the marketing team the Project and R&D teams also get an opportunity to understand consumers and receive direct, unfiltered, unedited feedback from them.

The Product and its Future

'You are only as good as your latest design' has become the mantra of the automotive industry, as consumers pile on to manufacturers for new shapes, sizes and engine capacities. And this is where an international partner calls the shots. Honda, one hears has 400 designs, which are ready to be unleashed on the Indian market whilst some others have over 150 waiting to be tested on Indian roads. And the TVS strategy of having a design capability of its own should stand it in good stead in the months and years ahead. The initial TVS mopeds may well have been an adaptation of a moped model called Batavis of Holland but TVS itself has been no slouch in the design department.

The Scooty, XL Super, Spectra and the most recent Victor, have all been developed by TVS. The totally indigenously-developed Victor, perhaps, might have provided the writing on the wall for the relationship with Suzuki. The learning for other joint ventures in a nebulous relationship such as this, is to prepare for the eventuality of a parting.

'You are only as good as your latest design'

TVS did two significant things to foster its design capability. One was a conscious decision to never outsource the design in its entirety, but to develop it in-house and use consultants to validate, test and critique the designs and suitably modify them. In fact, the company uses consultants extensively (someone said they come out of the woodwork). The company has used universities and specialist agencies as well. The strategy of getting the collective wisdom of specialists is an interesting one (if you can manage the relationship). The second is the recruitment of a few key designers from the Indian navy and organizations like Hindustan Aeronautics Ltd. Steve Jobs might well have said that it's better to be a pirate than join the navy but it's also a fact that the Indian navy has traditionally been known for its design capability. And though TVS may feel quite upbeat about its newfound liberation, a lot of its future success will revolve around its ability to turn around new products in as short a time frame as possible.

Research and customer feedback resulted in a superior product design for the TVS Victor, a significant factor behind the product's success. A customer for example spoke of how his stomach 'churned' when he drove the Max 100 R (a then-existing product) on a bad road. He didn't have a buyer's choice, and that set the design team thinking and eventually led to a new concept called 'Synchronized Suspension'. This undoubtedly made for superior riding comfort, in the worst of road conditions with minimum fatigue.

Many of us have had the experience of switching off the engine at signals and facing curses, honks and glares in the 30 seconds it takes for us to come to neutral and start again. The 30 seconds can feel like 3 days! The biggest advantage in the TVS Victor is that you press the clutch, kick-start and move, in any gear. This is because the initial torque of the vehicle is so high that it can be started without going through the routine, mentioned earlier.

The Indian consumer has always valued fuel economy. The Victor's fuel economy is the best in its class. A lot of work went into reducing the friction in the engine without compromising on the power. A significant drop in power makes it uninteresting to customers. So it is the ideal bike and is way more powerful than the competition and also much more fuel-efficient. The Victor gives better power and fuel economy because of the efforts made by the company to overcome the frictional elements.

Stability is always an important attribute in motorcycles. For greater stability the Victor has a square type swing, which is normally used for racing bikes, instead of the usual tubular swing. TVS, which maintains a racing team, used its experience in rallies to good effect here.

Brightness of lights is another important safety factor that customers seek and rarely get as original equipment. The Victor's lights were brighter than the rest and made it easy not only for the rider but also for the oncoming truck traffic to spot it from afar.

The TVS Victor was launched at a very sensible price between Rs.40,000 to 41,000. The pricing was competitive and on par with the market leader at that time. The market was still very price-sensitive around this point. Splendor, a Honda motor cycle, which was priced around this point, actually brought down the price by Rs.1000 and is now at a slightly lower price than the TVS Victor.

The Dealer Sells on Wheels

Companies do understand the role of the product in a brand's success, but the role of the trade in the same scenario though acknowledged publicly, tends to be sub-optimal. The TVS Victor owed a lot of its success to the dealer and an initiative called 'Sales on Wheels'. It is not unusual for dealer salesmen to be trained for the occasion, but this time around, dealers were also taken into confidence by the organization. The entire selling process was revamped. Earlier, if a prospect walked into the showroom, the sales person

'Word-of-mouth has been a powerful factor behind the brand's success'

would explain the working of the vehicle and the customer would take the test ride. This time around, the entire sales process took place while the customer was riding the bike, with the salesman perched on the pillion explaining every fascinating detail and nuance of the bike to the customer. This worked wonders for the brand. For a team of 1600 people (400 dealers and 4 salesmen with each dealer), it was a huge task to be explaining the features of the bike to two lakh customers who walked in, within the first two months. The word spread and of course, word-of-mouth has been a powerful factor behind the brand's success.

"No Problem" to "More Smiles per Hour"

Successful products are not only well-engineered but also well-positioned. TVS has always been known for its impeccable engineering, and as a consequence, the impression with consumers about any TVS vehicle is, that it is a 'No-problem Vehicle'. Actually this observation was featured in one of the earlier pieces of communication for another brand- the Suzuki Samurai. Crucial to the TVS Victor's success is that it is a better-quality product and superior to the Company's earlier offerings while being a cut above the competition. This resulted in a superior riding experience making the rider confident and comfortable while the fuel economy made him smile all the way to the bank. The magic of it all was encapsulated in the tag line: **'More Smiles Per hour'**

Come on Sachin Come on ....

The use of a celebrity is always interesting and for TVS this was the first time ever that a celebrity was being used to endorse the brand. The values of TVS have always been hard work, performance and humility. Sachin embodied all of these qualities. The fact that the TVS Victor had been highly certified by various labs in UK and Japan meant it was a world-class product. And, if it had to be endorsed by a celebrity, who better than a world-class Indian to endorse it? Sachin's understated performance and personality matched TVS Victor's brand values. There was a great build-up to the World Cup and, Sachin's

> 'Successful products are not only well-engineered but also well-positioned'

monumental performance in the 2003 World Cup helped TVS Victor ride higher in the market place than other brands endorsed by the little master.

Catch Me if You Can ....

A measure of TVS Victor's success can be gauged by the fact that the competition has come up with 9 similar offerings to try and catch up with it. The Victor's market share grew from 12.2 to 14.4% but the company has not sat on its laurels. It has launched several promos like the 'Victor Khaseedo Balla Ghumao' programme and has initiated numerous product upgrades which may not be path-breaking but are application-oriented innovations which have reinforced the overall consumer experience, and enhanced the 'no problem' image of the brand and the TVS range.

Think Long - Term

I have been observing the vicissitudes that TVS has been going through over the years and have always admired the company's long-range vision. A vision that enabled it to invest in an extremely modern plant and an excellent test track, coupled with the wisdom to continue in R&D for rapid prototyping, emission requirements, accelerated testing, even when the company was reeling under losses. Add to that the sharply-honed strategy of transforming the once-dowdy dealerships to state-of-the-art retail outlets that are quickly becoming landmarks, the heritage of quality which comes from Sundaram Clayton - another company headed by Venu Srinivasan, which won the prestigious Deming award in 1998 - and you have a company of class and success. And yet, no company can afford to sit back on its past. The greatest challenge for the future will be building recognition for the TVS brand.

> 'The three key rules of marketing are: brand recognition, brand recognition and brand recognition'

'The three key rules of marketing are: brand recognition, brand recognition and brand recognition'. Clearly the three letters TVS ought to have more value than that of a recognized symbol. Particularly, in the more complex and demanding markets of Northern India. The unambiguous focus on the future has to be brand building, for only a strong brand can withstand the onslaught of global majors with deep pockets.

Yes, the Victor for Now

TVS has silenced its critics and the cynics. It has demonstrated that Indian design can compete with global brands and that an Indian brand can compete with the best of the world. Yet, the bigger challenges remain.

- How to brand TVS as a "brand" in every sense of the word?

- How to broad base the portfolio of successes?

- How to correct perceptions that TVS is essentially a "South Indian" brand?

A good start is half the battle won. TVS Motor Company has won its first battle and demonstrated that it has the will and the ability to win the two-wheeler war. Will it pick up the gauntlet, is the red-hot question.

Although TVS Victor had a great launch - around 10,000 units of Victor were being sold per month in 2002 - it faced overwhelming competition from other two-wheeler brands. Bajaj Auto CT 100 and Hero Honda CD Dawn were soon neck-to-neck with TVS Victor. The times however have changed and TVS is now looking forward to the success of new products like Apache and others to keep it ahead of the pack.

"Your brand represents the sum of
all the minds and souls of
every single person that comes into
contact with your company over time"

- *Martin Lindstrom*

BRAND
MANAGEMENT

CHAPTER

A Very Good Paper But a Very Bad Habit

I have been reading *The Hindu* since 1959. I am not unique. Nor am I its most distinguished reader. I belong to a generation that started reading newspapers when it was young. Not surprisingly, many of that generation, like me, took to wearing spectacles early in life. And

not surprisingly, many of us still continue to be fiercely loyal and as passionate about the daily morning newspaper decades later, spectacles *et al*. In retrospect, I wish I had grown up as a conventional, normal news paper reader. I started reading the paper with the sports page then and still do. So I confuse and confound my clever friends in advertising who start with teaser ads on pages 7, 9 and 11 and end with a big, all encompassing ad on page 13 because of my propensity to begin my Monday morning reading, from page 15. Thankfully, my breed – the kind that reads the newspaper backwards - is only a small minority. But the readers of this 126-year-old 'brand', for that is certainly what it is, are no small minority. Today, the paper which never boasts, boasts of a circulation of 9,33,000. copies. And whilst all brands strive for loyalty, that is what the brand has easily acquired over the years from its readers.

Every brand has different facets and every newspaper different sections and each has its own appeal to different types of people: to me sports, to my uncle Carnatic music, to my cousin politics and to my children, entertainment. But the aspect of the newspaper which appealed to each of us, delivered the best within the category. If you read Fingleton you would find others wanting. I remember going to Bombay for my summer holidays in the midst of the English cricket season and agitatedly checking the hawkers and newspapers in Matunga for a copy of *The Hindu*. My life was incomplete, as I am sure is that of my son who studies in Pune today. I missed Fingleton and he misses Ted Corbett, but both of us, and several others miss *The Hindu* if we don't read it. In a sense, the statement of one of the readers during the 'strike days' (when the paper did not come out) might be turned around to say, that *The Hindu* is a pretty good newspaper, which has somehow become a very bad habit (a weakness, if you will) for several thousand people like me.

Today, Bangalore has 10 English newspapers, many of which come home, and I read *The Hindu* first. One of the indicators of a brand's strength is how incomplete the consumer's life is without the brand. I daresay *The Hindu* has to be a very strong brand, for many of our lives would have been incomplete without it. 'The Triplicane Six', as the founding fathers were called, created a legacy that reached further, much further than the original 80 readers who read it in its cyclostyled form.

> 'One of the strong pillars of *The Hindu* brand has been its technology'

One of the strong pillars of *The Hindu* brand has been its technology. I am one of those people who don't really care as much for the technology as to what technology can do for me. In the early days of desktops, my tentative and furtive attempts to guide the mouse into hitherto unexplored pastures provided great amusement to my family members who seemed like 'technowizards' in comparison to the technophobe that I was and steadfastly continue to be. And to me 'printing technology' or its advancement simply meant a better-printed newspaper, pleasant and easy on the eyes.

The Hindu has several technological innovations to its name, whether it was the facsimile edition in the old days or its own private aircraft to reach its readers before the rest of its tribe, today. And this has ensured that the brand has stayed ahead technologically,

> 'Maybe the greatest challenge for *The Hindu* is to make its newspaper a 'habitual choice' to advertisers and agency as well'

forcing its competition to continually play technological 'catch-up' with the paper of my choice, very often with limited, if any, success.

Another feature of successful brands is their ability to endure even as others bite the dust. Three years, or so the sage said, was the trial by fire for a newspaper brand in pre-Independence India. *The Hindu*, as it completes 126 years, has overcome several challenges successfully.

I am a great believer in the power of advertising, to build brands, including media brands. There exists a significant opportunity for *The Hindu* which has been described as 'a national voice with a Southern accent' to communicate. *The Hindu* could tell the truth freely, be humane, contribute to the social good and tell the world about it.

Howard Schultz, the Managing Director of Starbucks, said, *"A brand has to feel like a friend."* And *The Hindu* has a million friends in its readers. And yet any brand has multiple targets and customers. There is the user, the advertiser and the influencer, and recommender, the advertising agency. What do these people feel about *The Hindu*? There is no denying the `halo effect' that some clients and brands feel about their ad's presence in *The Hindu*.

In media, more than anywhere else, change is a process, not an event. And maybe the greatest challenge for *The Hindu* is to make its newspaper a 'habitual choice' of its advertisers and agencies. In its long, illustrious 125-year history, the 'Oracle of Mount Road' has faced several challenges, each one more daunting than the other. It just has to dig into the past to conquer the future. That would be the ultimate interplay of continuity and change.

How do brands continue to sustain their leadership even as generations change?

The era has witnessed tumultuous changes - bartering of editorial for advertising revenue, creeping corruption in journalism and negotiators with whom interaction is depressingly frustrating, avoidable even (given a choice), but inevitable.

Coke, arguably the most valuable brand in the world (notwithstanding the pesticide cloud), has demonstrated this globally. *The Hindu* has demonstrated this, albeit on a smaller, more local scale. But no brand can afford to sit back on its laurels in the continually shifting sands of consumer preferences. Old consumers die, new are born. Newer, younger, more exciting options appear everyday. The backpages of the competition of *The Hindu* are hardly made for healthy family reading. And yet, as lifestyles, preferences and consumers change, a brand too must change.

> 'As lifestyles, preferences and consumers change, a brand too must change'

126 Years Later the Look Changes...

"It takes a lot of courage to release the familiar and seemingly secure, to embrace the new. But there is no real security in what is no longer meaningful. There is more security in the adventurous and exciting, for in movement there is life, and in change there is power" said Alan Cohen.

The story of brands reinventing themselves is not exactly a new phenomenon. Just ask Hindustan Lever Limited. Brands keep changing their packaging, positioning and communication frequently to remain attractive to generations of emerging consumers. A newspaper however, is different to a cake of soap. More so, if the newspaper has the stature and standing of *The Hindu*, every word of which is read, analysed, dissected, very often with the help of a powerful microscope! They do say that brands belong to consumers, (in the final analysis). And a section of the owners (albeit a tiny one) might view the change as sacrilege. And yet the real owners of *The Hindu* must remember that its readers are getting younger, looking for a more vibrant offering and are now in large numbers outside Tamil Nadu. And as John F. Kennedy said, *"Change is the law of life. And those who look only to the past or present are certain to miss the future"*. Clearly this change in *The Hindu* is looking towards the future.

The Essence of the Brand

Very often when we talk of brands we are referring to the elements of the brand: its packaging, its physical appearance, its look and feel and so on. The same applies to newspapers as well. *The Hindu* in its new avatar has undergone a complete 'makeover', which has been masterminded by a designer of repute, Dr. Mario Garcia, who has redesigned no less than 450 newspapers around the world. Starting with the typography, which is more legible, the paper now has an efficient navigation system that makes it easy for the reader, who, in the words of the designer, is familiar with the Internet. The stories are laid out in a manner that

> 'What determines the very essence of a newspaper, and its character, is not the colour of the masthead, the typography or the font size but the editorial'

facilitates the eye movement of the reader. Supplements have a clear colour code – whilst they are from the same family, there is an element of distinctiveness about each one of the daily offerings. The visual elements are better organized with every page having a prominently displayed main photograph. The advertiser does not feel ignored with several more options for advertising to stand out from the clutter. And, last but not least, the space utilization has improved. Clearly a lot of thought, time and effort have gone into these changes.

And yet, notwithstanding the reverence that some of us hold this particular newspaper in, it is perhaps pertinent to remember just one fact. What determines the very essence of a newspaper, and its character, is not the colour of the masthead, the typography or the font size but the editorial. People read a newspaper for news and for its point of view. *The Hindu* has a point of view. And strange though it may seem in today's day and age, it is a paper where the editors (and not the marketing men) seem to call the shots. The average reader does not realize the value of this, but believe me this brings a lot of credibility to the brand. Packaging can only take you this far, whilst one realizes the value of packaging in certain product categories like perfumes, one must remember that what is at the heart of a successful brand, is a really, good product. *"The Hindu is a darn good paper to put it mildly"*, says one of its readers. I might read *The Hindu* for Peter Roebuck's column. And the fact that the column is set in

'Chronicle' a serif font is just an embellishment. Yes, however strange it may seem, it is the message that *The Hindu* carries to its readers that makes it the medium of choice for advertisers and, something to be savoured and read till the afternoon by its loyal readers, many of whom have access to slicker and decidedly more frivolous and flippant offerings.

If Wishes were Horses

If I had the opportunity of being the brand manager of *The Hindu*, I would do a few things

- Take a re-look at the 'Online Edition'. Every consumer has multiple touch points with the brand. I know thousands of my friends who live abroad who religiously go to this site. In fact my 92-year old uncle whose eyesight is failing uses a software called 'Text Up' (if my memory serves me right) to have the column read out to him. The online edition is yet to get the new look of *The Hindu*. If anything, considerable work needs to be done here.

- Take a look at the advertising, which is featured here. Whilst advertising is the very life-blood of the paper, supplements like the 'Golden Jubilee Celebrations of Sivaji Productions' which coincidentally came out on 14th April, take away from the prestige of the paper-not that too much can be done about it. Maybe the newspaper could offer to help one-time advertisers and those of a lower stature, design their ads?

- And finally, I would ask the readers what they felt about their favourite newspaper. What do they like? What don't they like? Design is one thing, but what about the very essence of the paper – its editorial. Is it the same 'outlook' with a new 'look'? Dissatisfied customers may just quietly walk away and that is clearly what the brand does not need.

If one were to borrow an analogy from cricket – the game has changed. Sometimes the purist may be offended by some of the innovations. And yet the game has benefited – whether it is coloured clothing, lights or third umpire interventions. *The Hindu* with its new and improved look is like modern day cricket. It has and will have a few detractors. But the glory of the game continues – innovations et al.

How does a brand contemporise without compromising on its basic value is the newspapers' ongoing challenge? In a quest to get new customers, no brand can afford to alienate its current loyal customers. Yes, 59 per cent of the population of India is below the age of 24. In my desire to reach out to them, I ought not to alienate someone who has been my reader of 59 years.

Who exactly is the *Hindu* reader? Is he a retired executive sitting in a grandfather's chair, savouring his filter coffee in a *dubarah* even as he reads the *Hindu*? Or an active, attractive, middle-aged socialite living on Boat Club Road? A brilliant engineer in NASA originally from Srirangam who reads its online edition or an MCA seeking a job? Probably all of these. For different reasons and sections. And yet the perception (I hope I am wrong on this) is the first. The *Hindu* reader is a 'Mylapore Mama'. Sadly enough, one of the few things that we know is that perception is reality. The *Rolling Stones* magazine addressed this wonderfully with its 'Perception Reality' campaign. So did *The Mail*, and David Abbott's much celebrated 'I never read *The Economist*' headline; below it in small print, was the clincher, 'Management trainee, age 42'). Or this one: 'Is your copy of *The Economist* always AWOL (Abducted while on lunch break)?'

CHAPTER

Titan: Managing a Brand Over Time

Titan is a brand close to Indian hearts. The company was incorporated in 1985 and launched in 1987. It has an integrated state-of-the art plant and several years later is the only profitable watch company in India. Understanding Titan and its performance over the years gives us an insight into managing brands over time and the challenges that come along with the task. If there is one quality that can be singled out from this much-admired Indian company with global aspirations, it would have to be innovation. Simply put, Titan changed the way watches were made in this country. It changed the way watches were looked at in India and changed the way watches were sold.

> 'Understanding Titan and its performance over the years gives us an insight into managing brands over time and the challenges that come along with the task'

A Sleeping Giant

Titan's entry into the Indian market was nothing short of sensational. HMT was a slumbering giant. The Indian consumer was just waiting to be wooed. He didn't really own an elegant watch and was used to wearing a veritable 'tawa' on his wrist.

Titan dazzled the Indian with a range of stunning quartz watches. These were watches you didn't have to go to Singapore to buy. Here, were watches you could confidently gift to your spouse; watches that did far more than just display the time; watches that made a fashion statement... HMT very easily lost share and eventually its way.

The Product

Crucial to Titan's success over the years has been its product range. Whether it was PSI 2000, a multi-functional watch, Fastrack, a mid-priced, large-sized range of casual watches aimed at the youth market, Sonata, a watch for the first time buyer of watches, Steel a contemporary, stylish and modern range, Titan Edge - the slimmest watch in the world, Dash for kids or Nebula, the high-end sophisticated range of solid gold watches...the Titan product range has enabled this company to stand out as the clear leader in the Indian context. Speaking of innovation, the launch of Titan Edge, 'the slimmest watch', made a major difference to Titan in more ways than one. It coincided with a period when the company was going through a slow, unexciting phase (mid - career if you will). The launch of this sophisticated watch (it's so light, you can hardly feel it), was a source of major excitement in the market place and equally within the company. Sometimes, we, who are in the business of marketing, are so focused on the customer that we hardly ever look inwards. It is a source of great motivation to people to be part of the team that produces the slimmest watch in the world. This is exactly what happened at Titan Industries Ltd.

Buyer Profile

The Titan buyer values style and the brand image that the brand brings, is influenced and guided by ads and is willing, to pay a premium. In startling contrast, the Sonata buyer is an active value seeker. He seeks functionality and utility at an affordable price.

The Fastrack buyer on the other hand is younger, seeking variety. He was probably born about the time Titan was launched and has grown up seeing his father wear a Titan watch.

Sonata, a Big Success

The mid 1990's saw an explosion in the watch market as large quantities of Citizen watch movements entered India. Centres like Rajkot with cheap labour spawned a number of Titan look-alikes who (sometimes illegally) were able to offer watches at half the price. It is perhaps fair to say that Titan underestimated the size of this market. Timex, which had a halting start, entered the market in the Rs.1000 price range as a consequence of the youth market remaining static. Then Titan and Timex parted ways. The small brands, to their credit, had created a huge demand and Titan was not really present at the lower price-end. The opportunity for Sonata really came from the steady growth in the budget customer segment. This was a huge market and for Titan, largely untapped. Sonata was launched to attract Titan-inclined customers who were daunted by the price. And in this segment HMT Lalit was doing very well. The company had the strategic option of launching a watch in this lower price range under the Titan umbrella. But to minimize 'cannibalisation' – a process where one product eats into the market share of another from the same manufacturer or company - it advertised itself as 'Sonata from Titan'. The brand promise was definitely 'acceptable quality at affordable prices'. And the most significant aspect was that the brand carried the reassurance of the Titan umbrella brand. The brand filled an important slot, fitted the consumer's wallet and captured the wrists of approximately 30 lakh customers and achieved a turnover of Rs.200 crores in 2000-2001. Once again, the dictum that the vast Indian middle class wants value, reassurance

and a reliable product, was proved. The numbers (as the figure suggests) are in the base of the triangle. Dominant players simultaneously seek volume and value. As an interesting strategy Timex (which has had its ups and downs) seems disinclined to look at this segment of the market. To quote the CEO, "it is for the young and the young at heart". The fact is that Kings, Ambassadors, Presidents, Hollywood stars, Sports persons and the captains of various industries sport Timex watches. Yet, one wonders if this aspiration may be just a step away for the average Indian. Time will provide answers. Sonata is becoming a stand-alone brand and is an integral part of Titan's overall success. Plastics and sub Rs.400 watches are very much on the cards.

The Domestic Watch Market

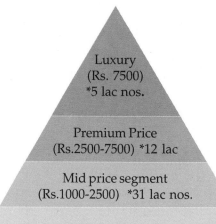

Luxury
(Rs. 7500)
*5 lac nos.

Premium Price
(Rs.2500-7500) *12 lac

Mid price segment
(Rs.1000-2500) *31 lac nos.

Budget segment
(Upto Rs. 1000) *302 lac nos.

Retailing Innovation

Pre Titan, watch distribution was still in the primitive era. Watch markets were concentrated in specific areas and the product display and merchandising were uninspiring. The terms of trade were varying and trade practices unethical. There was clearly the need for a store that was in keeping with Titan's stylish and premium image. It would be a store that would serve as a laboratory for a watch market and watch consumer and offer new levels of consumer satisfaction. Titan was the catalyst of the watch retailing revolution in the country. It set up a multi-tier retailing chain that accounts for

a substantial portion of revenue and watch sale. The multi-tier retailing chain included exclusive Titan show rooms branded 'The World of Titan', a chain of upgraded multi-brands stores for attracting the 'undecided' customers, Time Zone, the multi-brand dealers and Tanishq boutiques. The Time Zones had an interesting philosophy of getting the prominent multi-brand dealers into a long- term contractual tie-up.

At recent count, Titan was being sold in 1800 towns, 7000 outlets. Through 150 exclusive 'World of Titan' showrooms and 136 'Time Zones', 12 million customers have been served.

Titan Advertising

Titan's advertising campaigns have been among the most visible reasons behind its success. The initial catalogue style advertising showcased the all-new, attractive contemporary products. I have seen consumers come to showrooms with a cutting of the ad asking for specific models. The advertising was sophisticated. Mozart's 40th Symphony is widely recalled and actually a property of the Titan brand. In fact, it would be fair to say that Titan's was one of the most recalled advertising campaigns across brands and categories in

> 'Mozart's 40th Symphony is widely recalled and actually a property of the Titan brand'

the mid '90s. Over the years other categories and advertisers have overtaken it in 'share of mind' and 'share of voice'. And whilst the music, relationships, warmth and emotion are all widely recalled they have unfortunately given an element of predictability to the brands' advertising. The current Fastrack advertising which is more the 'In your face' genre of communication, attempts to lighten Titan's (more mature) brand image. Titan Slim on the other hand quite effectively promotes Titan's technological superiority.

Enter Aamir Khan

Aamir Khan, both as an actor and as a celebrity is different from the rest. He seems to choose his endorsements (and if one may add scripts) with care. He doesn't do commercials in droves like Amitabh nor choose products randomly like Shahrukh. Unconfirmed rumours suggest that the original Coca Cola scripts of 'Thanda Matlab' were his. So when Titan chose Aamir Khan as a celebrity it certainly appeared to be that it had made the right choice. More significantly, Titan fired its first serious salvo of nudging people towards matching their watches with their clothes with this commercial. Aamir, with the help of an initially bemused, and finally completely confused assistant, demonstrates how to match a watch with the clothes one wears. The initial commercial undoubtedly created an impact. Helping it was the fact that the company had brought out a superior range of watches offering people the option of upgrading their watch wardrobe. Aamir had clearly brought an edge to Titan advertising that had been missing of late.

Aamir Continues the Magic

Obviously the campaign seems to be working on parameters like brand salience and recall, not to forget market share. The more recent series of commercials feature Aamir, his now well-recognized assistant and a pretty girl trying to buy a dress. Of these, the one I like the most has a script (albeit a bit reminiscent of the scene from the Kamalahasan film 'Pushpak'), which follows the classic Bill Bernbach formula of 'Simplicity, surprise and a smile'. The star-struck girl thinks that Aamir is gifting her a watch, while he is actually buying one to give his mother who has a saree of the same colour as the girl's dress. Notwithstanding its reference to gifting, this commercial too is about matching watches with one's clothes. Titan, it is apparent, realizes that selling concepts like these cannot be done overnight. It is an interesting long-term strategy and Titan obviously has hopes that it will meet with the same success as its strategy of gifting.

Gifting

In the early and late '80s watches formed a minuscule position of the total gift segment. 'Gifting' happened almost accidentally in Titan's case, by way of 3 TV commercials concentrating on 'core' relationships. The focus was on emotions (not products) and was linked with special occasions. In 1995, 'Gifting' moved to 'Anytime Gifting'. Gifting has been a phenomenal success for Titan. It has added 'warmth' to the brand, built a bond with the customer and today accounts for more than 50% of Titan's sales. Gifting is a great idea and it has made a difference to the brand. What new ideas have you come up with recently which have the potential of becoming winners tomorrow".

> 'It has added "warmth" to the brand, built a bond with the customer...'

Bye Bye Titan, Hello Tata

The initial launch of Titan was 'Titan from Tata', and then came 'Timex from Tata'. Interestingly enough, 'Sonata from Titan' has now become 'Sonata from Tata' representing perhaps the closer synergy between the various Tata group companies and the increasing realization of the value of the Tata name. The Tata name which for generations has stood for reliability and trust should stand Sonata in good stead as it reaches out to wider cross-sections of the Indian market.

Challenges or Opportunities of the Future

Notwithstanding its phenomenal achievements in the Indian market, Titan's European foray has hurt its profitability and performance significantly. Thankfully Tanishq seems to be gaining in acceptance and brand recall. But the Titan brand today is facing competition from a better-prepared Citizen, Omega, TAG Heuer and a whole host of global brands. Affluent, middle class Indians who already own multiple watches will perhaps buy one more watch. But it is more likely to be an Omega or a Patek Philipe. Titan is no longer an 'aspirational' brand, for some Indians at least.

Even urban, upscale normally impulsive and usually compulsive shoppers don't buy watches on impulse. I could buy my Louis Philippe shirt for Rs. 1395/- (because someone likes me in checks) but I will not buy a watch on an impulse for Rs. 1295/- even if its elegant face makes my pulse race.

It is all very well to talk about technological innovations in watches. But in my opinion, customers are making cross-category comparisons. All the excitement seems to be in categories like mobile phones and laptops. Prices are dropping and features are multiplying. Are watches losing it?

Titan has 'matured' as a brand. It is no longer 'hot, hip and happening'. Titan may be likened to the Maruti Esteem. In the mid ' 90s the Esteem was the car to aspire for and to own. It was a good looking, well engineered and well-performing car. It also demonstrated to the world that you were successful and had arrived. You stood out from the Maruti 800s and the Zens. And yet where is the Esteem today? Whilst many of the functional attributes of the Maruti Esteem are still relevant, it suffers on image parameters and on perceptual biases. It is no longer 'the must have' car. In fact in the early 90's a Titan watch would have figured prominently in 'The Ten Things That I Must Own'. Today that may not hold good. Titan however is well aware of this problem and is well on the way to solving it since the first step in solving a problem, is an acceptance of the fact that there is one, and then to squarely address it.

> 'The first step in solving a problem, is an acceptance of the fact that there is one, and then to squarely address it'

And What of the Future?

Forecasting, as they say is difficult, particularly of the future! Will Titan succeed in its desire to move people towards ownership of multiple watches and actually prod them into matching them with their clothes? Will people buy into the concept of owning multiple watches from Titan and actually buy some other brand of watch? Will Aamir work equally successfully in markets like Tamil Nadu where even Coke used the actor Vijay? All of these are interesting questions and as cliché-ridden as it may sound, only time will tell. I believe though, that it is safe to predict that Titan will continue to be successful, even in the face of increasing competition. The reason is simple. You can either claim to be innovative or actually be innovative. That means the spirit of innovation has to extend to everything your company does in marketing, product design, advertising and distribution. These are not the best of times to sell Indian watches in India. But Titan it seems is more than equal to the task. And having Aamir Khan on your side is not exactly a disadvantage, is it?

"Colour creates emotion,
triggers memory, and gives sensation"

- *Gael Towey*

CHAPTER *3*

" Baggy green"- a Brand with a Difference

Why can't a cricket team be a brand? Particularly a hugely successful one? The usage and appreciation of branding as a concept have exploded in recent times. From conventional branding of products, services and companies to branding of social organisations to individuals to sports organisations and teams. Yes, branding has come a long way and perhaps the social and cultural climate is just right for team sport. Here is what Sepp Blatter, President of FIFA has to say, *"Team sport is very important today and will be in the future because the family no longer plays the role it should play"*. In fact Blatter's current obsession is developing the FIFA (Federation Internationale de Football Association) brand. He realises that others, like NBA, as a body and Manchester United have been there before and realised that whilst team sport is here to stay, a brand in this environment can't be content with merely staying put. Instead it must continually push itself, renew itself and break new ground, much like the present Australian Cricket team.

I am not sure if this is the opportune moment to write on the praises of the Australians who have just surrendered the Ashes to a resurgent England after 16 years. But you can trust people in advertising to be either way ahead of time (thereby seen as somewhat insane) or way behind deadlines (thereby seen as dull and slow). But the fact of the matter is while to even follow

basketball one needs to be seven feet tall, it has now become difficult to follow soccer because the English football fan has set such high standards of propriety and discipline, that it is impossible to emulate him or to write about the game easily. So I'll stay with cricket and the Australian cricket team with just one submission. People identify with brands that are linked to their dreams. So while I admire and can write about the Australian team. I have a dream: to beat them (again) in India. But we may have to wait for another time for that.

Successful Brands are Consistent

Successful brands are consistent. In quality, a bottle of Kissan sauce has to taste the same anytime, anywhere. Successful brands too, make profits, quarter after quarter, with monotonous regularity. Just ask Infosys. Cricket, one knows, is a gloriously uncertain game and is an even greater leveller. So it is in this context, that the Australian team winning 16 (yes 16) test matches in a row is proof of the brand's consistency. Success is all about winning. Be it in market share or test matches. And in all this media attention and noise it's perhaps worthwhile to remember that Australia is the current world champion of the shorter version of the game as well. Branding is all about experience. And in cricket our greatest achievement as spectators is to say, "I was there". I was there when G R Vishwanath scored 97 not out at Chepauk. I was there when Ramakant Desai yorked Harvey and O'Neill and I was there when Herschelle Gibbs dropped the World Cup vs Australia in 1999. But Australian cricket is bonding

> 'A brand's strength is measured to the degree that a consumer's life is incomplete without it'

spectators to the game in a far more broad-based and scientific way by ensuring that people are there with the game in every which way and not only in the stadium. Limited edition prints of the great moments of Australian cricket are marketed actively and frequently. Memorabilia are available on baggygreen.com au to relive the present through all time. 'Taylor's 334 not out', 'McGrath's 300th Test wicket', 'Shane Warne's 300th wicket', 'The record breakers'...you name it. Yes its possible to say that a brand's strength is measured to the degree that a consumer's life is incomplete without it. My guess is that many teenagers would feel life is incomplete without Pepsi, my mother's life would be incomplete without Sun TV and hundreds of thousands of Australians would lead less satisfying lives without their own favourite brand – the national cricket team.

Successful Brands Innovate

Marketing is all about innovation; companies that innovate win. Whether it's Dell or America Online. Australia was perhaps the first team to have 2 different teams for 2 different versions of the game. So whilst Slater struggles to get into the 'One Day' side and the 'helmeted Iguana' Michael Bevan prays that he will get a test call, the teams keep winning in their areas of respective core competence. The Australians now talk of banishing night watchmen and have more slip catchers than other teams even for One - Day games. They keep challenging the status quo, experimenting and winning. They put the opposition in (and on the spot), more often than any other team I know. And whilst they may still dither in a chase and struggle against England or South Africa they are far more exciting to watch and write about.

The Ugly Australian!

Australian cricketers have few friends outside their homeland. Their brand personality is pretty strong. You have to love them or hate them but you can't ignore them. They single out Artherton or Lara or Sachin aggressively for media attention and mid-wicket sledging. They are proud of 'Baggy Green' and the honour of playing for their country. They neither ask for, nor give any quarter. In 1968 when Bill Lawry's team was playing India at Chepauk, a ball slipped out of Prasanna's grasp while he was bowling. Instead of picking it up and handing it to the bowler, the pugnacious Australian captain struck the stationary ball for four! (Contrast this with our own G R Vishwanath recalling Bob Taylor in the Jubilee Test match against England). Oh yes, the Australians trade stare for stare and swear for swear. They don't give up. And they won't sit back on their laurels, because a place in the Australian cricket team is not guaranteed. Just ask Damien Martyn! And to my mind the brand personality of Australian cricket teams (in general) and this one (in particular) is the differentiator. The other teams (barring India and Pakistan to an extent) are boring and bland in attitude and demeanour. The 'brand feel' is something that you may not like but it's most certainly evident. Losers may brandish comments about 'The Land of Convicts', "What else do you expect?" and the like, but the Australians play a different brand of cricket. Way back in 1977 Kerry Packer's rival series had a tagline. "Big boys play at night". Today the big boys wear "Baggy Green".

Branding is All about Consumers

Where would brands be without consumers? Where would cricket be without spectators who pay to watch them and viewers who pay to view the telecast? The cricket lover is the boss. Australian cricket and the team have recognised this, in no uncertain terms. Whether it is Steve Waugh or Malcolm Speed they recognise that spectators matter. As part of media training, the cricketers mingle with the crowd, pose for photographs and shake hands with tiny tots. Contrast this with our own subcontinent where you may buy a ticket for Rs.3000/- but find your seat taken by a policeman, if you leave it for a few minutes.

The other key aspect is that a brand may have several endorsers serving it in different capacities. But all of them can further the brand - whether one is in the middle of the pitch playing, on top, in the commentators box speaking or laying the surface beneath the pitch as grounds man. Australian cricket has several people providing service to the brand.

I can't but end on this note. Branding is all about the mind and the heart. Simultaneously a brand must appeal to both. We as people tend to look at situations both from the mind and the heart. My mind says that this aggressive, focussed Australian team will continue on to the top. My heart hopes that it is India who will be the World Champions in 2007.

What, are the odds, mate?

> 'Branding is all about the mind
> and the heart'

"Brands are the express checkout
for people living their lives at ever
increasing speed"

– *Brandweek*

CHAPTER

How Cool is Your Brand?

Youth is more than a primary market for goods and services. That is a reality in the 21st century as it was in the last thirty years of the previous century. They are tremendous influencers on other 'family purchasers', and significantly enough, a major future market for a range of products and services. It is a 'no-brainer' to suggest that young people are changing, dramatically and the pattern of change differs from country to country and culture to culture.

Perhaps the first thing that needs to be said is that the generation is no longer the homogeneous market of the seventies and the early eighties. MTV in a study conducted some years ago, classifies youth as follows.

Homebodies –	who are traditional, collective and have low individuality.
Two-faced –	inwardly traditional, outwardly modern.
Wannabes –	those who show-off, are materialistic, desperate to be part of a crowd.
Rebels –	who want to 'think' and 'do' differently but who won't rebel overtly.
Cool guys –	who work hard, play hard, are confident, have strong individuality and are full of aspirations.

They (youth) seem to come in all shapes, sizes and attitudes. So before we market to youth, or anyone for that matter, we need to understand what makes them tick. "You must walk with them in your shoes, not walk on them in your shoes" is sage advice on how to deal with youth.

Wear Your Attitude

What distinguishes the youth of this generation is the fact that they wish to belong and don't wish to stand out overtly from the crowd. They exhibit a strong need to be accepted by their peers and they desire parental approval of their choices.

India is one of the few countries where you can see 16-year-old sons coming into jeans outlets accompanied by their mothers! They also have a strong need to be taken seriously by adults. If you treat the young with less than the seriousness they deserve, then you are failing both as a parent and as a marketer. (There's the adult in me surfacing – judgemental as ever). And yet, winds of change are blowing here too.

> 'If you treat the young with less than the seriousness they deserve, then you are failing both as a parent and as a marketer'

Here's what Aditi Bhatt (16) has to say to other young people like herself:

"Don't live up to anybody else's ambitions or dreams, you are your own person, live your own life".

"Don't go out of the way to be accepted, if people don't accept you for who you are, they are not worth the trouble".

Troubling as these words may seem to conservative parents and marketers, they still can't be ignored. Yes, youth has changed and continues to do so, by the day.

Blame it on The Times

We need to remember that men 'resemble the times' more than they do their fathers. To borrow an example from the U.S., the 'mature' generation (as classified by the Yankelovich report on generational marketing) could readily relate to the Timex watch line, which said 'It takes a licking and keeps on ticking'. That's how our generation's life has been – a lot of adversity seen through patiently. Similarly, our generation needs to understand and realize that it's a different set of kids out there whose experiences and expectations are different from ours. We run the risk of generational myopia if we expect today's 'Generation X' to behave in the way we did as kids. The most important need of the hour is research and understanding the youth mind set. Studies like the MTV research are important beginnings. It's also important to remember that they (youth) see life differently from you and me. They see it in raw terms. Raw is right. For starters, the MTV research says that they don't mind putting their parents in an old age home!

> 'We run the risk of generational myopia if we expect today's "Generation X" to behave in the way we did as kids'

The Latchkey Generation

I grew up in a household with mom, dad, grandma and granddad. My children are growing up with mom and dad. Who will their children grow up with ? Mom OR Dad? One hopes not. And yet, the important thing to remember is that parents are delegating (or is it abdicating) more and more of their decision-making to their children, who are growing stronger in confidence and richer in pocket money, at the same time. As a parent sheepishly once said, "Pocket money is certainly growing faster than inflation". Youth is increasing in importance and we are not merely talking economics here. There is also a significant shift in the growing up pattern of today's kids, which impacts their development and their subsequent behaviour. Many urban kids in India are growing up in households where both mom and dad are working. They let themselves into empty apartments with their own latchkeys. They are confident, albeit, a bit lonely. I guess they tend to be a lot more inward looking. They belong to 'met-opia' (a conjugation of metropolitan and myopia), which seems only to reaffirm their individual importance.

> 'They want to make their own choices, and be treated as intelligent. They want to feel that their opinions count'

'They want to make their own choices, and be treated as intelligent. They want to feel that their opinions count'. And the signal for communicators is fairly obvious. Appeal to the individual, don't aim at the lowest common denominator.

The Net seems a great opportunity. And maybe this generation will buy more from the Net than we ever did.

How Current is your Brand?

Many of us have grown up with brands. The most precious gift I received in 1968 for passing my school exams was an 'HMT' watch, 'Sona', priced at Rs. 110. My son who has long since passed his 10th standard wouldn't be caught dead wearing an HMT watch. Alas, many powerful Indian brands of yore have lost their lustre over the years. They have failed to spot the changes in the market and among consumers. Even more importantly, they have failed to upgrade their brand's image to a contemporary level. I am sure many of you recall dominant brands of your childhood, which are struggling now more than ever, against the onslaught of 'trendier' brands and attractive foreign labels.

The 'icon' of the 80's shrinks in popularity

Levi Strauss, one of the greatest American brands is suddenly in trouble. We, the Woodstock generation, yearned to own just one pair of Levi's jeans in our wardrobe. We eyed the visitors from abroad who flaunted their Levi's with envy barely conceived.

But what has happened to Levi's over the last few years? The Company is closing plants and laying-off thousands of employees. Since today's youth have moved on to trendier offerings like Old Navy, The Gap, Tommy Hillfiger, MUDD, and others. Levi's is considered 'stodgy' by today's western youth. Unthinkable? Sad, but true. "The only one I know who wears Levi's is my dad " says a 16 year-old derisively, reminding me of what Quentin Crisp, a British author and a film critic said way back in 1908. *"The young always have the same problem – how to rebel and conform at the same time. They have now solved this by defying their parents and copying one another."*

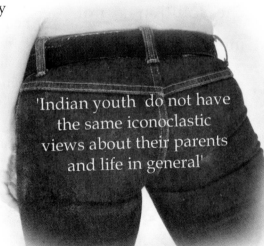

'Indian youth do not have the same iconoclastic views about their parents and life in general'

Arguably Indian youth do not have the same iconoclastic views about their parents and life in general. But what seems fairly clear is that parental approval notwithstanding; they will not align themselves with a 'stodgy' brand.

The Challenge of Being "With It"

In the Indian context, we have had several brands that have been dominant for many years. Brands like BPL, Philips, Godrej and Bajaj are those that we are familiar with. We as customers have patronised these brands and derived a fair amount of satisfaction from using them. Many of our houses have these brands. Our children who are now in their youth have grown up with them.

But in the near future when they fork out their own personal cash to buy one of these products like a TV or a music system, which brand would they buy? The ones their parents bought or a newer, trendier offering? I suspect the latter, unless the brands in question get intimate with today's youth.

> 'The solution is not merely producing 'youthful' advertising. Levi's did that, but it hasn't helped'

The solution is not merely producing 'youthful' advertising. Levi's did that, but it hasn't helped. Some years ago, they ran a new advertising campaign called '*What's true*' featuring teens wearing jeans in ways that fit their personal style. For instance, in one print ad, a dreadlock-sporting youth wears dark, baggy Levi's while standing on a sidewalk with a sign that reads 'Conformity breeds Mediocrity.'

The trick is to understand what kids (I use the word loosely here) want. If they want super, wide-bottom slacks or cargo pants with large pockets on the thighs, give it to them. Then, you are not seen as 'Dad's generation' but today's.

I used to diligently watch a program called 'Rangoli' on Doordarshan, the Indian national TV network, every Sunday morning. Whenever a song from a black and white film appeared, my son would turn to me and say, "Your favourite song, Daddy." Sad but true; it has to be black and white to be "Daddy's favourite". Is your brand 'black & white' in a young world of vibrant, kaleidoscopic colours?

A Company on the *'Fastrack'*

Titan, India's most successful watch brand was launched in 1987 and was an instant success. Titan, in 1987, was aimed at young, upwardly mobile executives. We bought into their concept of gifting and the ownership of multiple watches. Today, many of us own multiple watches (presumably Titan). What about our children, our nephews and our friends in the age group of 16-25? To them, Titan means a solid, reliable, high quality brand. Could it also mean 'fuddy-duddy'?

And the reality is that today's emerging customer is younger, trendier and guided more by his peers than his parents in his choice of brand. And this is where 'Fastrack' comes in. The images are 'cool' whether it is a mint, a cologne or a girl in a bikini and it's reinforced by a line which says 'Cool watches from Titan'.

'Today's emerging customer is younger, trendier and guided more by his peers than his parents in his choice of brand'

I believe that strategically it's a major departure - a conscious decision to move away from what Titan originally stood for, and focus on current trends. The brand properties continue, the signature tune is cheekily whistled and behind it all is the reassurance of the Titan name. The purist might question the validity of a multi-brand strategy but that argument can only be resolved in the market place.

I suspect it will be resolved in Titan's favour. Let me also reiterate that advertising is only one (important) part of the brand story. The product offering too is young. Strangely enough, Citizen had shot itself in the foot in India, at least in the launch phase, with a chunky product range that belongs to my father's time. The brand has thankfully, regained lost ground since then.

Youth in India is a mass niche and to quote from a recent seminar, "They (youth) have never wound a watch, dialled a telephone or plonked the keys of a manual typewriter. But they think nothing of burning a CD and downloading music off the Internet and... Yes, we need to get into their heads and understand how they think".

And more importantly, we need to think about our own brands. How appealing are they to today's youth?

Be Quick. Be Friendly. Be Gone

Many of us tend to lecture our children. I guess it comes with the territory, if not with the age. And yet, one needs to be reticent.

Just observe the expression on your teenager's face when your spouse lectures him or invite her to observe him when you rave and rant. That will give you an important pointer. Lecture only if you wish to lose your audience. Treat your young audience with respect and intelligence. And as equals! It's so easy to sound authoritarian or judgemental (and so boring in the bargain). Another important fact to be borne in mind whilst communicating with youth is to remember that their attention span seems to extend to mere nanoseconds. This makes communicating with them all the more challenging. And as Janet Kestia, Creative Director, Ogilvy and Mather says, *"They have a great bullshit meter, and they are very critical of advertising".* I am not sure if our youth is as critical or as cynical towards advertising. And yet, I am quite sure that we shouldn't communicate in stereotypes while talking to teens. And whilst we are on the subject of communication, lets not forget that "word of mouth" is perhaps the strongest endorsement for many products and services for young people. In a study conducted in Canada amongst students – 40.2% of the students polled, said they trusted 'word-of-mouth' over all other forms of advertising. Sounds familiar?

Catch'em Young

"One of the very advantages of youth, is you don't own any stock in anything. You have a good time and all the grief and trouble is with the other fellows". We are the 'other fellows' who could easily come to grief if we don't recognize the opportunities that the youth market presents. The youth represents a growing market. Today's niche can become tomorrow's mainstream. And savvy marketers who catch them young and hold on to them despite their

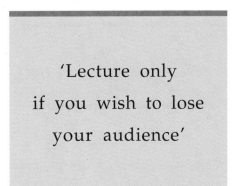

'Lecture only
if you wish to lose
your audience'

idiosyncrasies will reap enormous benefits. Imagine the lifetime value of a kid who opens a bank account at the age of 18 and stays with your bank for the next 50 years! As Lisa D'Innocenzo says, *"The belief is that if a brand can successfully seduce young consumers, it can forge a lifetime relationship with them"*. Just get them before your competitor does!

Youth can be exciting, exhilarating even. And yet, one wonders if marketers share the same excitement about marketing to youth. "Youth is too fickle", says a hardened marketer. "Its like entering a mine field" say a battle-scarred veteran. "How many successful youth brands are there in India?" asks another. The 'teens' is a funny phase. It's something that you are anxious to get into and equally desperate to get out of.

There is a point of view that there is a lot less heartburn and a lot more stability in targeting and marketing to 25 - 34 year olds for instance. But you need to be blind to ignore the sheer magnitude of the youth market, particularly in the Indian context.

India is a young country with 11 crore people in the age group of 15-19 years. Another 10 crores are between the age groups of 20-24, whilst a whopping 72% of our massive population is below the age of 35. So, the obvious inference is that a marketer ignores this huge potential at one's own peril. But neither can we ignore the nuances of this non-homogeneous mass and its preferences. The world over, marketers are grappling with the tremendous challenge and opportunity that is simultaneously being provided by this generation. Automakers in the West for example, are targeting youth aggressively. What should we do here in India to harness the enormous potential of youth? What works and what doesn't?

> 'Today's niche can become tomorrow's mainstream'

So what's the solution? A refresher course, perhaps?

On our young consumers: Not on the balanced scorecard but on how kids don't want a balanced life!

On vocabulary as well: "For heaven's sake, not cool!"

On haunts which thankfully seems to be the 'Coffee Day' outlet than the pub.

On their music, as alien it may sound to you.

'But neither can we ignore the nuances of this not so non-homogeneous mass and its preferences'

On their outfits, as outlandish they may appear to you.

On the programs they watch, as bizarre they may look at first viewing.

On their vocabulary when MSN bumps them off during chats.

On the lyrics of the music they hear which could make you blue in the face.

On their views on their parents and teachers, however difficult it may be to stomach.

Well, in management terms, we always say, "Walk the talk and talk the walk" don't we? Let's walk in step with today's young consumers if we can. Otherwise the generation which cut its teeth on 'marketing myopia' will find itself suffering from 'generational myopia'!

We can't look at today's youth with our biases, prejudices and blinkers of yesterday.

I heard another interesting comment from a different teenage girl who was explaining her mother's preoccupation with studies to a friend thus, "Mama is losing it", she said almost with pity. Let's not lose it. Then, we won't even deserve their pity.

M&M or Eminem

"M&M is truly AWESOME", gushed my friend's sweet sixteen-year old daughter. I stared at her, a bit perplexed. The only M&M I knew was Mahindra & Mahindra. And living as I do amidst brilliant kids, I thought here's a budding stock analyst predicting a winner. Unfortunately, I was wrong and I can hear you saying "As usual!". Well, she was referring to "Eminem", the current hot rapster whose name is Marshall Mathers. Does Linkin Park ring a bell? Or 8 Mile? Well, if it doesn't and if you are in marketing, you have a problem.

Let Me Ask You a Question

How old are you? Okay, maybe it isn't the most tactful question but it's still worth answering. If you are heading the marketing of a company, you are probably in your mid-forties. And if you are the CEO, you are probably closer to 50. You probably just celebrated the 'Thees Saal Baad' of your engineering college and the 'Pachees Saal Baad' of your management school. And there lies the rub. The customers for a whole lot of products and services in this country are young. 57% of the Indian population is below the age of 24 (IRS 2002). 24? When were you 24? I for one can't remember. So how am I going to sell products and services to today's youth to whom Chyna (no, I do know my spelling) is one of the divas of the World Wrestling Entertainment. And young American males watched more of her in 2000 than football! Now who is the young Indian watching? We need to understand this. And understand it fast.

CHAPTER

Yeh Dil Mange "More Consistency"

Last week, three of us were driving to Mangalore. A red Maruti van with tinted glass, blaring A.R. Rehman music with 2 big stickers at the back with the names Rahul and Smitha overtook us in a swirl of dust. We started playing our usual (brand) guessing game.

"Rajni style dark glasses" I said.

My Creative Director said, "Thick gold chain with a locket" (He actually said pulinagam in that wonderfully simple (!) language Tamil).

"Red T-shirt with both buttons open" said my Vice President.

"Gold bracelet" said I again.

Soon enough, we overtook the red Maruti van. Our anxious, eager and impolite stares were rewarded by the sight of a gentleman who matched our predictions, word for word. All our predictions and suppositions were based solely on the associations created by the red paint of the car, the music, the tinted glass and the stickers. The same associations apply to brands and their usage as well. What images come to your mind when you picture a Harley Davidson rider? And what images come to your mind when you think of a guy in a pony tail or a guy wearing a gold earring? (Agency types kindly bear with me!) Brands too, can become identifiers. Hence brand image and personality become extremely important in what is turning out to be a largely undifferentiated world. The brands people use (sometimes flaunt) send out strong signals of their preferences and personality type.

What sort of person in your opinion would wear an Armani suit, a Patek Philippe watch and drink Glenfiddich? And who buys pre-ripped jeans or brand new jeans with 'buckshot wounds'? Probably someone from a different planet but the key fact is you are actually saying a million things without saying a single thing, by choosing the brands you do. We rely more and more on brands to sum up others in our judgement.

All the World's the Same

Today, there is a proliferation of products across categories. Technology is another reason for similar-looking, similar-performing products. And technology can easily be replicated by the competition. We have entered the era of 'similarity marketing', if you will. So, it is important to recognise that in a world of parity products, the brand's personality may be the only factor that separates it from the competition. The other point to be borne in mind is that, when a purchase decision involves (or perhaps even depends on) an emotional response, a likeable personality might well provide that necessary emotional link. Keith Reinhard, a former copywriter and the chairman of DDB Needham says, *"When a customer identifies with the personality of a product and finds its behaviour attractive, he transfers that personality and behaviour to himself by buying and using that product. It's like putting on a badge and wearing it proudly".*

Change For the Sake of Change?

Agencies love to be different and create work that is different. Work, that stimulates and wins awards. 'Breakthrough' work that pushes creative teams to the brink. And yet, is change necessarily a good thing? Way back in 1955 at the AAAA conference, David Ogilvy asked, *"Have you noticed that Winston Churchill has been careful to wear the same ties and the same hats for fifty years – so as not to confuse us?"* True, it would be difficult to imagine Winston Churchill in a polka dot tie or Gandhiji in nifty sunglasses. Brands too are much the same. Agencies, in their anxiety to be creative and challenge the status quo run the risk of throwing the baby out with the bath water and losing some long-term brand properties. It's difficult to imagine, Liril without a girl and water, Vimal with a slogan different from 'Only Vimal', Rasna without an 'I love you Rasna', or Titan without the music track.

Every brand has properties and a tone of voice, which add up to personality. Could be the colours, the props, the jingle or anything which customers recall from your brand because it lends a dimension to its personality. Brand properties are built over time but lost easily. Perhaps the greatest threat is when clients change agencies. The agency has been chosen to bring about change and goes to town. After all, it must justify its appointment. I have no quarrel with that, but objectivity is called for in brand management and the brand must be viewed seriously. Norman Berry, Creative Director at Ogilvy & Mather, believes that the values in many brands have just been tossed away. The case in point is the pink rabbit in the Duracell commercial which was resurrected with great success after several years. If the audience didn't forget the rabbit, why should the agency? He went on to say, *"I believe we should resist the temptation to change great campaigns."* It is astonishing that a manufacturer turns over the brand, the most valuable asset he has, to a brand manager without telling him he has handed him an investment of millions of dollars worth of value spent in a franchise built over years with his consumer. Further, it is astonishing that he will allow that same person to change a campaign because it isn't `his'. It is equally ridiculous for an advertising agency to allow a 'new creative group' to do the same thing. What

'Which properties and associations can add to its personality and make it more attractive to our target consumers?'

nuggets lie within our brand waiting to be polished? Which properties and associations can add to its personality and make it more attractive to our target consumers?

Personality Differentiates a Cola

Pepsi is a classic case of how a brand with common features and benefits can set itself apart by personality. Coke in the 1970s was perceived as conservative, stodgy, republican, old and such whilst Pepsi on the other hand enjoyed an image of youth, fun, vibrancy and adventures among other personality traits. The advertising is creative and rewards the viewer. And yet, each and every piece of communication adds to the overall image of youth and youthfulness. Like the 'Shady Acres' commercial where a young-minded octogenarian man dances holding a can of Pepsi to rock 'n' roll music with a fiery septuagenarian woman, even as younger, bored and boring people play Bingo and drink Coke. It's not how old you are, says Pepsi, but how young you feel. (Just ask Amrish Puri who demonstrated this truism so precisely). Further, youth is long term. It demonstrates that every brand has a kernel. In this case, youth as the new generation and 'Generation Next' symbolizes the truth of the tone of voice, which adds to personality, which is 'youthful' and 'irreverent'. But this does not fetter creativity. If anything, the discipline fosters creativity and makes it more focussed, and youthful.

Building a brand and creating a personality is long term. But this should be done without losing sight of the present. As Jack Welch says, *"Anyone can manage in the short run and anyone can make money in the long run. The truly great ones are those who can manage both these simultaneously"*. The same applies to brand management as well. We live for today, even as we worry and plan for tomorrow.

How long-term is your brand thinking?

CHAPTER

Celebrities? Yeh Dil Mange "Less"

He brushes his teeth with Colgate toothpaste. He drinks Boost, which is the (worst kept) secret of his energy. He loves this beverage so much that he sometimes has a Boost moustache. He occasionally dips some Britannia biscuits into his beverage. He goes on to the field wearing Adidas shoes and carrying an MRF bat. During the drinks break, he swigs Pepsi in the company of Amitabh, Shah Rukh and his old schoolmate Kambli. He is the proud owner of a Benz but drives a Fiat Palio. It is

> 'How many people's expectations can he realize and what is perhaps more relevant to us, how many diverse products can he simultaneously endorse?'

rumoured that he is coming down in the world as he is contemplating riding a Suzuki motorcycle. He used to watch cricket on a Philips TV, but now seems to have given up, a commentary perhaps on the manner in which his teammates are playing. When he wants pocket change from the stock market, he logs on to home trade. If he wants to be hospitable to the Aussies (after first mauling them) he treats them and charges it to his Visa card. When he wishes to speak on his mobile phone (definitely not to bookies) he uses his Airtel Magic card. And if he feels like tyre tampering, he does it to his MRF ZVTS. And you don't need to be Harsha Bhogle to know that we are talking about Sachin Tendulkar, the darling of India, the man who will score more international runs than anyone else, the man who will earn more money than any other cricketer despite a weak rupee, the man who scored 35 test hundreds and the man who will endorse more products than any other cricketer. Yes, not only cricket-loving India but advertising India seems to be besotted with our 'little blaster'. Remember the Amul ad line 'Tendu, Ten don't'. That is as much a reflection of the dominance of the great batsman, as much as a reflection on the (often) hapless nature of his teammates. Yet, how many people's expectations can he match and, perhaps more relevant how many diverse products can he simultaneously endorse?

Mirror, Mirror on the Wall, Who is the Most Exposed of them All?

There has been divided opinion on the real value of using celebrities. As an expert said, "Celebrity endorsements are the recourse of someone who is bereft of ideas". True, there is an element of reality in that statement but perhaps it is an extreme view. Yes, brands like Lux, Pepsi and Nike have had incredible success using celebrities as part of their overall long-term strategy. And therein lies the rub. Many brands and brand managers do not seem to have a long-term strategy - celebrity or otherwise. One remembers Mayur suitings signing on Shah Rukh in his fledgling days and found to their chagrin that they were unable to afford him as he grew in both stature and price. Britannia in their early days seemed to be in favour of 'fringe cricketers' who were on the verge of becoming rich and famous like Sadagoppan Ramesh, Kanitkar and Robin Singh - an interesting strategy that can lead to disproportionate gains if the cricketer performs big time.

> 'Many brands and brand managers do not seem to have a long-term strategy - celebrity or otherwise'

To go back to this strategic decision of hiring a celebrity or not, one needs to carefully examine the costs and benefits of signing on a celebrity. And to add to the excitement, no one can predict the form and future of stars. When MRF signed on Steve Waugh, he was the batsman you would want to play for your life. A few months later, he no longer featured in the all-conquering Australian one-day side. Not for nothing did Terry Jenner refer to the Australian selectors (at one time) as a bunch of jokers!

Thankfully, for MRF, Sachin is going great guns leading us to wonder whether a company can balance its risk by having more than one celebrity. A strategy should have a contingency plan, as the fortunes of a company are dependent on or linked to the vagaries of people like selectors who often seem to belong to another planet. Imagine dropping Anil Kumble! And lack of form is just one of the imponderables. What happens to celebrities like Hansie Cronje, Mohammad Azharuddin and O J Simpson? Does your brand need that sort of undesirable attention and association? And today, one of the biggest threats facing sports celebrities is the very real threat of injuries that frighten, curtails and very often brings sporting careers to a premature end.

A few Questions worth Asking

Before we rush to sign on celebrities, it's worth asking a few questions.

Q. At what stage of the life cycle is the brand in? A celebrity can create tremendous awareness, rapidly. On the contrary, if you are a market leader, you wonder what a celebrity can do to your brand. A pre-KBC Amitabh was perhaps not the ideal choice for BPL TVs, which was already a market leader.

Q. Does your brand's personality fit the celebrity's? We can see a perfect fit between an action hero like Dharmendra and Bagpiper Whisky (or is it Club Soda). On the other hand, it is a struggle to find a match between a balding, bespectacled Harsha Bhogle and a Timex that takes a licking and keeps on ticking. I am certain that Harsha Bhogle is an excellent ambassador for Indian cricket, but I wonder if he is an equally excellent ambassador for Timex.

Q. Is a single celebrity endorsing multiple products of your company? It could lead to dilution of his credibility and diffusion of his identity.

"The number of products a celebrity endorses negatively influences consumers' perceptions of endorser credibility and likeability, as well as attitudes towards the ad." (Tripp et al 1994).

Q. Next question what is the purpose of the celebrity in the ad? Can he act, emote and dance? Saurav Ganguly's dancing for Hero Honda is extremely entertaining, but for all the wrong reasons. Sachin today seems to be a lot more relaxed in front of the camera in startling contrast to his early days. And I just hope that celebrities should reject scripts like film stars (claim to) do. The net result would be better commercials.

Q. Continually research your offering. What do consumers feel about your brand/celebrity? Do they see a fit at all?

Proceed with Care

It is relevant to look at this whole situation of celebrities carefully. It is important to remember that celebrities when used expertly can make a big difference to your brands' visibility and recall. And yet, they do cost you...sometimes an arm and a leg. Have you considered the costs and benefits? Have you considered other options? Have you considered other 'associations' or 'properties' that can be more effective? 'Lalitaji' used by Surf, was one of the most recalled continuing characters and became a celebrity in her own right. The 'Maharajah' as a mascot symbolized Air India's rich tradition, heritage and values. The moppet in the Amul butter ads is an endearing aspect of the brand that strikes a chord in all of us. Whilst evaluating strategy, do not merely reject the strategy because it is expensive, but look hard at what benefits you can get from the strategy. And one last word: reject the obvious strategy! And as difficult as it may be, think long-term.

> 'Whilst evaluating strategy, do not merely reject the strategy because it is expensive, but look hard at what benefits you can get from the strategy'

"A distinctive identity is worth nothing
unless you can protect it"

Roberta Jacobs - Meadway,
Ballard Spahr Andrews & Ingersoll

CHAPTER

Looking For a Celebrity? Look Outside India

Care for an interesting tidbit? Remember the cricket world cup in South Africa in March 2003? LG, one of the main sponsors of the world cup had run an interesting campaign titled "Cricket first" featuring all fourteen captains of the participating countries. A whopping, consolidated amount was paid to these fourteen captains. Rather than getting into Rupees and paise, let's just call this amount 'x' (after all the

> '...guess as to what Saurav Ganguly was paid and what the thirteen others were paid?'

nation which discovered the zero knows that beyond a certain limit, it has no value - at least for middle class Indians like you and me). Now hazard a guess as to what Saurav Ganguly was paid and what the thirteen others were paid. Well, our inimitable 'Prince of Kolkata' was paid .5x or 50% and the rest of the 13 captains – Ricky Ponting, Sanath Jayasuriya, Nasser Hussain, Stephen Fleming, Waqar Younis, Heath Streak combined got the remaining .5x or 50%.

And consider this: India before it started its campaign was a rank outsider, though our subsequent performance was outstanding. Now this is great news for our self-esteem, a pat on the back for our tremendous marketing abilities and a glowing tribute to our cricket-crazy millions who offer a captive audience and are also willing to buy the products their heart-throbs so readily endorse. The marketer is happy, the TV channel is happy, the celeb's marketing agency is happy and the advertising agency is happy. So what's the problem? Oh yes, there's a problem alright. And the problem boils down to the 0.5x or 50% I referred to earlier. Although one may argue that our cricketers provide as much enjoyment as David Beckham and Tiger Woods and should be paid like them, I hold a contrary view, purely on economics and affordability.

There is no getting away from an important fact - we in this country are cricket mad. (What a euphemism!). Cricketers enjoy top billing, command viewership and generally call the shots. They also seem to belong to ambitious (and possibly avaricious) marketing agents who seem to be hawking them - as if they are products - to sell brands. And the biggies (read MNCs) with deep pockets, are pushing the prices of celebrities way beyond the reach of many advertisers and brands. Whilst celebrity endorsements have their protagonists and detractors, ultimately it is a simple, cost-benefit analysis. How much does the celebrity cost? And how much will the brand benefit from using the celebrity?

> 'Whilst celebrity endorsements have their protagonists and detractors, ultimately it is a simple, cost-benefit analysis'

Let's assume that celebrity endorsements have both successes and failures, though not in equal measure. A judicious and creative use of celebrities as a long-term strategy can make a significant difference as Lux and Nike will tell you. Some of the most celebrated sportsmen of all time have been proud to endorse Nike. There is a method to this madness. Nike the ultimate 'attitude brand' chose celebrities who had an attitude of their own. They chose Ilie Nastase (appropriately nicknamed 'nasty'), the foul-mouthed. Jimmy Connors, the racket-throwing McEnroe, the irresponsible (and now, domestically-tamed) Agassi and the mercurial Shane Warne. Each one of these men, is more than a great sportsman. He is also a character who can thrill, amuse and shock. A perfect attitudinal fit with the brand. Sadly enough, other celebrity endorsements, are neither as judicious or as appropriate. And more worrisome is the fact that celebrities cost money, very often lots of money. That takes me on to the next big opportunity.

Is there an opening to capitalize on this madness that we have for the game, without losing an arm and a leg in the bargain? I believe there is. I refer to the usage of Brett Lee by Timex. Brett Lee is the emerging 'White Lightning'. He is young, sends female pulses racing and batsmen scurrying for cover and can play the guitar with elan. He gets tremendous visibility for Timex. He to my mind delivers value for his celebrity tag. And if the past is any indication, I suspect foreign players will cost less. I remember in 1987, Alan Border and Vivian Richards were each signed on for pocket change by Reliance Industries Ltd. And AB (as he is fondly referred to) proudly held up the World Cup at the Eden Gardens 18 years ago. The cricketer with the 'looks of a winner' as the ad said, actually was the unlikely winner. Indian sponsors have flirted with foreign sportsmen in the past: whether it was the disgraced Hansie Cronje or Glenn McGrath or more recently, Steve Waugh, who will also have a lot more to do with India in his new role as tourism ambassador.

I am sure the doomsayers will gloomily predict , "Everyone loves to hate the Aussies", "What if Brett Lee breaks the bones of a few Indian batsmen?" "What if Brett Lee is hammered like Shane Warne?" Well that's the wonderful thing about the future, isn't it? You just can't predict how it will pan out. And yet, if the media coverage for the launch of Timex with Brett Lee as its brand ambassador is any indication, the American company is on a good wicket. When India plays Australia, I will be solidly rooting for the 'Men in Blue', make no mistake about it. But I shall scan the Aussies and Kiwis and look for more exciting, better-looking, more charismatic celebrities, particularly since they will cost a whole lot less.

'Although one may argue that our cricketers provide as much enjoyment as David Beckham and Tiger Woods and should be paid like them, I hold a contrary view, purely on economics and affordability'

CORPORATE
BRANDING

"Any CEO who cannot clearly
articulate the intangible assets of his
brand and understand its connection
to customers, is in trouble"

- *Charlotte Beers*
US Under Secretary of State

CHAPTER

Is Your Company A Brand?

I am a raving fan of advertising. I believe advertising makes the cash register ring. I strongly subscribe to the view that advertising builds corporate image. And yet over the last few months, I have realised that advertising is not the only route to fame and fortune for a company. There are other ways

> 'Advertising is not the only route to fame and fortune for a company'

to build a brand. And, the company which enabled me to widen my horizons is a company that was ten years ago, unknown and unsung. Today this company is a leader, which symbolises the new breed of Indian companies. A company called Infosys, which is the company of choice to investors, employees, suppliers and customers; and which occupies a position easier to aspire to than to actually achieve. It is a position attained by smart strategy and not by glitzy advertising.

Is Advertising the Key to Corporate Recognition?

There is enough evidence to suggest that a strong corporate image helps technology companies to get into the considered set of prospective customers. A strong company image also helps the company charge a price premium for its products and services. It's hardly surprising that companies, which advertise regularly, and not in fits and starts, will have better stock prices. The interesting fact is that Infosys has shown the world that you can have a tremendous corporate image without any corporate image advertising whatsoever. I think (barring its recruitment advertising)

the only advertising the company has ever embarked on was several years ago to announce its public issue. Very simply put, Infosys has discarded the tried and tested advertising methodology and taken the public relations route to recognition and consequent riches. Successful people in companies are those who consistently challenge the status quo and come up with solutions that are different but potently effective. Pioneers, they say, usually get arrows in the back, but on occasion they strike gold. Well not only Infosys, but the pioneers who invested in the early days of Information Technology in the country, have since struck gold.

What's a Brand?

Enough esoteric theories have been espoused on the power of brands and the difference they make to people's lives and corporate bottom lines. Yet, it is possible to approach the question of brands and their success from a more down-to-earth, practical level. 'A brand is built when other people talk about it'. This is probably what is most evident from the Infosys example. Instead of the company making manufacturer's statements, the press has written about the companys enhancing credibility and in the bargain, its shareholder value.

The Strategy of a Winner?

A strategy, someone said is a careful devised plan to murder the competition. I am not sure who Infosys has murdered, but its

> 'A brand is built when other people talk about it'

carefully planned and executed strategy on image building is something that the competition might well learn from. Here's what I, for one, have learnt:

- Don't go to the press or analysts only when you need them; build an on-going relationship with them.

- The more you tell, the more you sell.

- Transparency can't be a mere slogan – it must be a way of life. This applies equally to corporate culture as it does to public relations.

- Accessibility (to the press) is important. But even more important is being articulate. Have a vision and communicate it – coverage will follow. Public relations is a senior management function.

It's better to be proactive than to be reactive. A few years ago, when Infosys lost the GE business, the company went to the press, was upfront about the scenario, and talked about it honestly. It outlined its strategy to counter the loss of business. A potential PR landmine was diffused.

It also helps if you have a social conscience. Companies operate in a given environment and the Indian environment has enough poverty and destitution around it. For a corporation to allocate a small percentage of its profits to social causes is laudable, and well worth writing about. It is newsworthy and does not make for shallow reading. Building a civic character, not just

> 'Building a civic character, not just a business character, in the company's work ethic can build interest, respect and loyalty'

a business character, in the company's work ethic can build interest, respect and loyalty. The interesting thing about Infosys is that the promoters have contributed their personal cash to social causes. This too has benefited Infosys.

The key is performance. Obviously you will get written about when you consistently perform well. If your management is thoroughly professional and embraces a global outlook, it would definitely help. Infosys is a classic example of like-minded professionals with a dream to make an impact not only in India but throughout the rest of the world as well.

PR is all about story angles. A series of 'firsts' from Infosys has given journalists differing angles – whether the results are displayed in a CD ROM format, high quality annual reports or views on corporate governance.

And yet, it is probably important enough to say that the same PR strategy may not deliver equal success for companies producing fast moving consumer goods or those who have a diverse product line.

And What About the Future?

The future as we all know is unknown and at once challenging. We do not have any proprietary data to predict its behaviour. Companies and brands might well have to redefine strategies even if they have been successful in the past. Strategies which will enable them to manage, cope and lead. While Infosys may clearly be geared to meet the challenges of the future, a few concerns must be stated:

'PR is all about story angles'

The answers to the future are not necessarily in the past.

Being open and transparent with the press is a wonderful strategy as long as things are going well. If unexpected events take place they might also get 'larger than life' mileage. Infosys is today, an image leader. And, journalistic reputations are built by taking pot shots at leaders.

Success is all about the power of the individual, and the value of the team, which shares a dream. Today's Infosys employee could well be different from the employee of the early '90s. The 'what's in it for me?' attitude, money, stock options and other monetary considerations come into the picture. The new Infosys employee is joining a leader. And that's a far cry from the company's situation of the early '90s. So communicating the shared visions and dreams of the company, internally, is key. A software company's assets go down the elevator every day and (hopefully) return the next day. The focus for Infosys in the future might well be internal communications. Attracting, recruiting and retaining talent will be crucial.

Infosys has withstood several challenges in the last decade. Something tells me that this company will be equal to the challenges that the future will throw up as well.

> 'A software company's assets go down the elevator every day and (hopefully) return the next day'

Is YOUR Company a Brand?

I believe that one can classify companies into three distinctive image types:

1. Companies that talk to the press about what they are going to do, before they actually do it. New companies fall into this category. And if the slew of promoters from Hyderabad that marketed granite and aquaculture during the '80s are any indication, this isn't a worthy classification type. Theses are companies that are anxious to **'inform'** about themselves before they are ready to even think of **'performance'** One wonders where those companies which sprung up out of nowhere, are today.

   Is your client keen to **'inform'** before he/she **'performs'**? Then your antennae, as a PR agency, must be up.

2. The second category is one we are all too familiar with. This is the category of companies that perhaps do not even use a PR agency. These companies have a good track record, are dependable but their management is low profile and their image is exceedingly low-key. They suffer from a multiplicity of problems, like the ones expressed below.

   "Why should I talk about my success, others should".
   "I don't want to reveal my strategies".
   "I can't be as loud as XYZ".

These are companies that are wary of the press. By and large, they don't get the credit that is justly due to them. Naturally, this impacts their image and their stock price negatively. Nor is the best talent attracted to them. Things could easily be better.

3. The third category is what one would describe as a 'dream client'. These are clients that perform and then keep the media and their publics well informed of their performance. The name that comes to mind in this category, without much prompting, is Infosys. The Company's success, its first, and several achievements have been given to the media and, by and large they have been given the recognition they deserve. Whilst it is perhaps difficult to find too many companies in this league, it is also a fact that several companies have significant achievements as well. The problem however seems to be that at times companies do not realize the significance (in media terms) of all their achievements. Share as much as you can with your PR Agency. It might surprise you to discover the nuggets that lie hidden under the mounds of data. No fact is too small to be ignored. Properly packaged, it can make a difference and will make its way to the pages of the daily newspaper.

"Image is everything"

- *Andre Agassi*

CHAPTER

Building an International Indian Brand

Mr. Narayana Murthy, Chairman and Chief Mentor of Infosys, one of India's most respected citizens and a principal builder of India's neo-economy and global status, candidly sets forth his views on the serious purpose of brand building in India.

Speaking with the author about Brand Infosys, Mr. Murthy talks about the philosophy behind the core beliefs that have placed it among the seven international companies chosen to be in the first annual list of 'Top Brands with a Conscience'. Infosys is the only Indian company to be part of this select group.

Ramanujam Sridhar (RS): You are the founder of Infosys and its fundamental driving force. How would you view your own accomplishments in and for the company? In your estimation how has Infosys influenced the IT industry in this country?

N.R. Narayana Murthy (NM): To me, the concept of a brand must begin and end with being a source of trust and comfort for the customer. We started working on establishing the brand early in the company's journey. It wasn't easy.

Between 1981-1990, government policies and their associated hindrances and restrictions set us back a few years. It took all of two years to import a computer and its components. And at that time the duty on all imported electronic items was 155%!

Around 1990 I realized, being called the largest company was important but the significance of that position was extremely transient.

In the early nineties the order of business was such that you could have been the No 1 corporation on one day and dislodged, without warning, by an MNC on the next, leaving you with nothing to show for your hard work and vision.

TCS was much larger than us in those years. Our mindset was still fearful and we operated under a burden of financial constraint. We knew there were companies that had large financial backing while we lacked any kind of financial support and assistance.

On similar lines, to be known as the best employer was a great affirmation of our position but, we worked and lived with the constant apprehension that the others who came into the picture after us, could offer our employees much more... and in a matter of time, we could be left with nothing on that front as well.

These were the contributing factors that triggered my thinking that if Infosys is positioned as the most respected company in the country, the value of its integrity would have a far greater impact on the customer and would have far-reaching consequences on its industrial stature. And this is of much greater value and significance than mererly accruing commercial and business value. My belief was, and still is, that people's perception of Infosys should be first and prima facie that this is a company they can implicitly trust. We were (and still are) passionate about that. Our desire was that the public would perceive this company as an entity, which would never engage in activity which was unethical or illegal.

We strived, and continue to do so, to be in the position where people and the industry would never talk ill of us.

And that positioning suited us very well because all of us came from middle-class backgrounds and so by nature, we were all very comfortable with the positioning of integrity and trust. In fact, we conducted a survey around that time and 149 out of 150 people said that 'respect' as a quality was what they valued the most. I also realized that if you have to be respected by the customer, you have to deliver the best quality, in time and within the budget. What is paramount is that the customer must never feel he has been short-changed. From the employers' point of view, I realized that if one is open, transparent and fair, employees **do** trust you. From the investor point of view, I realized that if you adhere to the highest principles of corporate governance, you enhance their trust. I remember, at NASSCOM 2002, somebody stood up and said that his company thought that the following year would be such and such. The reaction of the entire gathering was "No, no, let Infosys make a statement, then we will accept it".

'The concept of a brand must begin and end with being a source of trust and comfort for the customer'

My simple point is that by confirming to the finest principles of corporate governance and by not falling to the temptation of using corporate resources for personal benefits, our employees and the industry as a whole have learnt to trust us. Our investors too were enthused because they knew we were not creating asymmetry in benefits. From society's viewpoint, I understood, that if one makes a difference to the environment, the environment and society will open up to you and trust you.

It was with similar sentiments and with the same motivation that we created the Infosys Foundation. From the perspective of society, this organization made a huge difference to the credibility of Infosys as an emblem of respect, comfort and trust.

Sure, this whole value system has emerged from our viewpoint. It has emerged from our observations of people's observations of us.

RS: Today you are a global brand with thousands of employees. How do you view this challenge in terms of size?

> 'This whole value system has emerged from our viewpoint. It has emerged from our observations of people's observations of us'

NM: Things have changed on many levels. Brand Infosys is a known, respected and valued name in the IT business in India and to some extent across its borders too. But we have to move forward to establish an equally credible positioning in the United States, U.K, Germany, Singapore, and Japan.

We still have a long, long way to go. Our operations in these countries are small but very focussed. Right now they have a single-minded goal - sales and marketing. The senior staff work at almost the same jobs as do their junior colleagues. Everyone works with equal enthusiasm. And the challenge is to establish Infosys as a key player in the international IT arena.

Our next challenge is equally daunting. We must retain the same value system we had when we were a small company. It was easy to demonstrate our value system then, because there were less areas of operation, fewer people to manage, and the alchemy of unity, integrity and progress was not difficult to maintain. It was transparently evident in the market place.

Today it isn't that simple because the current professional environment is very complex with layers of managers and messengers. We must ensure that both the managers and messengers buy into these core ideas of the Infosys brand and that they 'walk the talk'. In other words, they too should be as articulate as the rest of us who started this organisation, when it comes to our value system and our code of beliefs.

The third challenge is for us to ensure that we know when our code of ethics and values is being debased. Again, that was a simple task when we were a small-sized company. Now, it's a different story. In 2002 the conduct of one of our Board members was out of line with the organisation's value system. The unfortunate part of it was that the organisation was ignorant of the facts and the activities but they happened, nevertheless. So the question remains, how do we ensure that an employee does not vitiate what the company stands for?

And the next challenge, I would say is to keep our focus on governance.

> 'So the question remains, how do you make sure that an employee does not vitiate what the company stands for?'

In 1991, strong governance, customer focus, quality, creating an excellent employee-oriented work place, were the governing steps for building our enterprise.

We have done all of that. Many people are doing today what we did then. So we have to think of newer ideas to ensure we reinforce the brand.

RS: As a brand, you have a very strong equity and your value is extremely high. How do you see yourself capitalizing on these factors?

NM: I think, the fact that today we own a premium among the top three Indian IT companies proves our industry standing. Mr. Premji has accepted this fact and so has TCS. This is, in itself, bold evidence that we are a highly respected company, which is reason enough to attract high quality employees.

To grow in this area is our earnest desire. The way to go about it, I believe, is to establish norms that will make the company stronger in the long term. We are looking at quantitative models to ascertain which part of our incremental revenue counts toward our brand image and value. We are working on how to establish our premium in customer retention as part of the same brand value. And we're trying to understand which of our incremental rates have contributed to the brand value today.

RS: What are the steps you have taken in moving up in the value chain?

NM: We have established our consulting group; we have created a domain competency where people are trained in specific domains of distribution and manufacturing, banking and financial services. Our leadership institute and software and engineering laboratories have created methodologies for undertaking requirement definition for influx of people. We have also created our own management development centres which train people in several different fields.

> 'We are working on how to establish our premium in customer retention as part of the same brand value'

At Chicago, we have established new services, system integration practice, package implementation and IT outsourcing - at that time at the lower end of the IT business spectrum. We can also make a modest claim to have initiated the IT- enabled services business.

Back in 1990, we decided this is easy for us because it came naturally. None of us needed to do anything different to what we were used to. I don't think there was any great strategy meeting. We just told each other that being middle-class people, we were comfortable with both the technology and lifestyle that suits this business.

I generally don't attend parties; again it is natural because that's just the way I am. And that's the way I'll continue to be. I will not do anything that makes me uncomfortable. This is not a contrived statement or decision. It just comes naturally.

RS: What is your perception of mentoring which people refer to so respectfully?

NM: Basically what we have said is that the most important attribute of a corporation is its longevity. If a corporation has been around for a long time, say a hundred years, it's a given that it must've experienced at least twelve – thirteen business cycles, and that would probably mean that it must have undergone thirteen periods of an economic downturn in a lack-lustre market place. Needless to add, the company would've also faced immense competition. And that must've occasioned tremendous self-sacrifice from the employees.

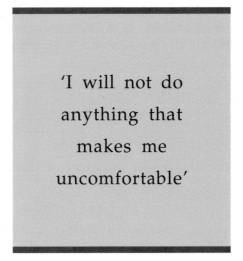

'I will not do anything that makes me uncomfortable'

So, the learning from this is that as the character of the company is strengthened, the brand is on more solid ground. The lesson from this is that if you want to be a long-term player, you need good and sustainable leadership. You need to create a new generation of good leaders, people who have high aspirations, people who are courageous and who have strong convictions.

So we believe that the biggest challenge for Infosys is to produce a new generation of leaders. That is the fundamental reason for founding the Infosys Leadership Institute at Mysore.

We also believe that mentoring is a good pursuit because it is, first of all, a voluntary office. It's therefore a very voluntary relationship where 2 people who want to work together, work together voluntarily, by choice.

Second, it's a private relationship. It's always one-to-one with the result you can be honest with each other. You're able to give feedback that you may not feel free to give someone else.

Third, mentoring is a good mechanism through which the mentor with the mentee can share experiential wisdom. Sometimes, the issue could be a concern which has to be dealt with over a period of time.

Being a voluntary relationship, and a private relationship it is also more objective.

All of us mentor in similar fashion. In fact, we have selected three tiers of leaders. Tier 1 has thirty people

> 'You need to create a new generation of good leaders, people who have high aspirations, people who are courageous and who have strong convictions'

mentored by the Board of Directors. Tier 1 mentors Tier 2. So, a person who is frustrated can just come and spill it all out at any level he chooses.

RS: What is your vision for your brand?

NM: The most important thing for me is for Infosys to be respected on a global basis, 5 years from now, if in the U.S, U.K and say, Japan, people are asked about what Infosys stands for and their response is respectability, trust, and decency; that for me is the accomplishment of my aspiration.

RS: From 91-2002, you have become the most respected and recognized person in business. What difference has this made to "Narayana Murthy the individual"? What changes do you see in the last 15 years, in yourself?

NM: Obviously I have a higher level of confidence. There is no doubt about that. Confidence comes from recognition and wealth but at the same time, I find that as you keep moving from one orbit to the next the issues you deal with get bigger and the picture you place yourself in, larger. Let's say, 10 years ago we were comparing ourselves with small companies. Today we compare ourselves with the bigger companies because we are now among the top 5 in the market.

In the last 4-5 years my orbit has grown to encompass factors connected with the global issues of society. In Infosys, we have a controlled environment where every employee is encouraged to grow. Incentives form an essential part of this activity. *

RS: What is your vision for India as a brand? How do you see Brand India in the new world compass?

This is where I feel very helpless. Only in this sense, I say, it causes a lot more heartburn for our people. When do people get angry? When they are frustrated.

Other than software, we don't have any 'Made-in-India' brand at all, unfortunately. Unless we can improve the quality of our hardware manufacture, I don't see a future in exports there. It pains me to see Colombian Coffee when we grow and process so much of coffee in India. It pains me to see Ceylon tea when we have so many tea plantations all over the country. We have failed in the arena of creating wealth. In the same way, regarding tourism, I would say we are not able to attract one-tenth of the people that travel to Thailand and Singapore. We need ministers and bureaucrats to nurture this industry and encourage the building of Indian brands for global tourists.

> 'Respectability, trust, and decency; that for me is the accomplishment of my aspiration'

CHAPTER 3

Who's Minding the Store?

'Bangalore is a one-horse town'. Presumably you too must have heard this comment from people who are (arguably) well-read and, widely-travelled. No longer. The 21st century has given Bangalore (and therefore India) top billing among world city rankings. And that's not surprising at all. Bangalore is driven by a single industry – software. The city lives, dreams and bills software and its related industries. That's great news for Indian software, exports of which have climbed to USD 9.2 billion in 2005, comprising up to 25% of India's total exports. The not-so-great news is for people in advertising who rue the fact that software despite its size, potential and profits is not advertising-driven. And why should it be, given the enthusiasm of journalists who seem to be preoccupied with software and its leaders and who cheerfully keep filing story after story on this industry in one newspaper after the other. However, there is a silver lining for the advertising industry in this scenario. Wednesdays and Fridays are good days for the advertising industry in South India and it smiles all the way to the bank, as it releases huge appointment ads for one high-tech company after the other.

Whether agencies have their heads in the clouds or not, they most certainly have their feet securely planted in the cash box. If there is someone who is happier than the advertising agency, it is the media. The media is ecstatic because it is sitting on a larger box of cash. And why wouldn't it be? The number of pages in the supplement sometimes rivals the main edition. The media too is getting creative in its marketing efforts as it markets the front page and the back page of each one of the supplements touting them as special positions! The Net gets clogged with resumes and the postal department too is happy as a lark because software engineers send in their applications in hordes.

A 'win-win' situation for all concerned, did you say? Yes and No. 'No' because while there is quantity here, what is lacking is quality. And whilst the one-time revenue on these appointment ads is high, the creativity is on an all time low. Yes, I know that the purpose of this advertising is to sell the company (to prospective employees) and not to win advertising awards. (Incidentally, sometime last year, I was the least eminent of 3 judges for the Advertising Club of Bangalore, who as a group, felt that the appointment ads category should go un-rewarded and un-awarded at the 'Big Bang' – the Awards Night of the Advertising Club of Bangalore). But awards or not, the fact of the matter is that a lot of these ads are similar looking, familiar sounding and cliché ridden. They are not differentiated, either by size or by the quality of the visuals. If you interchanged logos of two ads from two different companies, no one would be the wiser – the ads look so similar! While, two different ads from the same company look completely different in the choice of colours, typography and tone of voice! One ad is aggressive whilst another ad from a different product group of the same company is defensive. The problem is simple. Most high-tech companies view their recruitment advertising as a necessary evil. But today, these companies must advertise, to recruit. Fresh talent is necessary for them to survive and then to grow. Consequently, each piece of communication must be viewed as an opportunity to build the company as a brand. What are the company's values? How well are they being communicated in its recruitment advertising? What is the company's desired personality? Does the company's recruitment advertising reflect it? How integrated is this advertising with the other communication from the company? These are questions, which need to be

> '...the fact of the matter is that a lot of these ads are similar looking, familiar sounding and cliché ridden'

seriously addressed. And yet, it is rarely, if ever, done going by what one sees on Wednesdays.

Recruitment is back with a vengeance. Infosys is reported to have recruited close to 6,000 freshers through campus recruitment in the second and third quarters of 2005-2006 and 2,000 professionals during the fourth quarter of 2004-2005. Given the fact that recruitment advertising is perhaps the only advertising that most software companies do, it is critical for them to realize that every ad they release is an opportunity to build their corporate image. True, ads must pull and get qualitatively and quantitatively significant response but they can and should do more. They can help build the company's brand image. Companies would do well to remember that when one has a limited budget for advertising (is there a different category of budget?) every penny must count. The principles of appointment advertising are perhaps similar to successful corporate advertising. The most significant principle is that of consistency. Consistency matters. Consistency pays. And consistency works.

Consistency is King

Advertising people are trained to push the creative envelope, come to the edge, and consider normal as boring. But corporate branding at the risk of being boring is all about being consistent in the long run. I realized this the hard way, a small matter of 18 years ago. I used to handle a large consumer electronics brand and a small (uninteresting) part of the overall assignment included release of appointment ads. It was a nightmare. The company's head of marketing (unlike me) realized that an appointment ad was an important means of projecting the company's image and identity. He would carefully go through every word of the body copy with a fine toothcomb as I squirmed. He also decreed that all ads were to have a similar format (4 col. width) and use the typestyle of 'American typewriter'. My Creative Director bristled at this intrusion onto his turf and promptly abdicated his job (and responsibility) on these ads. Today, I am a lot older and perhaps just a little bit wiser. I realize the value of consistency in look and feel. I am not sure how many clients in the hi-tech world are as savvy as my erstwhile consumer electronics client, or as focused. The lesson I have learnt is fairly simple. Marketing people understand brands and their look and feel. Do human relations professionals who initiate a lot of recruitment advertising, possess the same competence or at least the interest to get the best out of the agency?

The trick is not to treat each appointment ad as an isolated 'stand-alone' but as one of a continuing campaign, separated by fairly long intervals of time, since a company may not release an ad a week.

Does She or Doesn't She?

Today's HR Manager is a very important part of hi-tech business. She has to recruit in hundreds. (Infosys reportedly has recruited 1500 people last quarter and the number is growing). She has to worry about attrition rate, hope stock market blues will not wipe the sheen off employee stock option plans, train people for superior performance, monitor the pulse of her people, and also approve appointment ads. You don't have to be a genius to figure out where her priorities lie. Perhaps she is making a few mistakes, which hurt the creative process and output, such as the following:

'The trick is not to treat each appointment ad as an isolated "stand-alone" but as one of a continuing campaign'

- Ropes in more people into the decision making process of approving ads. This results in chaos and compromise.

- "Has a dog and barks herself", as David Ogilvy would say by getting her technical people to write the body copy for the ads. (After all, how many advertising agencies understand digital signal processing or embedded systems?)

- Works on and gives unreasonable deadlines to the agency, which is finally relieved to get an(y) ad out on Wednesday.

- Is concerned more about correctness than creativity.

- Desperately needs support from marketing communication on branding issues. But very often, that resource is rarely, if ever available. And even if available, is found wanting in maturity and judgement.

Think Long Term. Think Brand

It's easy to let this degenerate into a tale of woe. But then that's a soft option. Advertising agencies must change their outlook towards this business and behave less like order-takers and more like consultants who advise their clients. I know that's easier said than done, but I also know for a fact, that a large client who was once a pathetic buyer of creative, buys outstanding creative today because he knows much better. Thanks to his agencies, he has grown on the job.

Very often, we rationalize our non-performance by making this familiar statement, "Every client gets what he deserves". Right? Wrong. I believe that many hi-tech clients do not understand what branding is all about. It's hi-touch, soft and emotional in startling contrast to the cold rationality of technology. But that's really what the agency should bring to the party: branding. We are, all of us, familiar with strategies for consumer brands and create a concept

Recruitment ads. that beat the clutter.   *Creative: brand-comm*

for our clients. But what about creating the strategy for corporate brands? Should we not articulate it and execute it, particularly if recruitment advertising is the only mass media communication that our client is engaged in ? Today, in the largely undifferentiated world, we live in, branding is critical and extends to every aspect of a company's activities. The way its staff answer the phone. The manner is which they respond to customer complaints. The visual identity it displays. The recruitment ad it releases. That's right! The first big step in the shift towards better advertising is the realization that advertising (even recruitment) is an investment in the company's future and not a mere cost or statistic. Maybe CEO's of hi-tech companies should shift their focus and look at their own brands. As Floathe Johnson said, *"The Road to Hell is paved with companies who developed their technology, but neglected their brand"*.

A few questions worth considering on the subject:

Q Is there a colour your corporation can appropriate? How distinct and unique is that colour? What colour comes to your mind when I say IBM?

Q Is there a typeface that you can call your own?

Q Is your logo strategically and visibly placed? Is it in the same position in all your ads?

Q Does your advertising tone of voice reflect your company's values?

Q What do you wish to be seen as – an aggressive company, a solid company, a company on the ball, a learning organization or what? Determine what your brand stands for, communicate that position and stay with it. Just ensure that the position you have chosen is achievable.

"The good news is if you own a strong position in the mind, you can milk that position forever. The bad news is, you can't easily change that position" - Al Ries and Jack Trout.

Now tell me, what does your brand stand for? And who is taking care of it?

And, by the way, happy Wednesday!

"A brand is a living entity - and it
is enriched or undermined
cumulatively over time, the product
of a thousand small gestures"

- Michael Eisner

CHAPTER

Do an Image Number!

When I first came into the advertising profession, just 23 years ago, I had an aversion to annual reports. My dislike was based on experiences that were both rational and emotional. On the rational front, getting an annual report ready for one's client meant late nights, hours of laborious proof -checking, buying the studio manager a quarter of rum, unending iterations and the sword of Damocles – 'fear of the sack' - over my head If you got one of the figures wrong, you would be better advised to figure out a 'new improved' career for yourself. On the emotional front, looking at an annual report meant looking at the salaries that some of our clients were earning (sec. 217 (2a) of the Companies Act 1956) which in itself was fairly depressing considering the abysmally low salaries people in advertising were earning then. In fact, by and large, advertising agencies tended to view the annual report as a necessary evil – a print job on which the agency made money. The tightness of the deadline meant that design and aesthetics were generally low on priority although cover design options were always provided by the

agency. Nobody bothered about building an image through this financial statement. But everybody was bothered about getting the miserable thing out of the agency into the client's office. Today, several years later, one has graduated from posting annual reports (for clients) to actually receiving reports in the mail – as an investor (albeit a 'small' or 'marginal' one). And yet one continues to see a few reports like the ones I supervised – functional, correct and boring. But it is extremely heartening to note that more and more companies are realising that the report is more than just a job which must be done. It is actually a means of communicating with the target publics and more importantly an opportunity to build the company's corporate image.

I need to quickly mention that this is not an exhaustive survey of all the annual reports printed in the country. It is rather, a flavour of my impressions as either a shareholder or an associate in the companies featured in this piece (and lest you think I'm rolling in 'ice', you might just wish to check the prices at which I bought some of these company's shares and compare them with the prices on 23.5.2005!)

A Few Observations On Annual Reports Today:

- The major improvement has been in the quality of printing, paper and overall aesthetic appeal not to forget the occasional CD of the entire contents, which comes with a few companies' annual reports.

- Discerning companies are using the pages of the annual report to espouse their philosophy and values.

- A section on corporate governance seems increasingly popular. There is an increasing realisation that corporate governance is about board performance and conformance. Global Telesystems, a momentum stock as CNBC will tell you, speaks of compliance with the Kumara Mangalam Birla committee, the Blue Ribbon committee and compliance with the CII's recommendations on corporate governance.

- Hughes Software throws light on its business to the investor by having FAQs on convergence and mobility and a glossary of telecom terms. An attempt to demystify technology if you will.

- Infosys holds a round table on the power of e-commerce and reproduces it in the annual report suggesting that could well be its future cash cow.

- There is a realisation that brands have value and more often than not, this is reflected in the annual report. Satyam has valued its brands with an earnings multiple of 23 whilst the Infosys intangible assets score sheet has its brand valuation multiple at 48.

- All companies seem to value their people. Hughes talks about the strategy of using appreciation as the tool of change, whilst Tata Elxsi gets its employees to share their experiences at the work place.

- The first rung software companies generally seem to have better brought out reports than their second rung counterparts.

- And if you thought finance companies were fuddy-duddy, think again. The annual reports of HDFC and ICICI reflect the fact that their image is contemporary. And their annual reports reflect the new economy wisdom and culture.

- Indian Shaving Products carries its big technological break through - the Mach III - on its annual report cover. A reinforcement of Gillette's commitment to "The Best a Man can Get". Yes, perhaps this report, more than anything else, demonstrates that you can benefit by integrating your brand message with your financial statement.

- BFL Software has an annual report, which attempts to beat the clutter by having an odd size. Its ratios include the needs of the industry it belongs to, by talking about attrition rate trends. Polaris' annual report clearly demonstrates its desire to be ahead of the pack.

- Some companies have differently executed annual reports – one for 'mass' and one to promote their class.

- A company like Silicon Automation Systems (SAS), although not a listed company still mails its annual report to suppliers and associates using this as a means of communication. Yes, companies are progressing from the 'have to' to the 'want to' stage with reference to sharing information. I am sure this was one of the reasons for the company (which subsequently changed its name to Sasken Communication Systems) having an IPO that was heavily oversubscribed.

- HLL, the marketing giant, speaks of connecting with the consumer and if one were to compare with its rival Colgate, it seems to be definitely a winner on the design front.

Yes, things have changed for the better, both in style and content. There is a strong urge to communicate more than mere numbers. There is a realisation that every piece of communication from the corporation contributes to building its image. It's perhaps relevant to reflect on what Wally Ollins, the identity expert has to say.

"A corporation's actions are indivisible, that how it behaves, what is says, how it treats people, what it makes and sells are parts of a single whole, that everything within the corporation has an effect on everything else; that everyone has an effect on everyone else".

And the annual report certainly has an effect on the way a company is perceived. Not only the annual report. Today, analysts, researchers and journalists are not waiting for the printed report, but accessing the company's website for gathering information.

That leads us to another important related question: How good is your website? Does it project your image effectively? Is your website's look and feel integrated with all your other channels of communication?

And yet, having been exposed to a variety of clients and situations, one does have a few questions, which companies might do well to think about.

> 'There is a realisation that every piece of communication from the corporation contributes to building its image'

Here's a quick check list

✓ Does your company see your annual report as a high-cost factor or an investment into the future?

✓ Is the primary decision maker on your company's annual report your head of finance, even if he has very limited competence in judging design?

✓ Do you believe that only 'actively traded' companies must have elegant and classy annual reports?

✓ Your annual report is well designed but it has no relation to what your company/brand stands for.

✓ You are a small company and this 'smallness' shows in the annual report.

If your response is "Yes" to even one of the above, then your company is ignoring a huge opportunity, to build its image.

"Your personal brand is a promise to your clients... a promise of quality, consistency, competency, and reliability"

- *Jason Hartman*

CHAPTER

Are you a Brand Champion?

It's 9.30 am on a Monday morning. The phone rings incessantly in a medium-sized organisation. The caller is persistent. He is waiting for someone to pick up the phone. On the 17th ring, the phone is picked up by a reluctant security guard who is standing in for the telephone operator (who's obviously been delayed).

'Ullo?' he asks gruffly. *"Avaru bandilla saar. Aamele phone madi"*, he says before putting the receiver down.

If you live in the 'Garden City', Bangalore's former nomenclature, this is clear indication, that the person you want to speak with is not in and you need to call later. I am sure some of us have been at the receiving end (in more ways than one) in situations like these. What is the image of the company we are left with, when something like this happens? 'Moment of truth'! Let's assume the caller is a customer or (heaven forbid) a prospective investor. Based on this point of contact, his views of the brand are unlikely to be very complimentary. And that throws up a fairly important point. It's easy to conceptualise branding as a 60-second TV commercial shot in Australia. It's easy to think of branding as glossy packaging and a slick display of the product in an up-market outlet. It's easy to think of branding as a strong visual identity. And yet, at the risk of repeating myself, I must say that branding is everything that your company does - not just what the CEO does. It is even how the security guard responds to a visitor or a caller. Speaking of security guards, it's sad that more and more companies as they move into the 'cost-cutting' mode, deploy security guards in place of receptionists. One of them sported the admirable name of Doberman! Imagine being welcomed by one!

> 'Branding is everything that your company does - not just what the CEO does'

The surest way to check your company's telephone manners is to ask your spouse to call your office. You may never hear the end of it but be prepared to get comments like "Nobody picks up the phone". "Why can't they transfer to the right extension?" "I am sick and tired of your jingle". Try to ensure that your organisation doesn't cause travails to your callers. It will eventually have a negative impact on your brand.

I remember visiting a large agency in Madison Avenue, a few years ago. The receptionist was a friendly middle-aged lady who, seeing that we had come all the way from India, was so very considerate and solicitous that the agency she worked for went up two notches in my esteem. People will be people and will make (seemingly) irrational decisions based on their own experiences. So, the point remains: are you putting your best 'voice' forward?

Brand Ambassadors vs Brand Champions

Consumer brands rely on brand ambassadors. Parker has Amitabh, Omega has Cindy Crawford, Taj Mahal tea has Zakir

> 'Are you putting your best 'voice' forward?'

Hussain, Santro has Shahrukh Khan and even the Economist had Kissinger. Of course, one is completely bewildered by the number of brands for which Sachin is the brand ambassador, but then, that is another story.

The common thread in all this is that communication is from the outside, and it is driven by mass media communication. The reality, however, is that these brand ambassadors may have very little to do with the company or its values. These ambassadors are used because marketers believe there is a strong fit between the brand ambassador's personality and the consumer's aspiration. While one recognises the need for brand ambassadors for some brands, it is perhaps important to understand that every corporate brand needs a champion. These champions are within the company. They are its employees. They impact, mould and convey the brand values to various target publics. Our employees are going to determine our brand's success or failure.

Whilst permutations, combinations and choices may exist in organizing brand management, there is no going away from one important factor: Every one who works for an organisation owns responsibility for the brand. After all, the best brand ambassador of a company is not Sachin Tendulkar, Aishwarya Rai, nor Shah Rukh

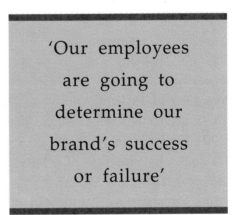

'Our employees are going to determine our brand's success or failure'

Khan - it's your employee. And how are you training her to be your brand ambassador ? By sharing the brand vision with everyone who works in an organisation. The solution is simple. Communication, communication...and more communication. Sadly, in terms of priorities, more corporations spend more time and energy communicating to the world outside than to their own employees.

Branding as I First Knew It

As anybody in Madras (as it was known then) will tell you, we all grew up on Horlicks. That was the great nourishing beverage of our time. Till, we graduated to South Indian 'kaapi'. This had other implications too. On the few days that I was helping out in the kitchen (read, my mother's 'kingdom'), or when I was fetching something from there I was confronted by rows and rows of Horlicks bottles collected painstakingly over the years. "Where is the sugar", I'd yell. "The third Horlicks bottle from the left", would be the answer. "Where is the salt?" "The first Horlicks bottle in the bottom row." And, the question-answer session would continue with a Horlicks bottle as the central point of the answer. Yes, consumer brands have multiple ways of remaining in our vision and in our memory. Not so for corporate or service brands. The challenge, as Mike Clasper, President of Procter and Gamble states it, is intriguing. Brands, he says, will need to win the battle for share of mind, not share of shelf.

Let me explain this with an interesting analogy. All of us men are familiar with Harley Davidson. We dreamt about it and yearned to ride it. And yet, there is an important fact about Harley, which is little known. Harley's image is determined as much by the people who ride it as the people who manufacture it. If the riders were staid and dowdy, it would certainly impact our perception of Harley. Similarly, our perceptions of companies by and large, are based on our observations of the people who work there.

Are they professional, competent and committed or apathetic, rude and ignorant? Are they champions of your brand or destroyers of its equity?

Enter the HR Manager

Some of my most formative, satisfying and challenging years were in Mudra in the late '80s and early '90s. The organisation was humming with activity and energy. The agency had buzz. It was a bit like standing at forward short leg when Bishen Singh Bedi was bowling. You could hear the spin even if you weren't watching the seam. Mudra had an important system in place. A livewire HR manager who was a sounding board, counselor, trainer and salesman all rolled into one. He displayed an infectious enthusiasm and a passion for the company. He was a true brand champion who shared the success stories of the agency with whomever he came into contact with. Here was a tremendous role model for the young people who would be the future leaders of the company.

> "It, is intriguing. Brands, he says, will need to win the battle for share of mind, not share of shelf"
>
> **- Mike Clasper**

Different organizations assign various responsibilities to different people when it comes to managing the brand. Additionally, marketing companies give the responsibility to brand managers for individual brands. Some of these managers may be at fairly junior levels in their respective organizations, which has its own implications. Savvy companies place the responsibility on the CEO and the Board of Directors. Some other companies like BMW have a special team to handle branding issues, and this team reports directly to the CEO and not to the marketing director.

Let's take this theory of *'Employee as Brand Ambassador'* a little further. Take the example of any corporation. How often would a middle manager be successful in communicating what the company stands for, to an outsider? And if one were to say junior management, the playback could become even more diffused. Hence, the role of the HR manager has acquired increasing importance in building the brand.

What is her job description? She identifies brand champions who feel strongly about the brand and unhesitatingly recommend it. Today, the HR manager's role is changing. It is no longer passive and supportive. It is extremely active and enables people to head in the direction we wish to take them. Today's HR manager is a coach cum cheerleader and much more than just the patient listener of yesteryear.

I am not devaluing the role of advertising, public relations and imagery in building a corporate brand; but merely including the employees' dimension. Let me give you an example from my own industry, the advertising industry. The account executive is often enough the face of the agency to the external world and the client. An efficient, organized, committed account executive says many favourable things about the agency. If he is laid back, disorganized and slow to respond, he encourages the client to believe that the agency has these qualities as well. Try extending the analogy to your organisation.

Who handles customers?
Who handles service?
Who handles applicants?
Who handles your website?
Who answers your phone (after office and during lunch)?

God is in the details; in the small things. A big brand has several facets and components to it. Are the people who are handling it responsible and responsive? And ticklish though the question may be, ask yourself this: "Have I empowered them?"

"Part of the requirement for a brand is passion", said Graham Mackay, Group Managing Director of South African Breweries. And this is what is

> 'Today's HR manager is a coach cum cheerleader and much more than the patient listener of yesteryear'

lacking in most organisations. Chief Executives, often enough, are passionate about their brands; but how about everybody else? A leader today has to be less of General Patton and more of John Buchanan (the coach of the Australian Cricket Team). He also has to be a cheerleader. We spend more than half of the day preparing for, going to, coming from and actually doing, work. If that is challenging and stimulating, then we can certainly be passionate about our place of work and communicate this to the rest of the world. So, today's organisations need human relations more than ever before. But it is more than recruitment training and compensation. It is about creating an environment for viewing the company as a brand.

Brand Types

Branding theory*classifies employees into four categories.

- Brand champions are storytellers who spread the brand idea.
- Brand agnostics are interested but not committed.
- Brand cynics are not involved with the brand idea.
- Brand saboteurs are working actively against the brand idea.

Clearly every organization needs brand champions. But, the tougher questions are like these:

Q. How well is the company's mission and vision communicated internally?

Q. How well have employees bought into this?

Q. Are the employees empowered?

Alisa Petchey, a flight attendant on Virgin Atlantic was organizing a wedding and understanding the travails of it. She felt it was easier to go to a one-stop shop, which would organize everything. She took the idea to Branson and the result was '**Virgin Brides**' - a chain of stores, which caters to everything the soon-to-be bride needs.

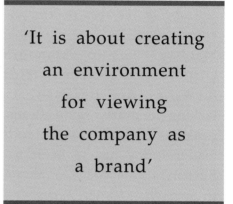

'It is about creating an environment for viewing the company as a brand'

Gary Hamel, the renowned management guru asks, *"Could this happen in your company? Could a 20 something first-time employee buttonhole the chairman and get permission to start a new business? Not a hope in hell! So the question is, are our employees empowered for them to be our champions?"*

Today, we know that people come in all sizes, shapes and attitudes. Whilst there may be strength in diversity, for an organisation, there must necessarily be, unity of vision on the brand and its values. So, having communicated your values, classify your employees who are your brand's champions. Reward them and ensure that they communicate the brand story to as wide as audience as possible. They are your winners. Difficult and painful, though it may be, identify the enemies of your brand and sack them. It may sound extreme but if they are allowed to hang around, they may damage your brand seriously.

Don't just Use the 'Branding' Word, Do the Actions

Most of us tend to take things easy. We believe that the brand is the CEO's baby, or the Brand Manager's, or the Human Relations Manager's. The reality, however, is that it belongs to all the employees. It has to be communicated, and even more difficult, it has to be internalized by them or appropriated as their own. As Rita Karakas, a consultant in organisational development, says, " ... *an organisation has to come to terms with how it actually owns branding as an attitude, as a presence, as a state of mind, a politique de presence, where everyone is a communicator and everyone is an embodiment of the essence of the organization. Every organization has a heart. The heart is not just on the outside. You need insiders to carry on feeding the heart.*"

Are your employees feeding or starving your brand?

'So the question is, are our employees empowered for them to be our champions?'

"Brands are not just about fulfilling basic consumer needs. Brands possess great power and the truly great brands will be those that learn to balance this power with responsibility"

- Susannah Hart, John Murphy

CHAPTER

Why Aren't You a Brand Yet?

What is common to Richard Branson, Bill Gates, Michael Dell, Jerry Yang and Jack Welch? No prizes for guessing the right answer. All these famous personalities made the Indian subcontinent their destination of choice in the recent past. Not so obvious but perhaps even more significant is the fact that each one of these are personal brands. They are the face of their respective companies. Though their individual brand equity could vary as

they belong to different countries and industries, there is no arguing the fact that these corporate giants would give their more beautiful counterparts in the entertainment world a run for their money when it comes to popularity, media attention and editorial space. An analogy is relevant, just as people would pay money to watch Brad Pitt perform, I imagine people would invest in Microsoft because Bill Gates owns it.

Yes, today's corporate world has its fair share of celebrities who make a difference to their own corporations, customers, employees and investors. People like Jack Welch formerly of GE, Richard Branson of Virgin and closer home Narayana Murthy of Infosys. Here is evidence to lend credence to my argument. In the fourth leadership study conducted by brand-comm with 12 prominent business schools in India, over 35% rated Mr. Narayana Murthy as the business leader they admired the most with Ratan Tata and

Azim Premji coming in second and third, in that order. The reasons are fairly obvious. They admire Mr. Murthy's leadership style, vision and entrepreneurial spirit. And they value his ethics. After all branding is all about consistency, coherence and long-term thinking. The same strategy applies to leaders who have the potential to be personal brands.

Today, however there is a subtle and important difference. People from the corporate world are rubbing shoulders with people from the world of entertainment in pages 2 and 3 of your local Indian newspaper. They are recognized and ofen mobbed. The important point is that in this manner, savvy corporate leaders are carefully and consciously building their personal and professional reputations. Why are they doing this? Simple really. By hitching their personal reputation to their corporation they grow the two synergistically. For instance if you were to ask which is the bigger brand, GE or Jack Welch, the answer could throw up a surprise. The analyst could well say GE whilst a management guru might well say Jack. But the reality is that both have benefited synergistically from each other's influence and achievements. Will GE be the same after Jack Welch? Can Jack Welch be the same after GE? One wonders.

And what about Richard Branson? He is a one-man PR army that can teach the whole world a trick or two about getting media coverage. How many Indian business leaders will dare try the bhangra in the airport or drive an auto in Connaught Place or ski naked down the Alps, fly a balloon over the English Channel or ride a tank down New York's busy streets? All front page stuff, stuff that had the biggies sweating be it British Airways or Coke. Branson identified lazy giants and took them on. His weapon? His own personal brand that united the entire gamut of products under the Virgin brand name. Nor has he been alone in this effort. Anita Roddick of Body Shop, Bill Gates of Microsoft and a host of corporate leaders are today realizing that they can be brands and further their own personal equity even as they build their corporation's equity.

A Brand? Who, Me?

I can almost hear you saying, "Here I am a hard working executive selling bank deposits, walking the floor in Food World, selling tea in Dharwad struggling to meet my stiff targets and you are raving about these Forbes millionaires and legends. Tell me something that is relevant to me". Yes, I hear you loud and clear and understand your concerns. All of us may not be extroverts like Richard Branson, as result oriented as Jack Welch, as visible as Narayana Murthy, as rich as Bill Gates or as brilliant in strategy as Michael Dell. These people are charismatic leaders. Let's face the fact that not all of us have charisma. And yet in the same breath let me state that all of us do have something within us which can help us become brands, perhaps on a smaller scale maybe limited to our own areas of competence and interest. For what is branding if not an opportunity to be unique and different? Branding enables us to stand out from the clutter at home, the Rotary, our place of work or charity. Each and every one of us has the opportunity to be a brand in our own right. Personal branding enables you to be recognized. Yes, you! To quote from Tom Peters' book *'The Brand You - 50'*, *"To be in business today, our most important job is to be head marketer for the brand called You"*.

> 'To be in business today, our most important job is to be head marketer for the brand called You'
>
> **- Tom Peters**

Let's get down to basics. What is a brand? A brand is unique and differentiated. So what is unique about you? How are you different? Do a useful realistic analysis of your own strengths and weaknesses. Ask your friend or spouse to give you feedback. And evolve a strategy. Crucial to this strategy is the answer to the question, "Who is my target audience?" Is it your boss, your competitor, your industry or your banker? There is an adage, which says, "You may not have a second opportunity to make a first impression". It's true. So how well dressed and presentable are you? Invest in a wardrobe and dress in a manner that is consistent and distinctive. Do you remember Winston Churchill? How was he dressed? In a tuxedo and a bowler hat. Can you imagine him in a yellow polka dot tie? What about Jawaharlal Nehru? Even Bill Gates' clothes reflect his affluence and unique standing in the technology business. Just give a little bit of thought to your personal grooming.

When did you last offer to do a project outside your job? "Good fortune", they say, "is when hard work meets opportunity". Successful people create opportunities to get noticed. And it's not easy. It may mean conquering your fear of the stage and getting up there to deliver a speech. Believe me, you can. I know the brightest and best, spending sleepless nights over delivering a 15-minute speech at the Rotary Club. Its no fun spending your weekends on a social cause - but if that will add a dimension to your brand's personality, why not ? How about an article in the newspaper? All around me are people with some unique qualities. 'The techie', 'The ideas man', 'The stock market wizard', 'The cricket statistician', 'The lord of the net' and so on. What is your own special quality that can make you remembered, sought out and recognized? Think about it.

Perception Is Reality

It's important to talk about something that I feel strongly about. None of us can be something that we are not. Not for long anyway. One of the most noticeable and outstanding qualities of Mr. Narayana Murthy are his simplicity and down-to-earth life style, despite his enormous wealth. A few Sundays back, I nearly choked on my idlis, when I saw him having breakfast at Adigas, a very popular place in Jayanagar, but hardly the Windsor Manor. Personal brands are real, genuine and true to life. All brands struggle to find one word that best describes them. What is the one word that best describes you? How can you build on this?

In any brand audit and re-engineering exercise, it is advantageous to begin with a realistic assessment of the present. How does the world view you? We can't be always objective about ourselves, can

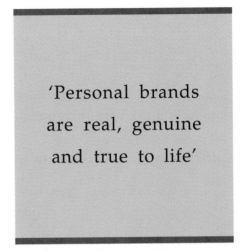

'Personal brands are real, genuine and true to life'

we? We are either too smug about ourselves or too critical about our failures or lack of success. If we actively seek feedback from those around us they could provide valuable insights as to where we stand and how we are perceived. Self assessment is an important first step in branding.

O wad some pow'r the giftie gie us

To see oursels as other see us !

It wad frae mony a blunder free us,

And foolish notion.

- Robert Burns in 'To a Louse'.

Will Powers used personal branding principles to improve his relationship (and standing) with an important customer, his wife by asking her to list out the most important attributes for an ideal husband. But he started by asking her what she thought of him. Similarly it is possible for us to clarify our strengths and weaknesses from our colleagues and customers. If people say you are 'responsive' or 'sensitive', 'reduce complex things to simple', then you are on a good wicket. You can use the feedback to actively seek projects that require these skills. Again, here is an opportunity to stand out and demonstrate your ability and show initiative. If you look at the big consumer and corporate brands, what are they doing? They continue to research with their target publics on what their brands mean to them, what they stand for and how they are perceived. Clearly the task at hand is to improve ourselves for the better. Research is a good beginning to build brands – most certainly personal brands.

Confidence. A Pillar for the Personal Brand

"I'm good. I know `cos God don't make rubbish!" said a small African boy in a religious broadcast in the BBC in the early 80's. The kid knew what he was talking about! This statement holds true in the new millenium as well. We are all born with confidence, but the trick is to hang on to it as the Jack Welchs of the world have done. Confidence comes from belief in oneself, from knowledge, experience and expertise. The core of confidence is self-esteem

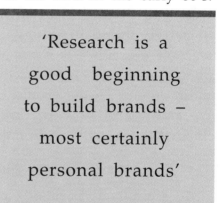

'Research is a good beginning to build brands – most certainly personal brands'

and what we believe about ourselves. The sort of confidence that comes with knowledge about one's industry, area of work and one's customer is perhaps a great source of strength. Knowledge can give confidence, power and enable us to differentiate ourselves from those within the company and without.

Lord Puttnam CBE Chairman, Enigma Productions says, *"The best and the most effective brands of the future will be built around knowledge."* You will be a truly effective personal brand if you "know". And you could take that further. Be visible in industry fora. Speak, write, offer your point of view. Most importantly have a sensible point of view. As Bill Bernbach said, *"If you stand for something, you will always find some people for you and some against you. If you stand for nothing, you will find nobody against you, and nobody for you".*

Packaging The Personal Brand

Bill Gates arguably the richest man in the world, has changed his image in recent times to be in sync with Microsoft's image. He looks the part of a successful CEO of the world's most dominant technology company. A far cry from the classic computer nerd of yesteryears appearing in dowdy suits and ungainly spectacles. And the (once) shyest man in the world, now trades jokes with David Letterman and builds a $50 million technologically perfect home. Yes, he has high visibility and has packaged himself for the noticeability that success brings. Everyone may not write 'The Road Ahead' but the way we present ourselves to the external world, the clothes we wear, are all part of branding and can take us ahead in life.

Consumer marketers know the value of brand associations. Remember the Titan music track? The Britannia 'Tin Tin Ti Din'? Or the Liril 'girl in the waterfall' (who has suddenly migrated to the desert)? Yes, associations are built consistently and irrevocably over time. The point I am making is fairly simple. Consumer marketing companies understand the value of brand associations and strive to build them. Corporations somehow seem to be (largely) unaware of the opportunities of associating their brand with a charismatic leader. Infosys has realized this and done this strategically.

The fact of the matter is that customers wish to deal with companies that have visible leaders. Investors wish to invest in companies that have ethical leaders. And management students wish to join companies that have dynamic leaders. And it is important to remember a few things.

- Personal branding is not only about media coverage.

- It is about having a point of view.

- It is about being seen at the right places.

- It is about thinking long term

- It is about having a clear strategy.

- It is about having execution and implementation of your strategy.

And yet a word of caution is perhaps relevant here. We talked about GE and Jack Welch. How many of us know the current Chairman and CEO, Jeff Immelt? What happens if you project the CEO, he stands for your company and (heaven forbid) leaves to join the competition? Yes, these are definitely areas of concern but not insurmountable obstacles. The old scout motto 'Be prepared' is perhaps relevant here too.

The Law Of The Personal Brand

Jason Hartman gives his seven laws of personal branding which makes interesting reading as he approaches this whole opportunity from the point of view of the individual. Here's his description of personal branding attributes – worth considering and internalising.

"I am significant and what I say has value"

"I become what I decide to be"

"Reputation is born of virtue"

"I am dependable"

"My name is my brand"

"Time is my friend"

"What I am lives on"

TECHNOBRANDING

"Branding is not about getting your prospects to
choose you over your competition;
it's about getting your prospects to see you
as the only solution to their problem"

- Rob Frankel

CHAPTER

Technology Today but Brands Forever

In 1982, Tim Bell, Managing Director of (the original) Saatchi and Saatchi agency, speaking at the Asian Advertising Congress at Delhi in 1982 recounted this story about problem solving.

"A colleague of mine was looking for a personal secretary, and had narrowed the field down to three young ladies all of whom were stunningly beautiful. So he tried to test their quick wits, and asked each of them what they would do if they were shipwrecked near an island inhabited by 40 husky men"

"I'd swim in the other direction", the first said.

"I'd find the strongest on the island, and get him to protect me", said the second.

From the third girl, no answer came. "So how would you solve the problem?", my colleague repeated impatiently.

"I hear the question", she replied. "But what's the problem?"

More recently, our problems seemed of a slightly different order. A survey conducted in 1999 by the Roper Organization, on behalf of America Online, revealed that a whopping 68% of people with access to the Internet, when asked which form of media they would choose if they were stranded on a desert island, answered the Internet! This choice far outweighed the telephone and the TV.

To my mind, two things became immediately apparent. The first slightly flippant observation on women seem more sensible than men! But the second more important (and yet obvious) observation is that the times are changing. And people of the Ice Age are warming towards technology. Nothing signifies this change more than one cold fact. 3 out of the top 5 brands of the world in the latest Interbrand study, are technology brands*. (See table at the end of this chapter). Nokia, the first European company in the list is in 6th place. The German car manufacturer Mercedes-Benz comes in 11th.

People want to buy the world more than a Coke. They want to stay connected and logged on to the Net, even as they are hooked onto technology. And yet, the reality is that branding seems to be more of a prerogative of consumer products. Technology brands are still to get the resources or the attention they deserve, unlike the Microsofts of this world. Here is what Steve Ballmer, CEO, Microsoft, has to say, *"In the hi-tech age, building and sustaining great brands are even more critical than ever. The strength of the brand is the only differentiator in a world of connected and knowledgeable customers"*. One does hope that this realization will spread, and soon.

> "The strength of the brand is the only differentiator in a world of connected and knowledgeable customers"
>
> **- Steve Ballmer,** CEO, Microsoft,

What Does the New Era Hold in Store for Us in Marketing and Advertising?

- In the case of technology brands, the reputation of companies will become increasingly important. Behind good brands lie good companies, companies that invest time and effort in their relationships. And brands are all about relationships. How good are your relationships with key constituents?

- Today is the day of 'Warp speed branding'. So brands have to be built quicker by more focussed efforts. Don't we all live in the world of 'quick fixes' and 'instant gratification'?

- Today's technology brands need more than brand managers. In the words of Agnieszka M. Winkler they need *"brand shepherds"*. A shepherd who keeps the flock intact and safe, who defines the core of the brand and evangelizes the brand strategy to all the constituents and all the stakeholders. Who is your company's brand shepherd?

- Branding is all about consistency. Technology is all about change and obsolescence. How do we retain the values of the brand even as we constantly renew ourselves and our technology, is a challenge that every technology company must face, today and tomorrow.

- There will be a lot more than advertising that will be necessary to sustain brands. Branding will encompass everything that companies do to manage their operations. This will become important and influence the way their target publics view them.

- In the words of Charles Handy, *"We've got to learn to live with chaos and uncertainty, try to be comfortable with it and not to look for certainty, where we won't get it."* The era of technology promises to be one of uncertainty. We all live in a non-linear world. How adequate will be our linear thinking?

- Brands will have both marketing and financial value. Perhaps the latter will be far more important than the former notwithstanding their interdependence and notwithstanding the vicissitudes of the Nasdaq.

Who Will Win ?

Whilst brands will rule, win and build value, there is a need to transform ourselves attitudinally and organizationally. In the words of Rowan Gibson *"The winners of the twenty-first century will be those who can transform their organization into something that more resembles a jeep – an all–wheel drive, all-terrain vehicle that is lean, mean and highly manoeuvrable".*

Given all this speed and transformation that is coming at us from all directions, one wonders about our mindset to handle all the monumental challenges by the 'Ice Economy'. Are we ready?

To move from technology to cricket and the Australian cricket team, which lost the 'Ashes' in September 2005 in a great contest, let me give a twist to this famous limerick of the 'Ashes' age to the 'ice' age.

"Ashes to Ashes

Dust to dust

If technology doesn't get you

then the brand must!"

*Interbrand's league table of the world's most valuable brands 2004.

The World's 10 most Valuable Brands

A newcomer, Toyota, breaks into the Top 10, while big-name consumer brands come under attack.

Rank	Brand	2004 Brand Value (Billions)
1	COCA-COLA	$67.39
2	MICROSOFT	61.37
3	IBM	53.79
4	GE	44.11
5	INTEL	33.50
6	DISNEY	27.11
7	McDONALD'S	25.00
8	NOKIA	24.04
9	TOYOTA	22.67
10	MARLBORO	22.13

Data : Interbrand Corp., J.P Chase & Co., Citigroup, Morgan Stanley

CHAPTER

Can Indian Industry Learn from Software?

I have been a passionate fan of the Indian Software industry, perhaps this is a consequence of my fortuitous investments in an undiscovered sector, at that time. I must quickly add however that much of these gains have since been negated thanks to prudent (?) further investments in the sector. Humour apart, one does realize that software too has gone through its share of ups and downs. What with September 11 2001, the slowdown in the US, people on the bench, consequent decline in market capitalization and the current furore created over unemployment as a result of outsourcing of jobs particularly in the USA. And yet, I think its important to address this question, which was posed to me at a seminar, "Does the highly successful way in which Indian Software companies have marketed themselves overseas, provide some learning for the marketers of other Indian products and services?" I, for one, strongly believe it does. If only we were to look around, we would find quite a few things worth understanding and emulating.

Just the Facts, Ma'am, Just the Facts

The software industry has had its fair share of friends. 'Suppliers of cheap labour', 'body shoppers', 'beneficiaries of Clinton's largesse', 'marginal players globally', 'where are the products?', 'when will we get beyond services?'...*ad infinitum, ad nauseum.* And here I was thinking, that this is the industry with the maximum number of friends! Software is easily India's third largest export commodity after gem-cutting and textiles. Those are the facts, plain and simple. The rest of India would be perhaps better advised to take a look at this success story, study it, perhaps emulate it, rather than be the wailers and whiners they have been. The preoccupations they have with 'levelling the playing field' and their clamour for protection notwithstanding the reality is that their track-record, globally, is hardly anything to set the Cauvery on fire. So how has the software industry achieved what the rest of Indian industry has so patently failed to achieve?

Necessity, the Mother of Invention

Charles Darwin said, *"It is not the strongest of the species that survive but that which best attempts to change"*. Software has changed with the times. Let's just go back to the state of the Indian market for software, a decade ago. The market was small, developing and relatively unsophisticated. This meant too that the Indian market could not support the prices, which the software industry (justifiably) claimed for the value it was bringing to the table. So, out of necessity, the software industry had to look overseas. And yet, a decade ago, it's perhaps relevant to look at the global perceptions about India. India was still the land of elephants and snake charmers and notwithstanding our being ruled by the British, the perception was that we could not speak English. The software industry addressed these problems and grew significantly. The software industry; going by my friend's words (a CEO in the making) developed 4 abilities – **credibility, reference ability, scalability and sustainability.** In the early stages, the industry made an initial breakthrough via contacts in key positions (often Indians)

'The software industry; going by my friend's words (a CEO in the making) developed 4 abilities – credibility, reference ability, scalability and sustainability' and used a clutch of solid manpower to do low-tech work with excellent results. They built credibility, slowly but surely and used these initial references to get better work, better rates and better clients. Today, nearly 50% of Fortune 500 companies are clients of the Indian Software industry. Clearly success has not only been scalable but also sustainable. And the reality when one looks at the rest of Indian industry is that the quality of products is still poor and the orientation process, suspect. Obviously, Indian brands and companies need to worry about this. If software can have dedicated development centres for Lucent, Nortel, GE, it can't be too long before other sectors follow suit. China has done this by supplying toys to majors like Hasbro and Mattel and are using tie-ups like these to overcome some of the low quality perceptions and biases which have been historical baggage in their case too.

World Wide Web, World Wide Customers

The website, as a marketing and strategic tool has been capitalized to a greater extent by the software industry than traditional industry. There was a time when a company was only as good as its latest advertising campaign. Now, more than ever, a company, particularly one that wishes to make its presence felt globally, must have a world-class website. It must be a site that has impact, is easy to navigate, with enough relevant data to attract the maximum number of relevant hits. Traditionally, industry too, has largely underestimated the importance of glossily produced marketing collateral. Their reliance on mass media advertising has shown a decline in the quality of important collateral.

Never Miss an Opportunity

Over the last few weeks, the postman carries heavy books addressed to my wife. They are the annual reports of companies like Infosys, Wipro, Satyam Computers and HCL Technologies. Our household is like any typical Indian household, in the sense that, all the assets are in the name of the wife, whilst all the liabilities are in the husband's name! (I shall resist the temptation to talk about that, for the present!). And all these annual reports are a lot better designed, are much more comprehensive, and give much more information than before, which is probably why they are bulkier too than ever before! Clearly there is a realization amongst discerning corporations that the investor is an important target segment - as important as employees and customers.

One of the most significantly discernible developments is the inclusion of the brand's value as an important part of the whole financial reporting process – a defensive move initiated by companies in the U.K, some of whom were doing badly. Today, most companies particularly in the software sector, include this important number in their financial reports. And whilst accountants may quibble about the subjective nature of brand valuation, there is no arguing about the need to portray the overall health and well being of a corporation. Incidentally, Infosys Technologies Ltd, has valued its brand in 2005, at Rs.14153 crores. Yes, brands have value, phenomenal value. Value that can soar higher than the physical value of the assets that the corporation owns. A brand's value shown along with its audited financial results will hopefully be the rule rather than the exception. And one hopes that it will not only be technology companies that will accomplish this.

In the early years, companies brought out their annual reports very properly and correctly; if not very creatively. Since, the decision makers in several companies were the accountants, when it came to financial statements, they tried to spend the bare minimum that was necessary, skimping on the design and the quality of the paper used. But today, there is the realization that mere parsimony is not economy. CEOs are realizing that a well-brought out annual report is an opportunity to project an image. And companies like Infosys, which led the way in design in the IT sector a few years ago, are finding that others are following suit. Today, if companies can play 'catch-up' in product design and technology, they certainly can catch up in aesthetics and creativity.

And yet, creativity whilst being important is not the only critical component in this activity. Equally imparting is information to shareholders. Companies want to take the 'transparency' and 'corporate governance' platform by giving comprehensive information. The most significant change in my opinion is attitudinal. Earlier companies gave information because they 'had to'. Today they give information because they 'want to'. No longer can companies operate within the framework of the Indian system alone. They must conform to global standards like GAAP, if they have any intentions of making a mark in the world. The software industry has discovered this. What about the rest of Indian industry? I do know that exceptions exist but ...

The Price of Fame Vs the Cost of Advertising

Traditionally, companies have used advertising as a means of building their corporate equity. Advertising whilst glamorous is also expensive, horrendously so, when you consider global media. Software has (re)-discovered the value of public relations as a strategic tool to innovatively build its image. The bottom line of course is to be innovative and consequently newsworthy. Interestingly, the software industry has used even the capital markets to garner more than resources. It has cornered media attention as well. Why would Reuters seek you out if you are not listed on the NASDAQ or NYSE? Clearly this is more than a strategy to raise money. It's a strategy to put your company on the global map.

'If companies can play "catch-up" in product design and technology, they certainly can catch up in aesthetics and creativity'

Here's another innovation. Infosys kicked off its Global

Internship Programme in step in 1999, when it got 300 applications for 14 positions, from all over the world. In 2005 the number of global applicants were over 9000 for 100 positions. Whilst it obviously made it to the newspapers, it also sent out a strong statement; if our students can go to Boston, why can't their students come to Bangalore to train and work? We must think globally and act globally if we are to compete globally.

Equity for the Firm Vs Equity for the Industry

Companies in general have bothered about building their own corporate identity and equity. But in the case of software, we have another interesting precedent. The players, collectively and visibly, and prestigious associations like NASSCOM have made software India's most written about, most glamorous and most sought after industry, whether its journalists or graduate engineers who are seeking its favour. So the industry's collective equity is greater than the sum of the individual firms' equities that constitute it. It is electronics and computers that hopeful students make a beeline for; and software companies like Wipro and Infosys are on campus from day 1. If an industry's success is going to depend on the sort of talent that it can attract, then the other industries do have a problem. They are no longer in the consideration set. Clearly, there is a problem here. And today, India too has been marketed as an IT destination. If Swedish and Japanese TV are covering India, what are they talking about? Software obviously.

> 'Software has (re)discovered the value of public relations as a strategic tool to innovatively build its image'

Think and Invest for the 'Long Term'

Indian business has this tendency to think short term and get confused between investments and costs. Nearly a decade ago, software companies invested in global offices as they realized that the only way to acquire customers is to be close to them, in more ways than one. People have been and will be software's cutting edge in a competitive world. After all, software companies have been and will be 'people-centric' whilst the rest of the world is 'product-centric'. Investments have to be long term. Investments have to be for the future. And the scary thing is investments have to be made in foreign currency. Here is what an experienced marketer has to say, *"Do not venture forth (globally) unless there is plenty of money for brand building and this money is available in appropriate currencies at the right time and that the domestic company's bottom line can accommodate the costs that go with brand building".* That's a sobering thought. And perhaps this explains the reticence of Indian industry to invest and harvest globally.

And Yet....

The reality, however is that software too has faced a correction in its path, which it was so unprepared for. Whether it was 9/11/2001 in New York or 7/7/2005 in London, tragedy has brought severe repercussions on the industry. The global slowdown has sharply thrown up some failings of the sector.

'The industry's collective equity is greater than the sum of the individual firms' equities that constitute it'

- The migration to higher value-added services like consulting did not happen quickly or effectively.

- Software companies are just realizing the need for branding and that it is an investment.

- Software has not scaled itself aggressively to address all the needs of the market. It still serves only a small percentage of the market.

- The industry is still struggling with the cultural integration of local employees on the global front, in marketing and selling.

- It went after the low hanging fruits alone, like the US market. Did not invest in developing European markets till slowdown happened (barring a few exceptions).

- Its general presence in the 'product space' is a big question mark.

Obviously, the software industry has miles to go before it sleeps. It can't look merely inwards. It must look at external examples that it can learn from. And, Indian industry, if it wishes to grow globally, can learn several things from software. That being so, we ought to still be aware that not so long ago, software's situation was very sobering.

Will software be satisfied with merely being much better than the mediocre rest-of-India? Or will it continue to be an icon that is absolutely capable of being a force not only in India but also globally. My heart tells me that it will be the latter. My mind however tells me that it will be a slow and arduous route. But, clearly the software industry and the rest of India don't have a choice. The world is up for grabs. That's both frightening and exciting. Let's grab the future before it is too late.

> 'Software companies have been and will be 'people-centric' whilst the rest of the world is 'product-centric''

CHAPTER

And What Software needs to Learn About Branding

On the 11th of March 1999, Infosys Technologies created history by becoming the first Indian company to be listed on the NASDAQ exchange. The very next day, Infosys Technologies made the headlines in every newspaper and business channel in the country. There are lessons in this for technology companies by and large.

All Software companies do not operate in the high technology space even if they believe they do. I believe it is important, critical in fact, for technology companies to address the issues of branding and its impact on a company's presence in the marketplace.

Technowizard or Technophobe

I am slightly in awe of technology. I could never get into engineering, a fact that my father never forgave me for. As an advertisement for GTE says:

'Some people are actually interested in how technology works. (Then there are the rest of us).'

I can be classified very easily as amongst 'The rest of us'. And this is precisely what some technology companies tend to overlook. My friends and clients are competent engineers and technologists. "We are a 'tech' company," they say, "Don't give us marketing jargon." The reality is that the rest of the world doesn't share the same enthusiasm (or is it passion?) for technology. Again, to quote a headline from another GTE advertisement.

"We operate under the rule that most people don't care how technology works (as long as it does)".

I am not suggesting that technology is declining in importance. It is very important, especially in the software industry where high achievers (prospective employees) want to work on 'cutting-edge' technology. So, if your company fails to emphasise its technological sophistry or competence, it will lose out on attracting the best talent. But in the same breath let me add, that companies are realising that they are also interacting with a wide cross-section of audiences simultaneously. Dell Computers had segmented its buyers into 7 different 'techno-types'.

TECHNO TYPES	
Techno Wizards	Thrive in a high-tech environment; the hotter and more challenging the technology, the better.
Techno-to-to	May already have a good knowledge base, but want a computer that's ready to run right out of the box and prefer to call a customer assistance line for help than to refer to a manual.
Techno-Boomers	May have started from ground zero, but studying hard to learn how computers can help them look smart.
Techno-Novices	Want to look smart, yet have no knowledge of, or experience with, technology.
Techno-Teamers	Chief interest in computers in how computers can improve their productivity at the office and how computers can make them more valuable members of the corporate team.

Techno-Critical	-	Rely on computers for more sophisticated applications critical to the job, such as computer-aided engineering or design.
Techno-Phobes	-	Avoid technology whenever possible. Pencil-and-paper types all the way !

As the table demonstrates 'Techno-wizards' and 'Technophobes' are at two ends of the spectrum.

So, what holds these two diverse people together? In a marketing situation, it is the power of the company's brand with the reassurance of high-end technology and the reliability that comes along with it.

But is Technology Alone Enough?

Savvy companies, the world over, are investing in brand building even as they upgrade their technology. Mere technology isn't enough. Companies who developed their technology and neglected their brand have long since dwindled into forgotten history.

It is, I believe, better to overreact to a threat than to under react. And, it is better to react sooner, than later. I believe that some technology companies are threatened today. The sooner technology companies realise the need to build themselves into brands, the better for themselves and their various target publics.

Is your Company's Image being Hijacked By the Bulls and the Bears?

For some time, **'Ice'** ruled the roost. For those (unfortunate) ones not initiated in to the stock market and the world of bulls and bears **'Ice'** refers to stocks in Infotech, Communication and Entertainment. These stocks were hogging the headlines; they were actively traded and PR managers were smiling all the way to the bank. Satyam, Infosys, Hughes Software, Zee Telefilms were all active in the stock market and even more active in the newspapers. I wondered then, whether that created a false sense of security in the minds of the people who here involved in safeguarding the interests of the brands of these respective companies. These companies were getting a tremendous amount of coverage and free publicity. But I have a question for them: "Should a company be satisfied with being the most actively traded stock?"

In short, every company would like to be a company of choice to consumers, investors and potential employees. Given this scenario, is it enough for a company to be merely traded actively on the stock market? Despite the tremendous importance of the stock market and the increasing interest in it by retail investors and the media, my submission is that the investing community in India is a very small percentage of the total target audience that any company would like to address. Is your company letting its performance/non-performance in the stock market be the sole determinant of its corporate image? Should your image be controlled by **you** or by analysts who give their views in newspapers?

> 'Should your image be controlled by you or by analysts who give their views in newspapers?'

Isn't it necessary for companies to guide their own destiny rather than leaving it to the Bulls and the Bears? Think about it.

Is Mere Publicity Enough

Today technology companies are created on the pages of business newspapers and on the covers of business magazines. The Wall Street Journal and Forbes Magazine launched some of the biggest technology companies like Microsoft, Dell, Compaq and Apple. And yet these companies have realized that publicity can take them only thus far and no further. They have realized that whilst a brand can be launched by publicity, it must be sustained by advertising. We have

> "Brands are like pieces of fine crystal – they take time to create and are easy to break"
>
> **- Mike Isaacson**

companies like Intel demonstrating the value of mass media. Would an **'Intel inside'** have worked as dramatically without the $250 million advertising budget that supported it way back in 1992? The mere fact that your brand is ahead of the pack does not necessarily mean that it will continue to be so forever. You need to tend to it carefully, nurture it with whatever it requires. To quote Mike Isaacson, director of Corporate Marketing, Sierra-On-Line, "Brands are like pieces of fine crystal – they take time to create and are easy to break."

And What about Internal Communication?

Advertising is glamorous and visible while Media Relations is noticeable. Both these play a vital role in corporate image building. And yet the role of internal communication is often ignored. In technology companies, the employee is an important if not a vital constituent. And yet how often is communication aimed directly at him? Internal communication is not glamorous. But, if strategically created, it can be effective and communicate not only news but corporate values to the employees. It costs a fraction of other media. Why is so little of that done? Simple. Advertising agencies are not turned on by it, because it is not on media. It will neither give them visibility nor revenue. And Public Relations agencies do not have creative resources at their disposal. And the harassed Marketing Communications Manager has too much on her plate. And the HR Manager is only hiring in droves. Companies would do well to go to a specialist for internal communications.

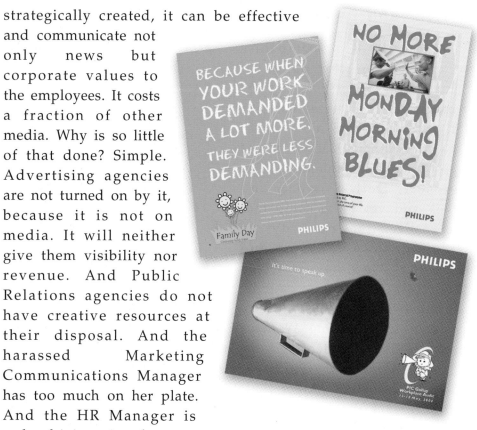

Internal Communication Posters.   *Creative: brand-comm*

So What's the Bottom Line?

I believe that technology companies are threatened today. The sooner technology companies realize the need to build themselves into brands, the better for themselves and their various target publics. They must have a clear strategy, think about their personality and evolve a well-orchestrated communications programme. The challenge becomes more daunting for smaller companies with even more scarce resources (for brand building). What must they do? They need to harness their technology without losing sight of what the company stands for. They need to communicate adequately with various publics. They need to build their company as a brand. And their sphere of recognition and influence will extend beyond the shores of this country. That will truly be great news for Indian software.

Finally, to return to our technology brand – Infosys. The brand has hardly done a thing wrong in the last few years. It serves as a beacon to aspirants and a benchmark for the industry. But, publicity can be a double-edged sword, and the position of leadership has its own share of problems. There must be enough and plenty of budding journalists waiting to make their reputations by sniping at Infosys in the future. And ridiculous though it may seem to Infosys today (with the media falling over themselves to write about the company), they must realise the value of a planned corporate communication programme and use mass media to inform and create a well-rounded personality. If today you were to ask questions about what people think about Infosys, one would expect responses like – performer, result-oriented, successful, ethical and so on. My own instinct suggests that their personality can become more comprehensive, more human, and complete with a well-orchestrated communications programme built around advertising.

If that is the case with India's most written about company, what should be the situation with similar albeit lesser-known companies. They need to harness their technology without losing sight of what the company stands for. They need to communicate adequately with various publics. They need to build their company as a brand. And soon enough you will find more and more companies being recognised, respected and even revered. Their sphere of recognition and influence will extend beyond the shores of this country. And that will create several, 'Red-letter days' for Indian industry, quite like the 11th of March 1999.

"In today's competitive world,
a name must function as a total messenger"

- Naseem Javed

CHAPTER

How to Make Your Brand "Buzz"

"If you like our service,

please tell your friends.

If not, then please tell us".

If your customers don't speak for you, who will? 'Word-of-mouth', as we know it, has been an important and often indispensable part of marketing. The reason for this is simple: people who are in a frame of mind to buy a product, tend to ask around before they shop.

> 'Word of mouth in its new avatar, has technology as a big pillar of support'

Would you buy a palm pilot without checking with someone? Would you buy a laptop without asking a friend about his experiences? How about a funky gizmo? Would you buy one without first checking with your friend in Dubai? Would you buy a new car without asking someone who bought it a few months ago? Would you sign on an ad agency without doing a 'credit-check' with its existing and former clients? Yes, 'Word of Mouth' has been alive and kicking from time immemorial (especially for those whose products do not live up to claims or expectations). But 'Word of Mouth' in its new avatar, has technology as a big pillar of support. It tries to go beyond passive responses to questions about the product or service to actually moulding opinion and creating 'buzz' about the brand. And 'buzz' is a recognition of the fact that the greatest advertising medium of them all is the human voice. To quote Steve Douty, former Vice President of hotmail, "Buzz" is 'Word-of-Mouth' on steroids".

Hot Mail buzzes and Palm Pilots a success story.

In 1995 when hotmail was in its infancy and doing the rounds of venture capital, Steve Jurvetson of DFC remembers Bhatia's projected number of users as being *"the most 'hallucinogenically' optimistic forecasts that you could imagine"*. But Bhatia's forecasts were proved right because word about the service started to spread, both electronically and as the result of face-to-face conversations. Hotmail was discussed at campus dorms, cafés and movie halls. And most significantly, it delivered. It was good word-of-mouth marketing, at Internet speed. Hotmail was not a heavy advertiser but as a PR expert said, *"Money can help, but 'word-of-mouth' rooted in a great user experience wins"*. You can say that again. And the opportunity to *"Get your free email at hotmail.com"* doesn't hurt either.

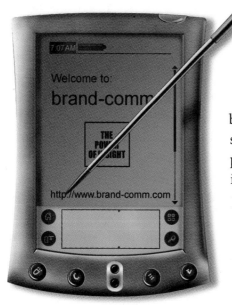

The Palm pilot, another big success, is an example of 'Humble marketing'. The company's credo was 'under-promise and over-deliver'. Whilst one has to concede the value of factors, such as, timing, technology and pricing, there is a big strategic factor behind its success. The Palm team let the product spread by itself through invisible networks, allowing people to discover the product, experience the excitement and tell their friends. They didn't push. And the rest as we all know is chronicled in history.

Network Hubs

All the world has experts, technology buffs and plain enthusiasts who can create 'buzz' around your product. Everyone knows what a mega hub like Oprah Winfrey can do. Her endorsement made 'Men are from Mars and Women are from Venus' a big hit. Today, a favourable review from Oprah is a 'hygiene factor' or absolutely necessary for success. But smart companies are realising that the spheres of influence are extending beyond the old parameters. You no longer have to hold centre stage to be of consequence. You could be sitting in the audience (perhaps in the front seats) and add your own sphere of influence to a brand's success. And the primary contributor to this scenario is the Internet. I, was for instance, pleasantly surprised to see a site called sierramaniac.com where a passionate car lover speaks about his Tata Sierra. He dwells on the celebrities who own the vehicle, their discussion boards and a forum not only to share experiences, but an opportunity to buy or sell Tata Sierras. Marketers want their brands to be an important and integral part of their consumer's lives. And if, a live consumer can describe his experiences with a brand to a whole lot of people, thanks to the Internet, it gives the whole exercise tremendous source credibility. Who can be passionate about your brand and create 'buzz'? Think about it.

It Works Both Ways

"The only thing greater than goodwill is ill-will" is something we should all remember.

In 1994, a college professor noticed a division error in Intel's Pentium chip, grabbed the microphone and spread it quickly on the Net. Intel's attempts to downplay the problem were unsuccessful, creating a stink in the press and ultimately, an adverse impact on the company's stock price. Companies have to listen lest they get hurt. Today, an unhappy customer need not quickly drift away as in yesteryears. He can harness the Net to demonstrate that he has been hurt and can actually hurt the company in many ways, like these;

- Email his experience to his friends

- Voice his disgruntlement at 'chats'

- Bombard the company's site with sarcastic remarks about their claims

- Publish the complaint on his own web site

- He can start a web site dedicated to the company. Only in this case, unlike the sierramaniac.com it would be a 'protest' site not a fan site

Yes, in a networked world, marketing is not easy. We must appreciate this and be well-equipped for the task.

I wish we could say that 'buzz' is the panacea to all our marketing problems. It isn't. But it can become a potent strategic tool provided we understand the buying influences prevalent in the market. Who are the people whose opinions (in the context of our brand) matter to prospects? How can we reach them and mobilise their support? What will make them passionate about our product? We already know that 'buzz' works for high involvement products. We know that people look for guidance and support in buying sophisticated technology products. And yet, we must recognise one important fact. Crucial to marketing success is a good product or service. Customers and enthusiasts do talk (mail) prolifically about a product or service that delivers on expectation and experience. So before we create 'buzz', lets ask ourselves one obvious question.

> 'In a networked world, marketing is not easy. We must appreciate this and be well-equipped for the task'

"How good is our product or service?"

ADVERTISING

"Successful branding programs are based on the concept of singularity. The objective is to create in the mind of the prospect the perception that there is no other product on the market quite like your product"

- Al Ries & Laura Ries

CHAPTER

You Went to IIM, for This?

Our world is full of brands. And what do brands represent? Brands represent freedom of choice. Every waking moment we are making choices, if you will forgive the exaggeration (people in advertising have this tendency to make things larger than life), and yet consider these choices.

Which car will you buy?

Which morning newspaper will you read?

What brand of coffee will have the privilege of being your first cup of the day?

Which drink will you order at the club in the evening?

Which brand of cigarette will you smoke (if you must)?

All these represent the choices available to us as consumers. And yet research suggests that people do not take these decisions lightly. Cars, newspapers, coffee, liquor are all high-involvement products. At the other end of the spectrum are products that we call low-involvement products. Which battery does your car run on? Which brand of chain does your two-wheeler possess? Which toothbrush do you use? Which brand of matches do you use to light your gas stove? Very often we do not know the answers to these questions, nor do we care as they are not very

> 'Advertising as a career option has become a low involvement profession for today's youth'

important to us. And this leads me to the purpose of this piece. Advertising as a career option has become a low-involvement profession for today's youth. And that could impact the very development of this industry.

Down Memory Lane:

I went to management school simply to study marketing and get into advertising. And I daresay I haven't looked back since. My concern is that today there are not too many young people beating a path to the doors of advertising agencies.

> 'Unlike manufacturing which values experience and gray hair, advertising actually values youth'

Just Consider these Figures:

In 1983 when I entered the advertising business it was a Rs. 170 crore industry. Today, it is over Rs. 9000 crores and yet the human resource base has not grown significantly in quality. But to go back to a basic situation of supply vs. demand of people, the hard reality is that not enough high quality young people want to enter the ad world of today. And that's the tragedy. It's perhaps critical to remember the nature of the advertising business. Unlike manufacturing which values experience and gray hair, advertising actually values youth. Because youth brings fresh ideas, new perspectives and objectivity. All of which is valuable. But which industries are today's young management graduates moving toward? It's software and therein lies the role model for the advertising business.

Who is the 'Narayana Murthy' of the Advertising Industry?

If you were to ask the average person on the street what comes to mind when you say software, he might well say "Narayana Murthy". And there is an important lesson here. Every industry needs a leader to champion its cause. A leader who will represent the industry, be visible as its spokesman and lobby for it, if need be. The software industry is the "industry of choice" to India's young minds. And I must mention here that this is no accident but a carefully planned and well-executed strategy. And one cannot ignore associations like NASSCOM and visionary leaders like the late Dewang Mehta who made their presence felt by making a difference. We can, in Bangalore at least, see the emergence of biotechnology as the next sunrise industry, whereas the advertising industry badly needs visibility. It needs leaders who are passionate about the business, leaders who will present their views articulately and with conviction, at visible fora.

> 'Every industry needs a leader or a champion for its cause'

Yes, there can and must be more to Indian industry than software. But then as an industry, if you are not even in the consideration set of young graduates, you are in trouble. I was amazed that, at one time, IIM Bangalore which is arguably the best management institute in the country did not offer advertising as a specialization in the 2nd year. Thankfully, that has since been rectified. Today's management graduates want to be venture capitalists, investment bankers, equity researchers and what have you...

Money, Money, Money It's a Rich Man's World

Today's kids are focused. They are pragmatic and know what they want. And they want to be paid what they are worth. And honestly they can deliver tremendous value. It's an obvious fact that if you pay peanuts you'll get only monkeys. Advertising which was one of the most well-paying industries has now slid down to the tail end of industries in terms of compensation. It's hardly surprising that in the Feedback – Mode study on 'Hot Jobs' that appeared in a weekly, young people spoke about becoming system administrators, call centre executives, insurance marketers, visual merchandisers and biotechnologists. There is no 'buzz' for advertising anymore. In a related field there is some excitement. There is a new breed of radio jockeys now, and video jockeys are discovering fame and perhaps riches. Good-looking kids want to walk the ramp, but not too many want to write ads and that's a source of worry, which leads me to a fairly important issue.

> 'They are pragmatic and know what they want. And they want to be paid what they are worth'

Let's Do Great Ads

The product of the advertising industry is really the press ads and the television commercials that we produce. That is how the world sees us. And that is how youngsters will determine whether our work is "cool" or whether it "sucks". I came into this business because I was turned on by the wonderful work of Madison Avenue although one had merely admired it from far. Our work for the brands that we advertise must 'turn-on' our youngsters. We need more Ericcsons, Cadburys, Fevicols, Pepsodents, Bajajs to capture the imagination of today's kids. Some of the problems like lack of money can be compensated by the opportunity for and the visibility from creating great ads. And the onus is on each one of us in marketing and advertising, to create an environment where great work can be produced, bought and released.

When I first came into advertising I was hard working (unlike now). I remember my mother waiting up for me late in the night to give me my dinner (it's not only in the movies that these things happen). Once she asked me "What do you actually do"? I launched into a major treatise on my job, my pressures and the stresses of being an account management person. And she asked me a simple question reflecting the down-to-earth wisdom and common sense of the earlier generation. "You went to IIM for this?" I didn't have an answer then, but I do, now. Each one of us has to be a "brand champion" of the advertising industry that has given us the limited success we enjoy. It is now our duty to propagate what this industry is and capable of becoming. Should we not make it more visible? Should we not make it "considered" by today's youth? Should we not put our shoulder to the wheel?

I am ready. Are you?

> 'Youngsters will determine whether our work is "cool" or whether it "sucks"'

"A brand is whatever
people think and feel it is"

- Sid Peimer

CHAPTER

Advertising that Rewards, Works

What is the purpose of advertising? A seemingly innocuous question. But I am sure the answers to such a question could be fairly complex. *"Advertising should merely inform"*, says a marketer supremely confident that he has produced a better mousetrap. *"It should induce trial"*, says a hard-nosed sales manager. *"It should win awards"*, says a creative director (privately). *"It should educate"*, says another.

Before we delve deeper into the controversy, let me quickly say that from whichever end of the spectrum one were to look at it, everyone would be in agreement with the statement that advertising must sell. This is what the advertiser wants and what the agency strives for. This point of view, although single-minded, is fairly narrow in focus as it misses out a key person in the whole process: the consumer. The consumer decides whether to buy or not, and any definition of advertising must include her.

> 'The consumer decides whether to buy or not, and any definition of advertising must include her'

Today, we have more information on the consumer than ever before. Her age. Her income. Her family size. Her possession of consumer durables. Her reading habits. Her buying preferences. You just name it. So advertisers and agencies work out the best strategy which they think will make the consumer buy; whether it is in blitzing her with 3 commercials a day, like Nirma, or asking her to be coldly rational like Lalithaji, or urging her to compare Rin with other detergents. All successful strategies, mind you, aiming to sell products and make advertising agency and advertiser very happy.

There are two conventional management approaches: one, a Theory "X", which looks at employees as lazy shirkers who must be pushed to the hilt, and another, a theory "Y" which treats its employees as mature adults who'll perform well with minimum controls. Advertising very often errs towards the former and tends to treat consumers as people with limited intelligence. Why does this happen? Normally advertisers and agencies, in attempting to reach the most number of people effectively, dangerously oversimplify their methodology. They follow certain tested formulae – brand name within the first 5 seconds, maximum repetition within 30 seconds, with video support, close-up of pack shot, and the check list goes on. This ensures that the lowest common multiple is being addressed. But the advertising, though hard-working, can be given a convenient miss as it doesn't reward the viewer.

I sincerely believe that consumers are smarter than we credit them to be. They are more demanding, and, what perhaps is even more critical, far more discerning. They are able to recognize and appreciate the finer things in movies, and casting in commercials. This probably explains why television commercials in India have (on occasion) better viewership than the television serials they intersperse. Is there a moral somewhere? I think we must try to treat the consumer as an individual with feelings and emotions rather than a demographic description who would respond mechanically to stimuli. This will lead to better and more effective advertising. This does not necessarily mean clever advertising, but advertising which rewards the viewer.

> 'Advertising must not only sell but also charm. It must reward the viewer'

It's obviously better to state our advertising proposition in a way that will touch and move the reader and viewer rather than bore her to death with the ordinary. And such advertising will reward the viewer and make him buy the product. Advertising history is full of such examples. The Volkswagen campaign with its self-deprecating style not only helped the brand but rewarded the reader. A "Hamara Bajaj" campaign not only helps the brand, it is also immensely satisfying to consumers. A Kelvinator commercial not only makes you smile but also makes you patronize 'the coolest one'. A "Kal bhi, Aaj bhi" not only mists your eyes but makes you want to buy. An "I love you Rasna" not only makes the cash register ring but also warms your heart. This, to my mind, is the true purpose of advertising. Advertising must not only sell but also charm. It must reward the viewer. And this becomes increasingly important, given today's clutter in both TV and press. As more and more ads fight for the consumer's attention, she'll soon see only those which reward her. And invariably what will work will be simplicity and an element of surprise which will bring a smile to her lips. And have no fears, she will buy.

I can very well hear an objection "Hey, listen, we are not in the entertainment business!" We most certainly aren't. We are in the business of selling and building brands. We can never forget this. But why can't we sell in style? Why must we tread the trodden path? I remember David Ogilvy saying "The consumer is not a moron, she's your wife". Don't you think she deserves a few rewards?

> "The consumer is not a moron, she's your wife"
>
> **- David Ogilvy**

"We're chasing our tails for 18 to 49 year old
idiots when 10,000 people are turning
50 everyday"

- former CBS President Howard Stringer

CHAPTER

Arriving at the Right Profile

Advertising runs the risk of falling into that genre of industries that are on the verge of becoming a numbers game. Terms like 'OTS' and 'Reach', which have tremendous value in the realm of analysis, sometimes prevent us from looking at the obvious, that good advertising is a highly personal communication between two persons – the sender and the receiver. And if advertising is to be a 'highly personal communication between two persons', the receiver must be described as a person, not as a male/female, 25-34 years old.

The 'Old Reliable' – Demographics

Most account management, marketing and media people are solid, no-nonsense professionals who go by hard facts. They need the support of demographics – the age of the prospective receiver, her educational qualifications and the classification of her town. All of this is necessary and relevant, particularly in the environment of the categories of media information available in the 21st century. But today's consumer is more than a

> 'Good advertising is a highly personal communication between two persons – the sender and the receiver'

> '**It's these images of the prospective consumer rather than a bland demographic profile which make for more focused communication**'

female of 25-34 years, with a degree, living in Bangalore. She is a person with feelings, emotions and distinct preferences. Let's describe her further. She has two children, possesses a driving licence, loves junk food, eats out at a big restaurant once a month, likes ghazals and prefers a churidar to a sari. It's these images of the prospective consumer rather than a bland demographic profile which make for more focused communication.

Are Grace Slick and Tricia Nixon Cox the same person?

An article by John E. O'Toole in the Journal of Advertising published in 1973 addresses this problem and is equally relevant today as at the time it was written. If one were to describe the prospect in demographic terms, it would be that of a woman of 25-35 years, a college graduate, with a family income of over $15,000.

On the face of it, this is a pretty comprehensive description. But, who really is this prospect? It's Tricia Nixon Cox whose father belonged to the Republication Party. She gets married in a beautiful White House ceremony and exemplifies the straight life. But it is also Grace Slick, of Jefferson Airplane – who isn't into marriage but gave birth two years ago, to a daughter who was originally named God, but whom Ms. Slick now refers to as China. Obviously, if one were to look primarily at demographics, one would run into problems of oversimplification.

Does She or Doesn't She?

A few years ago, we were struggling to arrive at different advertising stances for two kinds of sanitary napkins, one with a belt and the other belt-less. The task at hand became relatively simpler once we had clear, distinct descriptions of the two prospects, both demographically and psycho-graphically.

One was traditional, conservative, married, probably living in a joint family, with children, most likely a housewife.

The other was aggressive, sophisticated, single, holding her own in a world of men, calling the shots, leading an active social life, knew what she wanted and how to get it.

These two distinct types led to two distinct images/role models: The lady using a sanitary napkin with a belt was like Jaya Pradha, a traditional South Indian screen actress of the eighties while the belt-less user was more in the mould of Meryl Streep.

Smooth Days Begin This Way

When we were designing the advertising for Wilman II shaving systems (a brand taken over by Gillette in India) we realised that significant differences exist between the users of conventional double-edge blades and twin blades. In demographic and psychographics terms, we defined the twin-blade user as young, urbane, sophisticated, and a denizen of the metros, upwardly mobile and with aspirations to the strong outdoor life. And in current times, whilst modern offerings like the Mach III and the Sensor have made their appearance, the Indian male is still traditional in his shaving habits.

Oh, Weary Traveller!

The following description, of a business traveller, found in a DDB Needham strategy document, seems to me to be ideal: "Business travellers, who are likely to stay at a mid-price hotel, have an annual income of $25,000 to $50,000. Eighty percent are males. They choose mid-price accommodations because they are paying their own way, or because their expense accounts are limited".

Why Fly when You can Take a Train?

When the purpose of advertising is to persuade frequent travellers between New York and Washington to take the Amtrak instead of a plane, it is better to describe the target audience as follows:

Frequent New York-Washington travellers are likely to be well-educated white-collar professionals conducting a day's business in either city. The nearly 10,000 people who fly daily between New York and Washington have grown accustomed to no-frills service, crowded seating and 'cattle-car' conditions.

Given images like these, it is certainly possible to design more relevant advertising, which the prospect can relate to. It means more research, more qualitative inputs and more meaningful questions. It is not going to make our job easier, but will definitely make our advertising better. So the next time you see a Plans Board or a Brand Review or an Annual Campaign discussion getting out of hand, just pause significantly and say "Excuse me, but just whom are we talking to?"

I promise you that will work.

> 'It means more research, more qualitative inputs and more meaningful questions'

CHAPTER

Good Brief or Good Grief ?

"No amount of planning can ever replace dumb luck". Sounds familiar? As much as this dictum applies to Kaun Banega Crorepati, I am reasonably certain that great advertising is produced not by chance or accident (although the odd exception will always be there) but by a good creative brief which is based on

> 'A good brief can result in stunning creative that can make a remarkable difference to a brand'

understanding the consumer. A good brief can result in stunning creative that can make a remarkable difference to a brand. Quite often the key to the entire process of providing an exciting creative brief is the role of the account planner. A good account planner can go beyond the research and provide a key insight to the creative team resulting in great advertising.

Who is this animal, the 'Account Planner'?

"A planner is the one who thinks all the time like the consumer of advertising rather than an advertising person".

"A planner is essentially the account team's contact with the outside world".

"The planner could well be the objective conscience of the brand".

Michael S. Lewellyn Williams, Director of Account Planning at Ketchum, says that a planner is a hunter looking for the *"grit for the pearls in the oyster"*. And advertising agencies in the UK (the country which invented the process of account planning) could well describe the planner as one who introduces single-minded focus in creative. But perhaps the best definition is this given by a Boase Massimi Pollit (BMP) director, *"Account planning is the discipline that brings the consumer into the*

> 'Account planning is the discipline that brings the consumer into the process of developing advertising'

process of developing advertising. To be truly effective, advertising must be both distinctive and relevant, and planning helps on both counts". Distinctive, relevant, consumer focus: all of these factors are important and familiar to us in advertising. Rarely however, do they find exciting creative representation. Account planning helps make breakthrough creative possible. Indian advertising could benefit from this.

The Threatened Account Executive.

One of the biggest stumbling blocks to the development of account planning as a discipline is perhaps the thin dividing line between research and account planning. People tend to view both these specialities as the same, but there are plenty of differences.

A researcher is data driven. The planner is information driven. More dramatically the researcher is passionate about research whilst the planner is passionate about advertising. And most significantly, the planner is someone who talks in the language of advertising and marketing, not of research; someone who is a sensitive contributor to the creative process, not just an evaluator of it.

But a greater impediment to the future of account planning securing a place under the sun is the account executive who feels threatened. The obvious question that any account executive could ask about the account planner is obvious, "Isn't this my job?" The other crib could well be "Why should I do the dirty operational work alone when someone else does the interesting strategy part?" Somehow, planning seems to connect with the head, whilst servicing seems to have more to do with the hands. Emotion notwithstanding, the fact of the matter is that the average account executive has his hands so full that he could do with some help. I used to be an account executive myself (and a pretty harried one at that). I'd have a "to-do" list, which could be pretty disconcerting and, at times, frightening. I ferreted out one of my old job lists which had 25 items. I am reproducing a few of these, to prove a point.

List of Things To Do

- [ ] Ask for voucher copy from Dhainik Bhaskar

- [ ] Prepare travel statement for last trip.

- [ ] Prepare for collection meeting.

- [ ] Send flowers to client's secy. on her birthday.

- [ ] Remove key no. in that lousy ad written by client.

- [ ] Give creative brief for new campaign

- [ ] Proof read annual report.

- [ ] Check whether banners were delivered at conference venue

- [ ] Get VHS copy of 15 sec edit.

- [ ] Pay house electricity bill (if you want dinner tonight!!)

And the list went on. And more often than not, "Write brief for the new campaign" was something that one had to get out of the way to reduce the items on the to-do list. Clearly I could have done with some help of the account planning type. Someone who would analyse all the research, talk to consumers and the trade and come up with a key insight which would lead to an incisive creative brief resulting in some outstanding work. In retrospect, it all boiled down to protection of "one's turf". I didn't want someone encroaching into my area even though deep down, I knew I couldn't do justice to this aspect of my job.

A good Creative Brief enables a Creative Leap

One of the few things that I learnt in my fleeting association with computers was the term, "Garbage in, Garbage out". Sadly, it holds true for advertising as well. A lot of mediocre work is churned out because not enough time goes into providing direction to creative. It need not necessarily be a competence issue. More often than not, the problem lies with the account executive grappling with multiple tasks, being pulled in different directions, with only 24 hours in his day. Here are a couple of examples of creative briefs (one bizarre, one not), which tell you how time and effort (not to forget, competence) can make a difference to briefs and brands.

Example 1: A new Sony camcorder was being launched. It had a very powerful zoom lens and also a new CCD imager with thousand more pixels than the competition, leading to a brief and creative direction at BMP which read like this:

'A lot of mediocre work is churned out because not enough time goes into providing direction to creative'

"The powerful zoom lens allows you to spot a bee's balls from ten paces. And the thousand pixel CCD imager gives you a picture so sharp that you can't just see his balls, you can count the number of hairs on them". The analogy helps in explaining the technology in as interesting a fashion as possible. The creative team found other expressions for mass consumption using the essence of the product.

Example 2: An ad for a Trooper, a sports utility vehicle, which read like this:

"Trooper is exactly the right equipment for life's great expedition.... it's the Swiss Army Knife of SUVs".

Yes, great briefs make the task of producing timeless advertising possible. The question is "do we have the time?"

Relationship the Name of the Game

It's fairly clear that Indian advertising could do with a lot of planning inputs. Significant benefits can accrue from the planning process. Agency management would do well to realise that planning is a line function, independent of account management and the creative departments. It is therefore on the frontline, sharing responsibility for the quality of the team's work on challenging the account. The onus is on the client servicing person to marshal the additional planning resource for his client's and brand's benefit. The client servicing person is after all the catalyst, bringing together resources for the common good. The planner and account executives can and must work together to produce a great brief. It's not "either" "or" but "together". As a famous advertising personality said, "In most cases, it would be absurd to say to a creative team, "Who had that idea?" Equally, a great brief can come from a working relationship (between planner and account executive) that makes it irrelevant to debate who was the writer of the brief. And everyone has a role to play, the creative, the client service person and the planner. And everyone has ownership. Wouldn't this be a win-win situation if you could hear the following conversation:

Creative director – *"It's my ad"*

Account director – *"It's my client"*

Account planner – *"It's my consumer"*

> 'The onus is on the client service person to marshal the additional planning resource for his client's and brand's benefit'

Less is more

Remember Bill Bernbach? Well at the risk of carrying coal to New Castle, I must tell you that he is arguably the greatest advertising writer of all times. Once he was asked to work out an all-encompassing commercial for Alka-Seltzer. "What else is it good for besides indigestion?" Mr. Bernbach asked. "Headaches, hangovers, depression, everything", said the helpful client. "Good", Mr. Bernbach shot back, "Next time I have everything I'll take some".

Unfortunately, few, if any advertising professionals today, have the stature of Bill Bernbach. Nor are advertising agencies able to stand up to their clients, some of whom believe that they and their brands can be everything to everybody. This is what a client would say, "We have state-of-the-art technology", "Global collaborations", "ISO 9002", "Modern plants", "The best team", "Transparency and ethics" and the list goes on. I can almost hear the reader saying, "So what?" And that's absolutely right. Today as readers, viewers and consumers, we suffer from information-overkill, whether it is a website, a newspaper, a magazine, your car radio, a hoarding or your favourite TV channel, everybody wants to communicate with the prospective consumer.

And yet in our anxiety to communicate, we end up bombarding the consumer with too many messages in one ad, thereby confusing her and causing her to switch off. Sometimes we forget that the consumer has millions of things to do and isn't actually waiting in high anticipation for our ad. Some of the best ads I have seen have actually said one thing and said it dramatically. Duracell said, "The longest lasting battery", Kelvinator said, "The coolest one", Polo said, "Mint with a hole", Spectrawide said, "the widest tyre" and Coca Cola hammered home the price as it just said, "Paanch". All of these ads could have said more than they did, but their success is due to the fact that they said "less" but said it interestingly.

Whilst agencies often take credit for great advertising, as they must, the client must get his fair share of bouquets as well. Both client and agency must work together to separate the chaff from the grain. It calls for hard work, discipline and an element of ruthlessness as well. Tim Bell, an integral part of the original Saatchi & Saatchi team (in fact he was referred to as the third Saatchi) said this at the "Adgrow" in Delhi in 1982, "Great advertising is produced by a single-minded thought which comes alive in a compelling way".

How single-minded is your advertising?

"Tell me short, and show me true,
or else, my dear, to hell with you"

- Old Irish saying

CHAPTER

Can You Recognize a Great Ad?

Guess which is the most abused word in the corporate world? The word gets throws at you by every level of management at every venue – the boardroom, the canteen or the corridor. It's the word 'strategy'. "A strategy", someone said, "is a carefully devised plan to murder the competition".

How do you get the better of your competition? You don't necessarily have to murder them, although that has its merits, but you most certainly have to produce ads that are better than theirs. And how do you do that? By creating ads that are strategically sound. There's that word again! Okay, let me try to steer clear of jargon and explain this whole process to you.

So, How Do you Create Better Ads?

There are two components to producing advertisements. The first is the 'strategy' or more simply 'what is to be said in the ad'. Now that doesn't sound too complex, does it? And yet, I have seen enough clients and agencies struggling with these tasks for a variety of products and services. And why is there a problem? The problem is because, very often in life, we have to create ads for products that are depressingly similar to what

'Very often in life, we have to create ads for products that are depressingly similar to what the competition produces' the competition produces. Someone once said that "even the most technologically advanced and sophisticated new product entry has just the advantage of a few weeks before a similar looking and similar performing product takes its place alongside it on the shelves". If that is the case with technology products, imagine the plight of ordinary consumer products. Yes, the reality is that products are woefully similar to each other.

There are too many "me-too" products in the shelves of 'kirana shops' in India and supermarkets across the world. So it becomes increasingly difficult to say something that will make your brand stand out. When Hero Honda launched their 100 cc bike, they offered 80 kms per litre, which an economy conscious Indian population lapped up. Once the "what" was clear, it was simple to say, "Fill it, shut it, forget it". It was effectively able to shut out the competition for some time at least. An analyst report suggests that only 1 out of 671 new product ideas ever makes it to the market and hits its sale or profit targets. That tells you how difficult our job can be. Have you done your homework?

Having said that, I need to also mention that on many an occasion, hard work can help us ferret out facts, which can give us a direction on 'what' needs to be said. One of the earliest Western examples is of "Bottles that were washed in steam". Someone in the agency or at the client's end had obviously done his homework and acquired a sharp competitive advantage for the brand.

> 'Someone in the agency or at the client's end had obviously done his homework and acquired a sharp competitive advantage for the brand'

The Indian example of Promise toothpaste is oft quoted. Whilst clove is an ingredient in every toothpaste, Promise chose to major on it and reaped handsome rewards, and that too very early on in the product cycle. I remember working with a very gifted copywriter who has won more awards than he can remember.

We were to do a campaign for The Oberoi Hotel in Delhi and were stuck for ideas. The writer wasn't getting clear direction from the account management team. So he asked to be put up at the Oberoi to soak himself in the experience. Whilst I thought he was generally having a good time in a five star environment, he was actually putting in a lot of work.

He noticed that the glass in the bathroom mirrors were of a special type. The glass didn't mist even after the guest came out of a steaming hot shower; a clear advantage and the beginning of an outstanding campaign. So the question we need to ask ourselves is this: Do I know everything I possibly can about my product? Am I living dreaming and soaking in my product? As I've mentioned in an earlier

'Do I know everything I possibly can about my product? Am I living dreaming and soaking in my product?'

chapter, when you walk into a shoe store, observe the shoe salesman as he drops his eyes to your shoes, sizes you up and assesses your preferences, makes a judgment about the state of your shoes, and all of it as he walks up to you. Shoes are his passion. That's probably why some brand managers are such boring company as they are obsessed with their brands. But there is a learning here which will help us unearth some hidden treasure about the products we advertise.

Execution that will Make you Sit Up

You may have a great idea, but it will need a lot of planning and effort before it becomes a great ad. As Bill Bernbach said, "Finding out what to say is the beginning of the communication process. How you say it makes people look, listen and believe. And if you are not successful at that, you have wasted all the work and intelligence and skill that went into discovering what you should say". Think of some great ads and you will probably remember the words, the visuals and the music (kids remember commercials frame by frame and enact it to the pride of doting parents and the embarrassment of guests). And when it comes to making great ads, Bill Bernbach and his agency were no slouches either. His campaign 'Think small' for Volkswagen was voted by Advertising Age as the "Campaign of the last Century". No mean achievement. Again, 'The what' and 'The how'

worked in synergy. David Ogilvy's campaign line *'At 60 miles an hour the loudest noise in this new Rolls Royce comes from the electric clock'* made history for what it said and how it was being said.

Today, we live in a world of television. A world of heady images, exotic locales and captivating music. The solution to great execution is not merely to rush off to Switzerland or Italy (I am told New Zealand is a current favourite) to produce the film, but to see how distinctive the execution can be.

> "Finding out what to say is the beginning of the communication process. How you say it makes people look, listen and believe"
>
> **- Bill Bernbach**

The Ericsson commercial with the line, "One black coffee please" had a simple enough execution, but it got the agency, and the brand, visibility and recognition, globally. So, it's not the size of the budget as much as the power of the execution.

I am sure many of my readers watch advertising. After all, don't we watch cricket, football and soaps in between commercials? So tell me, which are the ads that fascinate you? Ads that say what they have to say effectively, creatively and interestingly? Ads that are top of mind? Ads that will make you switch on your computer and write?

> 'So it's not the size of the budget as much as the power of the execution'

"The three key rules of marketing
are brand recognition,
brand recognition, brand recognition"

- *Anonymous*

CHAPTER

7

Look Who's Buying

Remember your visit to a shoe store? What does the salesman do? He looks at your feet and then proceeds to determine their size, whether they're broad or narrow, the shape of your current footwear and anything else that may concern your feet. He is doing this even as he walks up to you. A shoe salesman is obsessed with feet. The cynic might even say, he has a foot fetish. Well, people in

> 'People in marketing must be obsessed with their customers and spend as much time as possible in understanding their needs'

marketing must be obsessed with their customers and spend as much time as possible in understanding their needs. It has been said (half in jest), that product managers tend to spend a lot of time with their products (sometimes more than with their spouses). So they are inclined to get very attached to them (the products, I mean!). My submission is that we need to understand more about consumers, too. How do they use our products? What do they feel about it? What makes them tick? Can we get under their skins?

I remember working on a campaign for a premium dish-washing liquid a few years ago. It was a superior product and would be soft on the affluent housewife's hands. An interesting proposition leading to a warm commercial, featuring a wife with soft hands and an admiring husband. And yet, when I sat in on 'focus groups', we discussed something else. These were affluent housewives. They were not doing the dishes. Their maids were. So how powerful was the allure of soft hands? Unless the husband had dubious intentions on the maid! Yes, who is your customer? An obvious question, with a not-so-obvious answer.

The solution is to continually keep in touch with your consumers. If you are selling detergents, understand and experience how women wash clothes. If you are selling beer, understand where your customer drinks. I suspect that more beer will be drunk at the "Addah" than in the pub. If you are selling cement, figure out who the decision maker is. If you are selling cars, find out what the family – not just the husband - thinks of your car. If you are selling music systems, what do teenagers (who can make or break your brand) think of your brand, even if they don't have a rupee in their pockets. Talk of "pester-power" if not paisa power. Teenagers will volunteer opinions, views and decisions even when not asked.

The solution to marketers is simple. Manage by wandering about at your outlet; at home where your product is being consumed. Look for opportunities to ask questions. I know the MD of a big durable company who comes to teach my MBA students and spends valuable time understanding what they feel about his brand. I know how busy he is yet he feels it is important that he gives of his time to these students. They are his window to the world. So too must we look for opportunities. Remember we live in a changing world. Tastes change, preferences vary, new customers enter and old customers exit. And how do we manage? Just remember our trusted Bata shoe salesman. Don't miss the obvious. Don't lose touch with your customers. They are your life-line.

> 'The solution to marketers is simple.
> Manage by wandering about at your outlet'

CHAPTER

Are You Waiting for Opportunity to Knock?

In the summer of 1975, I left the city of Madras (as it was known then) for a job in unknown territory. To someone who had lived a sheltered (and often) pampered life, it was quite an experience and even more, a startling revelation.

I started my work life in a small town called Manipal in South Kanara, which has since become famous for its opportunities in education. My entire exposure thus far had been to similar-thinking, similar-speaking people. The experience of meeting so many different people (all from the same country) with so many diverse customs, languages and eating and drinking habits, was quite an eye opener. Imagine my horror the following morning, when I saw one of my batch mates (who was from Tallegaon*) dipping his biscuit into his cup of tea! I looked at him as though he were an alien. This seemed to me even more crass than drinking tea from a saucer! Thirty years later, I know that lots of Indians dip their biscuits into their "chai" while sipping it. And my years in advertising have taught me that if you strike a chord in your prospect's mind, you are home and dry. And the Britannia Marigold commercial hits home with incredible rapport and perception.

The riveting commercial of the wife asking for the biscuit to dip into her "chai" and the husband dashing to get the biscuit and then, in a heroic effort, handing it over to her

> 'If you strike a chord in your prospect's mind, you are home and dry'

* **A tiny town in Maharashtra**

even as he misses the train to the amusement of the porters, is cute and is loaded with recall value. "Dip nahi kiya tho chaai kya piya" says the line. Thankfully, the writer was not being judgmental about consumers like I was in my own experience of witnessing this "biscuit – dipping - into - tea" behaviour. Instead, he observed what they did and, used this information to reach out to them. How often do we observe life around us? And how often does it reflect in advertising concepts and ideas?

You can See a Lot just by Observing

People in advertising very often get carried away by the power of their own rhetoric. They tend to complicate simple things. And because their clients jargonize, they too believe that is the only way to go. They talk about key consumer insights and glamorise it. *"People are spending more"*. They state the fact as though it were a revelation! How profound! How incisive!

Insight or otherwise, the key to producing memorable, advertising is observation of human behaviour. As Yogi Berra said, *"you can observe a lot just by watching"*. And my advice to young writers and creative wannabes is to observe people around you, simplistic though that may sound. Look all around including at what happens to you. And you could have the beginning of a great commercial, which is anchored in experience.

'Insight or otherwise, the key to producing memorable, advertising is observation of human behaviour'

Retire from Work, not from Life

The commercial for ICICI Prudential addresses this yearning that most of us have to take it easy and to take a sabbatical from the fast lane if we can. Have

We cover you. At every step in life.

you recently met someone who is 45 years old? Invariably people of this age group are tired. You can hear them saying, *"I am tired of this rat race"*. *"If only I had the money I'd retire"*. *"You need 2 crores to hang up your boots..."* *"I want to teach..."* *"I want to do community service"*. Sounds familiar? Peaceful retirement hinges on financial security that comes with judicious investment and careful, (not extravagant) spending. It means quality time with family, time for indulging in childlike pursuits and generally living without a care in the world because you are secure - financially. The ICICI Prudential captures this deep desire of every professional in its charming tag line "Retire from work, not from life". It encapsulates the aspirations of a lot of people and it demonstrates an observation of human behaviour at work. ICICI Prudential is a warm TV commercial that strikes at the heart with someone like me, who yearns, desperately, to retire.

Do you have a Titanic 'paunch'?

What is the first thing that you notice about another male? Quite clearly, his paunch. Today, paunches come in all sizes, shapes and dimensions and this is what the Supreme Oil commercials depict. Looking at the

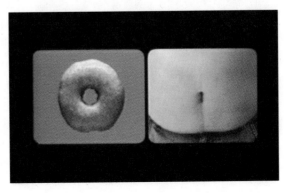

commercial, I am hard pressed to figure out which one is mine! (I am sure my wife has a point of view on the subject!) And that is the point about the commercial – it addresses wives who have a role to play in (the reduction) of the husband's paunch. Cholesterol and heart disease have been done to death (forgive the pun). The paunch is the most visible part of a person, often the most embarrassing. Can you cue health in a light–hearted and effective way? Or must you bludgeon the prospect with fear? It's a no-brainer if you go by the two commercials for Supreme Oil. I loved them and maybe next time around you will see a leaner, meaner me writing vitriolic columns!

Different Sardar same Savitri!

There is this cute Sardar kid who shrieks, "Stop the bus" in Tamil. He enters the house where he used to live in his previous "janam" (birth), recognizes the ancient table in which he used to write which even has "Savitri's" name inscribed on it. Strands of M K Thyagaraja Bhagavadar style music blend with images of his being curled on a grandfather chair in this single-minded commercial for "Greenply". Reincarnation is an Indian concept as old as the hills. While films like the "Reincarnation of Peter Proud" and "Karz" (sorry, my time) have popularised it and books like

"Many Lives, Many Masters" (by Brian L. Weiss) have all put reincarnation top-of-mind, it is something that most Indians are familiar with. The seemingly incongruous match of a Sardar boy with a conservative Tamilian is perhaps the charm of this commercial, but the key brand thought is the longevity of the plywood.

Are you missing an opportunity?

William Faulkner wrote *"A writer needs three things, experience, observation and imagination, any two of which, at times one of which, can supply the lack of the others"*. Soak in experiences. See how you can use them. Your experiences, properly presented can strike a chord in your consumer's mind. Unfortunately many of us are like this patient on a couch telling his psychiatrist *"Opportunity paged me, beeped me, linked me, e-mailed me, faxed me and spammed me, but I was expecting it to knock"*. I am sure you will create your own opportunities and not wait for them to knock.

> "A writer needs three things, experience, observation and imagination, any two of which, at times one of which, can supply the lack of the others"
>
> **- William Faulkner**

"A Brand is a complex symbol. It is the intangible sum of a product's attributes, its name, packaging, and price, its history, reputation, and the way it's advertised. A Brand is also defined by consumers' impressions of the people who use it, as well as their own experience"

- David Ogilvy

CHAPTER

The Power of TV Advertising

Television has invaded our drawing rooms, over-run our bedrooms, captured the minds of our children and even woken up Doordarshan. Some of the finest work we saw, admired and talked about related to the world of print. The power of a U.K. poster once helped overthrow a government. Today, the scene is different. People are not exactly waiting for your ad on TV. Whether it is print or TV,

> 'In a TV commercial you are being watched by millions of people and yet you are talking to one individual'

the first principle is to know whom you are talking to. In a TV commercial you are being watched by millions of people and yet you are talking to one individual. One individual who will make or mar your brand. So the first step is a clear definition of the target audience in demographic and psychographic terms. The following description of a business traveler seems to me to be the ideal. *'Business travelers, who are likely to stay in a mid-price hotel, have an annual income of Rs. 3 lacs to Rs. 6 lacs. 90 per cent are males, they choose mid-price accommodations because they are paying their own way. Or because their 'expense accounts' are limited.* Images like these which are borne out by research and not a figment of a writer's imagination, leads to focused communication.

In advertising (and may I add, in life) we are concerned about perceptions. And the management of perceptions. A company is perceived to be professional whilst it probably is extremely different, a person is seen as dynamic merely because he knots his tie well or is considerate because he is supporting his secretary's arm. Unfortunately we have to come to terms with perceptions. As they are very real.

The First Principle is That Your Advertising must be truly Hard Hitting

I remember reading somewhere that the only rule in advertising is that there are no rules. But before you reject them you must first know them. We reject guidelines – which is considered okay – but without knowing why – which is certainly not okay. Yet, let's not forget that 'Rules are what the artist breaks; the memorable never emerged from a formula'.

Today, TV has improved in popularity and importance. And yet it is only one of the many activities, which people indulge in. They read the newspaper, shout at kids, answer the phone and also watch TV. They are not waiting with bated breath for your commercial. So the first principle is that your advertising must be truly hard-hitting. In more ways than one.

The problem with many of us in advertising (and I suspect clients are guiltier in this regard) is that we wish to say everything possible. Our product is the most durable, most economical, most reliable and whatever else you can say about it. This militates against great advertising. The critical thing is to separate the grain from the chaff and focus

> "If you have a clear idea you must be able to write it on the back of your calling card"
>
> **- David Belasco**

on the bare essentials. David Belasco said, "If you have a clear idea you must be able to write it on the back of your calling card".

Bill Bernbach said, *"A great ad campaign will make a bad product fail faster. It will get more people to know it's bad".* The truly sustaining advantage has to be the product's performance.

Claude Hopkins once thundered. *"People don't buy from a clown".* Humour in advertising was taboo. And David Ogilvy too frowned on all those commercials which

> 'The greatest advertising is that which is simple, surprises the viewer and makes him smile'

made people laugh. Today we have developed a better attitude towards humour. Carefully used, it can be a clever device to gain attention, build a favourable disposition and even induce purchase.

Emotion is again a potent tool. Property handled it can make a tremendous impact. Bill Bernbach (again) said *"I can put down on a page a picture of a man crying, and it's just a picture of a man crying; or I can put him down in such a way as to make you want to cry. The difference is artistry – the intangible things that business distrusts".* The greatest advertising is that which is simple, surprises the viewer and makes him smile. It is probably easier said that done. In India, at least, we have a scenario where the TV set is on in the living room, while the housewife is busy in the kitchen. It probably makes sense to have a jingle, so that even if the viewer is unable to watch the commercial, she can at least hear the brand name being sung.

The human race has always had a weakness for cute kids. They cut across age, language and cultural barriers. This emotional appeal is what clever script writers have used over the years to get attention, mould opinion and build brands.

It is important to have a format for your commercial which is distinctive. And the critical thing is that your commercial is not merely competing within the product category, but with all commercials which any viewer is being exposed to.

The testimonial as a route is probably as old as the hills. It's been used quite effectively before and will probably continue to be used much in the future. But some questions which we need to answer are: How relevant to the target is this testimonial? How powerful is the testimonial? Does the ambassador overshadow the product? Is he/she being overused?

We have been looking at the ideal scenario: TV for brands and large budgets. Now, however with the proliferation of channels and options available to the advertiser, it is possible to look at TV even for simpler things. The only constraint as always, is our imagination.

> 'Great advertising evolves from people who are students of life, and not so much from students of advertising'

Great advertising evolves from people who are students of life, and not so much from students of advertising. Films often reflect life in our society. Which explains the reasons why films and commercials borrow from each other.

The greatest advertising cuts across language barriers. One must also expect some magic in the final film which can't be seen from the story board.

Whilst there will always be big budget, high technical value commercials, a simple powerful thought can be equally effective. Execution is important but not at the cost of an idea as these commercials hopefully confirm. The important thing in advertising is to not lose out on a brand's existing property or values. It is critical that we continue the tradition of excellence, which a brand has acquired, over the years. I can assure you that sometimes these high standards are difficult to maintain. Two cases in point are the Rasna and Red Eveready commercials. Sadly though, both these brands seem to have lost their way through advertising in recent years. Ideally, great advertising stems from genuine product advantage. Bill Bernbach evaluated, *"No matter how skilled you are, you can't invent a product advantage that doesn't exist, and if you do, and it's just a gimmick, it's going to fall apart anyway"*.

> "No matter how skilled you are, you can't invent a product advantage that doesn't exist, and if you do, and it's just a gimmick, it's going to fall apart anyway"
>
> **- Bill Bernbach**

"Your brand's power lies in dominance.
It is better to have 50% of one market,
instead of 10% of five markets"

- Al Ries

CHAPTER 10

Humorous Ads? Are you Joking?

Have you ever tried telling a joke to a large, somewhat disinterested audience? I have. And believe me, the experience is not funny. I guess people who come to these functions seem preoccupied. They are probably worrying about their next EMI payment for their house or wondering how they can make it to the door attracting minimum attention, or forwarding a joke by SMS to a colleague. I am sure you get the picture. If that is the case with 50 people who are educated and intelligent, imagine our plight when we talk to 50 million people, across the length and the breath of this vast country, using humour as a communication tool. It can be a daunting task. Just imagine this. It's 8.30 p.m. in a normal TV watching household. This is prime time viewing. The telephone is ringing (nobody wants to pick it up), the door bell chimes which makes the dog bark in a high crescendo, the children are fighting (remember I said normal household) and the wife is yelling out to her husband asking him whether the pressure cooker has whistled twice or thrice. Now this is the setting for viewership of my new commercial. Do I have a hope in hell of this family watching and liking my commercial and acting upon it? Whilst all of us are familiar with commercial clutter, this is domestic clutter. And if your commercial

'Humour although difficult to conceive and execute can, when properly handled, make you laugh all the way to the bank'

message is cute or clever or funny, then God save you. Does that mean that humour is a no-no? No it doesn't. Humour although difficult to conceive and execute can, when properly handled, make you laugh all the way to the bank. Just ask Fevicol, Ericsson or Spice. Yes many brands have successfully used humour over the years consistently. But they are still a minority.

What do the Experts say?

Opinion on the use of humour as an advertising tool has been divided. And it has changed over the years. The great advertising doyen, Claude Hopkins had strong views on this subject. (I suspect he had a strong view on many subjects under the sun). *"People don't buy from a clown"*, he thundered. David Ogilvy who

> 'Opinion on the use of humour as an advertising tool has been divided'

was influenced by him said, *"I deplore the current fashion of using clergymen, monks and angels as comic figures in advertising. It may amuse you, but it shocks a lot of people"*. However towards the later part of his career and life, David Ogilvy realized the need to hold the audience's interest and attention and hence said, *"You can't save souls in an empty church"*. These were the people who made rules in advertising. And yet, I go by what Bill Bernbach said, *"Rules are what the artist breaks; the memorable never emerged from a formula"*. So much for westerners and their point of view. What can we say about India and Indians in this context?

Be Indian. Think in an Indian language.

I think it's important to remember that India is divided by languages, culture and religion. So you better not tread on anybody's toes. I am sure there are enough people who can hitchhike their way to recognition and media attention by decrying your commercial and saying it offends the sensibilities and sensitivities of this or that religious group. Also what you may find as uproariously funny may only be moderately so for someone else. We must also remember that people will not make an effort to understand commercials that are funny but difficult to comprehend. They may just skip the channel. A similar fate awaits humour, which is based on an English turn of phrase or (heaven forbid) a pun. How will that original English humorous expression work when translated to Marathi or Gujarati? Let me remind you, at the risk of repeating myself that the Queen's English despite its charm and beauty is still an alien language for millions of Indians.

Having raised some doubts about humour and its efficacy let me also talk about the times when humour actually works.

- Humour generally works better for urbane, sophisticated audiences who are younger. Aren't the Cola commercials a lot more fun to watch? They are, because they are cheeky, irreverent, humorous and hugely popular aimed as they are at young people. One wonders, if humour works equally effectively for older, more sober audiences who are quick to frown and slow to smile.

- Humour works better on TV and radio. Whilst magazines have shelf life and newspapers are passed along, it is a fact that creating humorously for the print medium is a lot more challenging. Can you remember an amusing print ad?

- Humour has to fit in with your brand's personality. If you are a proper, stiff upper lip sort of personality, then humour may not just fit your overall brand's strategy. Humour or otherwise, consistency is key.

- Humour clearly works better for consumer products and services, not necessarily for industrial products. Corporate communication is very often emotive, factual or serious.

- Humour enables you to make a competitive brand statement. Rather than a boring comparison, one can make a cheeky humorous comparison.

- Humour helps brand name registration and associations.

- Humour may not add to source credibility.

And yet, the crucial question one needs to ask is "Do we have the ability to create funny commercials?" The point made by John Caples several decades ago, is still relevant. *"I must warn you that very few writers can write funny commercials which are actually funny. Unless you are one of the few, don't try"*. I can see enough evidence of writers who obviously can't write humorously, still struggling to do so and emerging the losers.

And when I talk of humour, I am not talking about slapstick. I am talking about commercials that entertain. Commercials that make you smile. However, it is important to remember that we are not in the entertainment business. We are in the business of selling products and services through communication. So whether your commercial is humorous or not, the product has to be the hero. If you can handle humour well, you can sell with style however difficult that is. Stan Freberg said, *"Humour in advertising is like a gun in the hands of a child. You have to know how to use it. Otherwise, it can blow up on you."*

Don't put a gun to my head. Just make me smile. And then, buy.

> "Humour in advertising is like a gun in the hands of a child. You have to know how to use it. Otherwise, it can blow up on you"
> **- Stan Freberg**

CHAPTER 11

For Better or for Worse?

I have always hated comparisons. A throwback to my experiences at school. I was at best, an indifferent student who had the good fortune (!) of having an elder brother who was 4 years older than me, and went to the same school as I did. He was efficient, organized and (sigh!) a pet of the teacher. His uniform was always pressed, his tie knotted perfectly, shoes polished, and he would remember to wear the school badge everyday. It's not over yet. As shocking as it may seem, he would do his homework every single day. What chance did I have with someone like this? The odds were clearly stacked against me. And often enough, simple sins of omission such as not carrying the school diary invited the wrath of my harassed teachers and produced unsolicited comparisons that were invariably unfavourable: "Your brother was so organised!" "Being Kasthuri's brother how could you do this?" "Are you really his brother?" Oh, the travails of being a younger brother, particularly, if one is normal! And yet the reality is that people tend to make comparisons. A child tends to compare his grades and toys, a student tends to compare his cycle and the growth of his stubble, an adult tends to compare jobs and raises, a cricket writer tends to compare Sachin, Lara and Waugh and a husband (one suspects), tends to quietly compare his spouse (usually unfavourably) with his friend's.

> 'Does it make strategic sense for brands to compare their respective merits with those of the competition?'

Yes, comparisons are odious but the human race has not lost its preoccupation with it. Why can't brands take advantage of this phenomenon that is all around us? This also leads us to a few related questions. Does it make strategic sense for brands to compare their respective merits with those of the competition? How do consumers react to comparative claims? Which product categories are best suited to comparisons? Are certain audiences likely to respond better to comparative claims than others?

Don't be a "Bandar", just steal Someone Else's Thunder

Traditionally the Cola marketers have been those who have had no qualms about comparisons, some of which have made the other guy blink. Pepsi Cola a formulation created by Caleb Bradham in 1898, has been an aggressive challenger not only over the years but over several decades. Conventional wisdom seems to suggest that leaders are better-off not being drawn into a war of copy and yet multi-brand companies use the other brands in their stable to hit out at the competition. Leaders do not usually get into street fights. Or, at least they should not be seen as getting into street fights. Hence a Coke uses Thums Up and Sprite to take pot shots at Pepsi and the global challenger is being challenged, at least in the subcontinent. Pepsi who created ripples with its "Nothing official about it" campaign in 1996 saw itself becoming the official sponsor for the 1999 World Cup which enabled Sprite to raise a few laughs (and hackles) with its "Kabhi Official, Kabhi unofficial". TV spot. Cola drinkers are young and hence comparative commercials that make them laugh (and on occasion, think) can work. Urbane, upscale audiences receive humour and comparison better. And yet, Thums Up whose earlier "Don't be a bhandar, taste the thunder" campaign made consumers chuckle, now seems to be taking itself too seriously with its "Grow Up" campaign featuring the celebrity endorsement of Salman Khan. It is pertinent to mention here too that every brand has a personality. Companies should not only understand their current personalities but also predict what they can reasonably hope to be. So if you are perceived to be stodgy, slow and apathetic you need to wonder whether comparative advertising is really your cup of cola, at least for consumer goods.

Every Comparison may have an Equal and Opposite Reaction

One of the classic advertising campaigns of all time relates to Avis the No.2 car rental company. Their manifesto was that they were No.2 and hence had to try harder, pay greater attention to detail and serve their consumers better. Their advertising based on research talked about their cars having clean ashtrays and although the Avis campaign was wonderful, the response from Hertz was equally effective. "For years Avis has been telling you Hertz is No.1. Now we're going to tell you why " said their ad. And even better was the response to the ashtray, with a human admission "Who's perfect?".

The point that you need to consider here is fairly simple though some of us may tend to overlook it. Taking on a leader can be exciting. Head to head comparisons may be heady, (forgive the pun). But the leader can react very tellingly. Like Hertz did. Naming your competitor can also be another interesting strategy that Apple adopted. It ran an ad with the

'The bottom line is that companies that take on the leader and their advertising, need to be prepared'

Headline "Welcome IBM.. Seriously". The ad suggested that Apple was a large player, welcoming an equally large player to the world of personal computers and the task of enhancing individual productivity. The bottom line is that companies that take on the leader and their advertising, need to be prepared....for retaliation. So, before you unleash that comparative campaign just think.

Cleverer by Half?

Very often many of us bring our own backgrounds, prejudices, biases and English speaking ability to the party. We assume that consumers are as interested in the brand as we are and are as educated as we are (mind you, they are decidedly more intelligent), Consumers are not waiting with bated breath for our ads. They may be confused as to which brand is superior if two brands are compared in one commercial. This is perhaps why some companies prefer "brand X" to mentioning the competing brand's name. Also, if the message is clever and the comparison difficult to understand then consumers will not make an attempt to understand it. They may just switch off. Consider the characteristics of the target audience and the characteristics of the product. Is it a high- involvement product category like cars or motorcycles? Comparisons will not work in low involvement products. They might work in products that enhance productivity at the work place. So whilst one can't be clever with the creative, it is important that we choose the product category where we can apply it, smartly.

> 'If the message is clever and the comparison difficult to understand then consumers will not make an attempt to understand it'

Dual Role

It's perhaps worthwhile to remember the social role that advertising can play. Advertising must do more than sell products and services. It must inform consumers. And properly executed comparative advertising can improve product knowledge and the methodology of usage. Many consumers are intimidated by technology and paranoid about instruction manuals. Hence they look for help and guidance to understand products, know their respective strengths vis-à-vis the competition, and how to use them. The responsibility of the ad agency goes beyond the mere creation of the ad. It has to ensure that what it portrays in the advertising is true. "Truth" that elusive word has a role to play in advertising. And that role becomes even more crucial in the realm of comparative advertising. In the Western world false and misleading advertising can lead to criminal and civil prosecution. In India, we live in a world of self-regulation and we all know how regulated we actually are when we're left on our own! And yet even as we fulfil our responsibilities to our client by using comparative advertising, we must recognize the rights of consumers to be told the truth and nothing but the truth. If we fulfil this duty then comparisons and comparative advertising need not be odious.

> 'We must recognize the rights of consumers to be told the truth and nothing but the truth'

"A branding program should be designed to differentiate your cow from all the other cattle on the range. Even if all the cattle on the range look pretty much alike"

- Al Ries

CHAPTER

Present Persuasively or Perish

'You don't get a second opportunity to make a first impression'. That's a familiar expression to most of us. People who are in the business of selling products and services strive to produce presentations that sparkle. Presentations that not only get noticed but actually result in sales. This skill is perhaps even more important for people who are in the communication business. And yet, often enough there seems to be little appreciation of the

> "The thinking human being, not able to express himself, stands at the same level as those who cannot think"
>
> **- Pericles**

theory behind powerful presentations and an even hazier understanding of the practice. Pericles said, "The thinking human being, not able to express himself, stands at the same level as those who cannot think".

Think about your presentation skills. How good are you when you talk to consumers, at a management seminar or an industry forum? How persuasive are your presentations? Do they measure up in style and substance?

Communication that Moves Hearts and Nations

Crucial to persuasion is communication. And that's hardly restricted to the world of business. Here's a quick example of some of the finest pieces of communication that the world has been exposed to.

"Friends. Romans. Countrymen.
Lend me your ears".

Mark Anthony after the assassination of Caesar

"Of the people,

by the people,

for the people".

Abraham Lincoln in the Gettysburg Address of 1863

"Ask not what your country can do for you.

Ask what you can do for your country".

John Fitzgerald Kennedy in his inaugural speech.

"One small step for man;

A giant leap for mankind".

Neil Armstrong after landing on the Moon.

"To be.

Or not to be.

That is the question".

Hamlet, while debating whether or not to kill his father

"Never in the field of human conflict has so much

Been owed by so many to so few".

Winston Churchill in his famous address to the House of Commons of the British Parliament on August 20, 1940, at the height of the Battle of Britain, often viewed as the most critical turning point of World War II.

Communication like the above is unforgettable. These excerpts of dialogues have become immortal because they appeal simultaneously to the mind and to the heart. They are simple. Simplicity, in essence, is the key to communication that wins hearts and (if one may add) votes. Simplicity, in the world of business gets attention and, more importantly, gets business.

> 'Simplicity, in the world of business gets attention and, more importantly, gets business'

Are we Forgetting the Past?

Persuasion is an ability that we have always had. As kids we persuaded our parents to sign our shoddy report cards (subtly hinting that ours were better than theirs). As teenagers we persuaded our parents to part with increased pocket money. At management school, we persuaded our teachers to give us more time for our term papers (after all weren't we offering them a Harvard Business Review classic?) As youth, we persuaded our girlfriends to go one step further. As a boss we could persuade our subordinate to go to Timbuktu saying that it would be the best thing that ever happened to him. The art of persuasion, which we have used so effectively over the years, suddenly deserts us when we make a presentation for business. And that could certainly affect our career prospects. People who present and present persuasively will grow faster in their careers.

Are you Passionate?

Crucial to success is passion. How passionate are you about what you are selling? People, research tells us, are persuaded more by the depth of a communication than by the height of its logic. They are persuaded more by your enthusiasm than the proof of your success. How desperately do you want to get the business that you are making a presentation for? Does your body language reflect this? Professor Albert Mehrabian of the University of California in an amazing discovery records that 55% of the impact of your presentation is caused by

> 'An amazing discovery records that 55% of the impact of your presentation is caused by non-verbal cues'

non-verbal cues. Are you establishing eye contact with your audience? Is your keenness coming through in your body language?

Content is 'King'

There is divided opinion on the power of words in presentations. Experts have tended to underplay its importance. But in my opinion and experience, what you say is as important (if not more important) than how you say it. In the world of business, people still value the rational and the tangible. They would like to know how your offering can make a difference to their function? How it will make a difference to their top and bottom lines. So whilst you certainly need to package your offering, you need to worry about your offering too.

> 'You cannot offer style at the cost of substance; rather substance needs to be cosmetically adorned with style'

You cannot offer style at the cost of substance; rather substance needs to be cosmetically adorned with style.

Be quick. Be friendly. Be gone.

Successful presenters know the value of the listener's time. *"The time to stop talking is when the other person nods his head affirmatively but says nothing"* says Henry S. Haskins The trouble is that some of us outstay our welcome and sometimes run the risk of letting our audience nod off into slumber. When you are presenting to senior management you need to understand the value of their time. I have also found that the attention span of CEOs is limited. (A few nanoseconds, may be?) So you had better 'go for the jugular', whilst the decision maker is awake and interested. In presenting for success, it's important to know your audience. Who will be present? Will the decision maker be present during your entire pitch? What are the various power dynamics in the group who is listening to your presentation? Is there something that you have missed? What is the culture of the organisation? Is it hierarchical or informal? How does your client dress? And remember this simple tip, *"You're never fully dressed without a smile"*.

> "The time to stop talking is when the other person nods his head affirmatively but says nothing"
>
> **- Henry S. Haskins**

Expect the Worst

In the old days we had the 35mm slide projector. Advertising agencies had their own dark rooms where they produced slides for presentation. We used to carry stand-by projectors and spare bulbs. At times even reams of paper to darken the windowpanes in clients' conference halls. Any equipment that is mechanical in nature can fail. And from experience, let me tell you that it will fail. We all know the story of the presenter whose slide tray was left behind on the plane. What is your contingency plan? Is alternative equipment going to be available for you at your time of need?

Some presentations insult the audience's intelligence. But others test its eyesight. How good is your presentation material? It is not only retail that is in the detail. Are your slides readable? What about the font-size? Remember the audience may have people who are above 40. Are your slides too heavy? How smooth is the transition? Are you using charts? We all know that English is an alien language and sometimes the way we speak it a sounds mangled and jarring. If you listen to Navjoth Singh Sidhu, you soon realize that the loudness of his turban can match the colour of his expression. But then, he is in exalted company. None other than George W.Bush, who whilst speaking of the American economy, spoke of the need to make the pie higher when lesser mortals normally speak of the pie becoming bigger. Watch your metaphor.

Close with a Bang

All meetings have an objective. What do we want at the end of our exercise? Successful salesmen close deals. They don't leave them hanging in mid air. Similarly, successful presenters achieve the desired results at the end of the presentation. They get action. Remember, when Aeschines spoke, they said, *"How well he speaks"*. But when Demosthenes spoke, they said, *"Let us march against Philip"*. Power presentations close with powerful statements; statements like these.

"Where you are today is the result of choices you made yesterday. But where you will be tomorrow will be the result of decisions you will make today. Make a smart decision today that will improve your tomorrow. Choose us".

How's that for a closure?

CHAPTER

Media, Where's the Big Idea?

In the early 80's whilst I was still wet behind my advertising ears, Media Planning (and if I may add, life) was a lot easier. Even, a lowly servicing person like me whose only vocation in life was to lug artworks from the agency to the client's office, could (when it came to the pinch), work out a media plan (preposterous as it may seem now). After all, large advertisers used a 30 second TV commercial with 3 double spread colour ads with black & white adaptations. So all one had to do was book spots in Chitrahaar, use India Today and take the mainline dailies. Today the challenges are a lot more complex. And seem to be actually mind-boggling when you think of what is available. There are publications and TV channels simultaneously providing a choice to the consumer and chaos in the media planner's life.

I know that I am unashamedly committing the same mistake, that many of us do of using the past to predict the future. And I am sure anyone who has had the misfortune of putting money in the stock market as I have done, will realize the futility of using past trends for predicting future earnings. The media challenge to my mind is even more complex. Instead of being drowned in this complexity, let me raise a few

'There are publications and TV channels simultaneously providing a choice to the consumer and chaos in the media planner's life'

examples of how media issues are being side-tracked and how the woods are being missed for individual trees.

PRESS vs TV

This is a debate as old as the hills, which surfaces once in a while lest we progress in life. I believe enough columns have been devoted to this over the years. Let's end the issue once and for all by saying that both have a vital role to play and let's examine something exciting – like a media idea.

'When was the last time you heard of a breakthrough idea in media?'

People in advertising (including myself) wax eloquent on the subject of creative ideas. In fact every campaign has a creative idea. Some brilliant, like the Volkswagen. Some merely good. Many mediocre and quite a few downright bad. But the starting point is an idea. And some have the beginnings of a campaign idea. But when was the last time you heard of a breakthrough idea in media? An idea which captivated your imagination and captured your consumer's mind. An idea, which extended the gamut of media used for the campign with dramatic results.

Before we get into a post mortem on the entire scenario, let me raise some practical issues which though not in the nature of challenges will probably put things in a proper perspective.

Clients have several meetings with their advertising agencies on size of logo, color of skin, Sharpline Vs Illustration, Helvetica Vs American typewriter, Girl Vs Boy, You Vs me.

Q. How many discussions are there on the media strategy? I do realize that people argue endlessly over specific media vehicles but rarely the strategy. The better companies however do. And will do so at greater length in future.

Q. When was the last time the agency viewed its creative product by channel? The viewers of Channel V are very different from the viewers of Sun TV. Earlier, advertising used to have language versions. Will we now need a channel version?

Q. Why should even large companies do only brand reviews? Why can't media reviews be an integral part of account reviews? Where honest, unbiased information is disseminated on money spent, channels chosen and objectives achieved. Honestly, today both clients and agencies are groping in the dark. The need of the hour is objectivity and the desire to be critical of one's own functioning.

Q. Why should the publications or channels be willing to the negotiate on their rates be a major influencing factor on media choices? A beaten-down rate may be very satisfying but maybe but the publication may not be the right one in the first place.

Q. Why do we realize that we don't have a big budget for the job, after the entire campaign is finished. We create an ad in 200 col. cms but release it in 20 col. cms. What a waste! And yet, media planners aren't getting an opportunity to work closely with creative and account management from the early stages of campaign development.

Q. Today, we have information. Lots of it available everywhere. And yet, most analysis degenerates into number-crunching. How about cutting-edge media strategy?

But the biggest challenge to my mind is our attitude to Media. Media must become not merely the other creative department but **THE** creative department. Campaigns can no longer be evaluated merely for their creative content. They need to be evaluated on the ability to work in synergy with media to produce results in the market place. Campaigns need to have a 'Media Idea' which

> 'Media must become not merely the other creative department but **THE** creative department'

sets them apart. A media idea, which is new, innovative and which beats the clutter. Like the very memorable earlier Polo campaign of 10 second commercials. But then how many such memorable campaigns have we seen? One realizes, too, that with the emergence of stand-alone media agencies the challenges of co-ordination here become even more pronounced. The onus is on clients to get the creative agency and the media planning and buying agency to produce magic.

David Ogilvy speaks of the needs to recognize a big idea and says you must ask yourself these questions.

- Is it unique?

- Did it make me gasp when I first saw it?

- Does it fit the strategy to perfection?

I think the time is right for a big media idea. A big idea, which is not built on the past but transforms the future. An idea, which will put media rightly where it belongs. On top. That to my mind is the ultimate challenge. Why wait for some auspicious day in the future? I am in a hurry. Shouldn't you be too?

CHAPTER

Radio is Hot. Are you Tuning In?

Everyone has a little bit of genius, that is, they do really listen. They can listen and talk at the same time. Then they grow a little older and many of them get tired and listen less and less. But very few continue to listen. (Just ask any one who is married!) And finally, they get very old and they do not listen anymore. *"That is very sad, let us not talk about it"*, said Gertrude Stein.

In a way, what happened to radio in this country was very sad. People stopped listening to each other and also to the radio, a wonderful medium of our time. And then came the great "come-back" of the "second-class medium".

Radio is on... as an advertising medium; as a means of entertainment and as a possible vehicle to involve the listener with your message and your brand. And a whole new generation of youngsters is suddenly rediscovering this means of entertainment, which many people in my generation were reared on. I am fond of repeating this real life incident, which happened a few years ago. For a long time my son (and I suspect several others of his generation) did not know that one of the twin functions of a 'Two-in-one' was a radio. We were watching a one-day international on TV when the power went off. (In Bangalore, the more things change, the more they stay the same). So, I switched on the radio,

'A whole new generation of youngsters is suddenly rediscovering this means of entertainment'

which was on batteries and Tendulkar, as he was likely to do, hit a six. I called my son, excitedly shouting, " Tendulkar's hit a six". He came racing in and planted himself strategically in front of the radio and kept looking at it, anxiously waiting for an action replay! And today, this same son who was 18 in June 2005, alternates between all the FM stations available. Yes, a whole generation of youngsters is taking to this medium, which is good news for advertisers, radio stations and advertising agencies as well. This represents a sea change from its earlier second-class status. I remember David Ogilvy calling radio "The Cinderella medium", and it could well turn out to be the "belle of the ball".

But let's go back for a bit to those woeful days when radio was the "second-class" medium.

Theatre of the Mind

I grew up on radio, unlike the next generation, which was reared on the picture tube. My prized possession was a Philips transistor, which I literally went to sleep with, provoking my father to sarcastically ask, "Are you going to get married to that silly transistor?" But then, one's life can't be music and cricket only, can it? My day would begin at 5.30 am with the ABC (Australian Broadcasting Corporation) and end at 11.30 pm with the sports round-up on the BBC, punctuated by Binaca Geetmala, Radio Ceylon and Vividh Bharati, Alan McGilvray Brian Johnston, Ameen Sayani and V.C. Chakrapani were honoured guests. John Arlott was unforgettable. Who can forget his description of a male streaker in a test match with the following comment: *"Old women in the stadium are seeing something they haven't seen for a long time."* Radio enabled us to imagine and dream. We had never seen Dennis Lillee bowl but thanks to John Arlott, we knew and relished the experience. Something, which the current generation has probably missed by and large.

The advertising industry too gave this medium a convenient bypass and few, if any, had the competence to create advertising for this medium. But now, the increasing congestion, commuting distances, proliferation of vehicles on city roads and emergence of FM radio makes one believe radio has now made a comeback. Living as I do in Bangalore, it's been a pleasure to watch and listen to the popularity of FM stations with today's youth. Clearly, its future as an important niche medium is gaining ground.

I saw You on Radio!

Today, thanks to the emergence and popularity of Radio City and other FM stations, a host of small advertisers are making it to the medium. Mind you, radio is a relatively cheaper medium than television. And yet, one feels for these small advertisers. They believe that they have arrived simply because they are using this medium. They get so excited at hearing their brand name on radio that they forget the larger picture. Repetition of the brand name is fine, but you have the opportunity to do more. Much more. Remember the production cost of a radio commercial is a very small percentage of the overall media spend. Saving a few thousand rupees will most certainly not get the best bang for your media buck. So try to produce a good commercial, which will not only get you mileage in branding but will also, make you stand out from the clutter of other messages. You don't need to go to Hawaii to produce your radio commercials but you can transport your listener to Hawaii with the power of your message. It is images such as these that charm and sell.

'You don't need to go to Hawaii to produce your radio commercials but you can transport your listener to Hawaii with the power of your message'

One recalls the Radio Advertising Bureau's promotion of the power of sound with its slogan, 'I saw it on radio'. Not for nothing is radio called "the theatre of the mind". Can you get your audience to imagine things? Go back to your own childhood before 1982. Can't you imagine Bjorn Borg's serve, or how John McEnroe flung his racket down, how Sunil Gavaskar batted or how Dennis Lillee bowled. You certainly can because at that time you were seeing it through the radio. Now, in a similar manner, you can make your listeners imagine a few things. Evoke pictures...a cup of steaming "chai" on a wintry morning, a glass of deliciously chilled beer on a scorching afternoon, the extra five minutes in bed on a Monday morning....

Radio enables you not only to visualize but to also create imagery in the listener's mind, this medium calls for domain knowledge of both consumers and the medium and, the skills as well, to create for the medium, of which one sees too little evidence currently. But there's something else to cheer about: there are an emerging lot of mini celebrities who are making a name for themselves as radio jockeys. Some of them are already topics of conversation at pubs and campuses. Maybe they will in turn breed a generation of writers who will create and make waves in this medium.

The erstwhile Cinderella Medium

It was not only radio that had been sidelined. The "Cinderella" medium was neither as active as print, nor as dramatic as television, nor was it an exciting medium for agency creative prima donnas. After all, creating television commercials according to creative "hot shots" is the road to recognition and riches. Nevertheless, scriptwriters would do well to recognize the challenge of the ultimate one-to-one medium. As Marshall McLuhan observed, "Radio affects people intimately, person to person, offering a world of unspoken communication between the writer, speaker and the listener – a private experience."

Consider this commercial talking to business travellers who are looking for a no-frills room for the night: *"When you stay at Motel 6, you'll have to turn the bed down all by yourself, and go without that little piece of chocolate those fancy hotels leave on your pillow. Well, I know it's a lot to ask, but for around 20 bucks, the lowest price of any national chain, well you can't expect the moon, can you?"* The commercial goes on to end on a rather evocative note. *"And we'll leave the light on for you."*

> "Radio affects people intimately, person to person, offering a world of unspoken communication between the writer, speaker and the listener – a private experience"
>
> **- Marshall McLuhan**

Right time. Right place. Right message.

One of the greatest advantages of radio is the opportunity to be with the consumer at the right time to cue behaviour and purchase flexibility which TV and print may not offer. Some of us are familiar with media aperture and the timing of the message at the time most appropriate to the target audience. A message for blades at 7 am, pepperoni and pineapple pizza at 12.30 pm or mouth-watering ice-creams at 9.30 pm are all opportunities. The production costs for radio are so friendly that one can and must think of multiple executions.

The drug Contac, for example, tied its advertising to the pollen count, addressing allergy sufferers. As an aside, I must comment on certain Spice commercials on Radio City, Bangalore, which ridicule a certain sect of people – I am allergic to them. It reminds me of the disastrous Hindi movie comedy of the Padosan day and age where the Tamilian was the butt of inane jokes. FM radio audiences are young, urbane and upscale. So obviously humour works; but not of this genre.

Renaissance of Radio

One feels this time is right for radio to be rediscovered, particularly for certain products and services - products for youth, for instance, or retail and local services. So agencies have to understand this medium, weave messages specifically for this medium and market it to clients. For too long, radio has been a passive reminder medium. It has the potential to be an interactive, response-driven medium.

> 'It has the potential to be an interactive, response-driven medium'

I remember listening to BBC radio on the day of the India-Pakistan one-day cricket match at Edgbaston in 1999, and the entire morning was devoted to listeners who called in, to give their views and good wishes.

That made me realize that communication need not pass us by. It can involve the consumer. Radio can do that. And that's a big opportunity. But there's also a bigger question. Will Indian advertising tune in?

The Power of Radio Jockeys

The growth of radio as a medium has spawned a whole breed of successful, young radio jockeys who have become icons in their own right. They have entered your car, your study and your children's bedroom. If the radio jockey reads your advertising message in his own voice, at his pace, in tune with the mood of his programme, it might make a difference. Celebrity advertising is all about cashing in on the image, appeal and value of aspiration that a successful person provides. And most of today's RJs provide that. Is there an opportunity here?

Integrate, Innovate or Pack your Bags

Radio very often is not a stand-alone medium in the media planner's schedule. Many brands use multiple media and radio is just one of them. And yet, often enough I have found that the radio message has no relevance to what is being said in other media. Or, it could be that it appears to be a duplicate of the TV commercial in audio form, and is hence unsuited to this medium? The best way to create radio spots would be perhaps to specifically create them for the medium of radio and integrate them with the other brand properties. Take Titan for instance. Its television commercials are visually rewarding. And yet, its music is a brand property. This could be used in radio with messaging that is tailor-made for the medium. What is your brand property? And how will you integrate it when you use radio?

Do you Know your Audience?

It's important to know your audience and certainly it is possible for radio to have niche audiences. There is this old joke about radio programmers, which says, *"Even though we don't have very good ratings, we're number one in men, in the 18-24 segment, who have hair loss."* Yes, it is an audience that may be finely segmented. This means that your message can be sharply tuned (forgive the pun) and finely focused. The audience is young for FM radio and don't mind cheeky, irreverent and at times, whacky messages like this international commercial (being reproduced in parts) which was a big hit in the U.S.

"Hello, have you heard about this rather unusual English candy....

And its made by an English firm called Callard and Bowser.... And, I say, it is English. So please buy it because we need the money in England at the moment. I mean we are all as poor as church mice now. Servants are unbelievably expensive and our industry's practically disappeared.... So please do us a favour and just try the Callard and Bowser candy... and after all, I mean we did fight on your side in the war and we always let you beat us at golf and incidentally, let's not forget you pinched our language... so please buy Callard and Bowsers rather sophisticated English candy and help England back on its feet, frankly I think it's the least you can do".

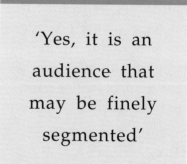

'Yes, it is an audience that may be finely segmented'

A series of commercials like these were well appreciated by the target audience. Why can't we think of a series of radio spots for our brand? All of which appeal to our target audience. It won't cost the earth to produce them.

Get the Customer to Act

Historically, we have viewed radio as a passive, reminder medium. It has always been a support medium. And yet, if you listen to Radio City 91 FM today, you have thousands of callers who either page or call in for requests, points of view and so on. So there is a captive audience out there who can actually be made to respond to your message and made to act! They can be made to call you, visit a place or buy your product. And yet, most of our messages are merely reminder messages. We all know the power of radio when Levis has a sale! I think there is a great opportunity to innovate on radio as a medium itself and change the type of messages. Involve the audience. And remember radio is the ultimate one-to-one medium. Each listener is in her own private world.

Radio Advertising that Works

Advertising has two functions. One to sell products; the second to reward its listeners. Since listening is a dying art one needs to work extra hard to deliver messages that I heard. Remember people don't give radio their undivided attention. People (very often) listen to the radio as they are driving, talking or watching the cop. So radio advertising must ask itself a few questions.

Q. Does the message attract the listener's attention?

Q. Does it appeal to the listener's self-interest?

Q. Do the words paint pictures?

Q. Does it give the listener a reason to act now?

Q. Does it say too much and mean too little?

Q. Does it use music to enhance or cue advertising in other media?

And One Thought for the Day

Radio is back with a bang. Sadly, it seems to be an "add-on" medium still and most media planners are yet reluctant to look at it seriously as a potent medium for advertising. Creative writers too seem keener to create for television. Maybe the medium needs account management people to champion it and use its potential while it is still affordable.

Just think about it.

"Branding adds spirit and a soul to
what would otherwise be a robotic,
automated, generic price-value proposition.
If branding is ultimately about the creation of
human meaning, it follows logically that it is the
humans who must ultimately provide it"

- David Aaker

CHAPTER

If you Pay Peanuts...

I came in to advertising in 1983. A small matter of 22 years ago. My mother whose greatest achievement was sending all her four children to college even if she hadn't been there herself, asked me to explain my job to her. I launched into a treatise on the roles and responsibilities of the account executive in the agency and the value of his inputs to the whole advertising business. She listened to me patiently and finally asked me a question that shut me up for the present and got me to worry about the future. She asked if all my learning at IIM had resulted in this, more sympathetically than sarcastically. Today, I still retain my association with the IIMs and the other management schools in the country and, things if anything, have become worse for advertising. It's hardly a career of choice to the bright young men and women who head towards software, marketing fast-moving consumer goods, investment banking and perhaps even aquaculture, but not advertising. I can almost hear you saying, "who says that the MBA is God's gift to mankind" and the cynic might even give you the cheeky definition that the MBA is the "Murderer of Brand Assets" who is certainly not required in the advertising business. My views on the subject are slightly different and stem from my own positive associations with advertising, aided (and abetted) by management education. But I find that my students in

'Our business needs top flight talent – MBA or not. And it's currently not attracting it on the account management side'

management school do not share my fervour for this exciting profession. And that's a cold fact. Our business needs top flight talent – MBA or not. And it's currently not attracting it on the account management side.

What about 'Creative'?

In 1987, a young, talented, intense Masters in Computer Sciences, walked into my office in Mudra to start life as a copy trainee. His name was Balakrishnan (Balki). 18 years later, he is Creative Director of Lintas Lowe India, after creating a stunning portfolio for Mudra on brands like Wilman, Van Heusen and BPL and an even more dazzling showcase for Kissan, Britannia, Titan and Wills at Lintas Lowe. And yet, this low-profile, high-achievement creative powerhouse is worried because the best creative minds are not coming into this business. Certainly the advertising business has a major problem on its hands, if, today's young Indians, are not turned on by advertising. We are a young nation, (our greatest batsman achieved most of his laurels by the time he reached 26) and we need young creative people to write and visualise in a manner that's appealing to youth. But the young creative people too are looking elsewhere.

> 'We need young creative people to write and visualise in a manner that's appealing to youth'

Advertising has become 'Low - Involvement'

People in advertising specialise in glamourising products that are low-involvement for consumers such as car batteries, toothbrushes, blades, automotive brake linings. Tyres similar in category, have moved up the consumers' "interest ladder", thanks to some consistent and forceful advertising over the years. Advertising as an industry of choice has become a low involvement product to today's Indian youth. How do we make it the 'destination of choice' to the best minds of today, is really the problem facing us. I wish it were as simple

> 'Today's "Generation Next" is pragmatic, knows its own value and worth and the importance of money'

as producing a 'problem - solution' commercial for a detergent. But the answer seems to have more gray areas than ever. Still, the problem is acute enough to worry about and to offer some solutions to. Let me make a few suggestions, which are tentative in nature. The advertising industry, as one voice, has to come up with its own aggressive solution as its employee attrition rate is a lot higher than it should be.

The first problem that needs to be addressed is the salary structure of the profession. In my view the pay in advertising must make coal miners feel like a pampered lot.

Today's "Generation Next" is pragmatic, knows its own value and worth and the importance of money. It's all very well to say that money can't be the only motivator, but money matters and how! I can almost hear the finance guys saying *"To which planet, does this clown belong? My 15% commission is under threat, my outstandings are the only things which are going up and this guy is talking about hikes?"* Yes, I know and understand the pressures of running an agency and reporting to Hong Kong and New York and I know margins are under serious pressure. I think agencies need to carefully assess and redefine their own structures.

> 'Agency business must soul-search and understand that its core competence is creativity not a range of services'

What is the core competence of the agency business? It's about great ideas that produce stunning work and build big brands. That's where the revenue will come from. It is the layers of people in areas that can be outsourced or dispensed with that drains resources and shrinks the profit pie. I expect that the agency business must soul-search and understand that its core competence is creativity not a range of services. Get the best creative teams and pay them the earth if you must. Get young creative talent whom you can pay more than the other industries can and train them for posterity. At least, this way if talent does not beat a path to your door, it will at least come in larger numbers than before. But let's realise that people who bring in the bacon must be rewarded far more, than the ones who cut it into tiny slivers. Let's learn too from our clients. In software, there is a clear difference between the guys (or is it the girls) who produce software (and US$) and the guys in finance and support. Sorry, we live in an unfair world.

Stunning Creative will Get People In

Today, there is very little aura or mysticism around advertising. The work too very often does not excite or entice. I know for a fact that lots of people came into a world of advertising which boasted of classics like the 'Avis campaign', the 'Volkswagen lemon' and the 'Hathaway Shirt'. I still believe the 'pregnant man' did more for the industry than several full-page ads released for other brands. The advertising business needs a few blockbuster TV commercials and press campaigns, which will bring it back on track in the mainstream and into the reckoning. Just look at what Kaun Banega Crorepati has done to television viewership in this country. Interest (or is it greed) has surged, bringing people back to their living rooms. Yes, great TV commercials will not only make the cash register ring but also make people think about advertising as a career.

Whither Leadership?

Today, Mr. Narayana Murthy is on every forum and in every newspaper. (He is probably tremendously over-exposed, but that's another story). The fact of the matter is that his company and industry are in the forefront. Software gets whatever concessions it wants from the government because someone is speaking up for it. Who is the Narayana Murthy of the advertising industry? Who is ensuring that it gets its fair share from the media and the world at large? Are our agency heads able to think beyond the tiny boundaries of their respective agencies? People like Mr. R.K. Swamy gave their competence, time and passion to the industry and its causes. Yes, the Indian advertising industry needs "a few good men" who will selflessly lead it in the new millenium to its rightful place under the sun.

'Who is the Narayana Murthy
of the advertising industry?'

"Managing brands is going to be more
and more about trying to manage
everything that your company does"

- *Lee Clow*

CHAPTER

Is your Ad Agency Truly your Partner?

"Quick, tell me, what makes for a successful marriage?" If you are a cynic, you might well say, "living separately". But thankfully, most of us are not cynics but optimists. And here is what Nannette Newman, a British actress (yes, actress) has to say. "A good marriage is at least 80 percent good luck in finding the right person at the right time. The rest is trust"- the magic word. But let me not jump the gun. I will address the need for this wonderful quality at the appropriate time and try to address your unspoken question: What caused my sudden interest in the institution of marriage? The answer is simple really. I strongly believe that a successful client-agency relationship is very much like a marriage, where two people with differing skill sets come together, complement each other's efforts and stand by each other in good times and bad. It may sound romantic in this day and age, when divorce rates seem to be going up as much as prices, but it is hard reality as well. And yet, it is perhaps relevant to say that very often client-agency relationships go through a fair amount of trauma, which is perhaps avoidable.

The question now is : How do we make this partnership work?

> 'A successful client-agency relationship is very much like a marriage, where two people with differing skill sets come together, complement each other's efforts and stand by each other in good times and bad'

It's All in the Mind

John Maynard Keynes said, *"In the long run, we are all dead"*. This is the precise sentiment that's hurting our business. We seem to be completely preoccupied with the short and immediate term. And yet, people like my parents who celebrated their sixtieth wedding anniversary last year, believe otherwise. And worldwide, client-agency relations when truly successful are anchored for decades together, whether it's Pepsi and BBDO worldwide, Volkswagen and DDB Needham, Horlicks and HTA (now JWT), Surf and Lintas (now Lowe) or Rasna and Mudra. Successful brands have healthy long-term client-agency relations. I remember reading somewhere that HTA handled Iodex for over 80 years! Imagine the sort of knowledge that an agency acquires when it works for such a long time on a brand. The agency knows more than young brand managers can ever know about the brand and the consumer. So the important learning for us is to think long-term. The agency too on its part can invest in time, people and technology, if it knows that the relationship is not going to be under review every quarter. And yet, if there is a silver lining for the agency business, it is that advertising agencies seem to be better off than market research agencies who keep quoting on a project-to-project basis without knowing if they will get it. Yet, to repeat, the starting point is the attitude that just as branding is long-term, so too must be the relationship of client and agency that builds the brand.

> 'The agency too on its part can invest in time, people and technology, if it knows that the relationship is not going to be under review every quarter'

Don't do, Delegate

Many of us know that success in management comes not from doing it all ourselves but from getting things done. The success of brand managers comes from getting the agency to do superior work and not by attempting to do the work themselves. Let me explain. Advertising seems to be so simple from the outside that anyone (including the managing director's wife) can lay claim to an idea. And some of us who

'Truly great work happens when the agency feels electrically-charged about the client and his brand'

have written the odd article for the school magazine believe we are capable of writing advertising copy. Technology clients believe that the ad agency does not understand high technology and hence they write the copy themselves. Whilst this perhaps makes the agency's job easier in the short run, in the long run, it affects the agency's morale. Truly great work happens when the agency feels electrically-charged about the client and his brand. And this will not happen, *"If the client has a dog and barks himself"* as David *Ogilvy succinctly put it.* One of the great challenges that a client has to face is agency motivation. How does one keep the agency motivated? The answer is in giving clear strategic direction, by pushing them to do great work, recognizing them and rewarding them and not by doing their work for them. And as an aside, "don't do, delegate" seems a wonderful policy for husbands as well on the home front! (I just hope my wife is not reading this!)

What the Brand Needs or what the Client Wants?

Advertising has one major distinguishing feature. The agency's client is its customer. He is the source of all benefits, business and livelihood even. And yet, the advertising is created for the client's customers who are quite different and this intriguing scenario often creates uncertainty and compromises. The agency ends up giving the client what he wants. The reality, however, is that what the client wants may not be what the brand needs. And this is why savvy clients are so valuable and rare. They

> 'The reality, however, is that what the client wants may not be what the brand needs'

continually put themselves in the end-consumer's shoes and evaluate advertising (very often with the help of research) from her point of view. I would like to proffer a word of advice here to advertising agencies. Advertising is a service business. Thus does an agency need to provide "service with servitude"? Shouldn't the agency be viewed as a consultant and not as a mere supplier or an order-taker. This in turn means that the agency too must continue to provide value, consistently. Remember another aspect of marital harmony – mutual respect. I, as an advertising professional, respect your ability in marketing. You as a marketing authority, need to respect my ability in communication. Both of us, mutually, must be worthy of respect.

Invest in the Relationship

"All marriages are happy. It's the living together afterwards that is difficult". Equally true of client-agency relationships. Clients sign on agencies with great fanfare and soon find that things are souring. Any successful relationship needs the investment of time for one partner to understand the other, making adjustments where necessary and being optimistic, always, about the future. And the most important quality is commitment. Commitment from the agency to the brand's success and commitment from the client to the agency, to allowing it an open mind and an opportunity to build successful brands. Mark Twain said, *"Always do right. This will gratify some people and astonish the rest"*. Yes, both the client and agency must do the right thing. By each other. And by the brand. To cut a long story short, whether you are client or agency, just ask yourself these simple questions about your marriage.

Do you trust each other?

Are you committed?

Are you thinking long - term?

Are you considerate?

Do you communicate with each other?

And finally, perhaps here is a question easier to ask than to answer.

Are you having fun?

"Extraordinary work is done
for extraordinary clients"

- *Milton Glaser*

CHAPTER

Learning from Your Client

The advertising business belongs to clients. Clients are the source of business, profits and (if one may add) heartburn. Good clients help agencies create advertising history while bad clients make them a part of history. But let me quickly tell you that I'm not setting my sights on the client bashing welterweight title! I'm too old (and bruised) for that. I strongly believe that clients provide agencies with tremendous opportunities to learn about brands, processes, technologies and management practices. To an agency, the

> 'Clients provide agencies with tremendous opportunities to learn about brands, processes, technologies and management practices'

client is benefactor, boss, tyrant and God rolled in one. The question in my mind is simple: Why can't this all–powerful individual be a source of learning as well to the advertising agency and its people?

Look Beyond your Own Navel

I am fond of repeating what Gary Hamel said, *"If a company is interested in finding the future – most of what it needs to learn it must learn outside of its own industry"*. And the typical ad agency has exposure to a variety of diverse and complex industries (and problems). Let me explain. On the same day, the agency as an organisation could be grappling with GPRS (without sounding superior, I can tell you that is General Packet Radio Service), computing GRPs (you don't need me to tell you that is Gross Rating Points), wondering about the poor off-take of sanitary towels in Sathyamangalam and the disproportionate guzzling of orange (as a drink) in Tenali. Yes, there's never a dull moment in advertising. And the reason why several of us have come to advertising is because of the variety, the challenge and the opportunity to learn about clients, brands and their businesses. So clearly, advertising agencies and the people in them have the capacity to learn, absorb and internalise. Yes, we are experts in floor cleaning liquids, stain removing detergents, quick mixing concrete and pain-killing placebos by choice. But how expert are we in understanding our client's management philosophy and practices, which being of far greater significance can largely impact the way we run our business?

Here are a few aspects that I have observed about clients, which are well worth studying and emulating.

- A few years ago, I used to head a medium sized advertising agency and I was amazed that while I used to travel business class even in the domestic sector, I used to see the likes of Venu Srinivasan, cheerily waving to me from the economy section. We admire Infosys, but their Directors still travel 'economy', whilst I see that several agency types (and I am not referring to agency heads here) travel 'business'. Is there a lesson for us in this?

- I had a client who is an industrial heavy weight with a huge budget and a corner office. He was a large buyer of media and a big customer for several publications. But when someone from the media (sometimes even a lowly rep) had an appointment with him, he would personally escort him to and from his room to the elevator. The rep would be his fan for life. I also know of some agency people of the lower ranks who treat representatives of the media almost like a piece of dirt. Agencies must learn to be more courteous.

- Agencies help their clients recruit top talent from business schools with attractive pre-placement posters, brochures and glitzy presentations, but when it comes to their own placements, they are found wanting in style and substance. They worry more about the culture in clients' offices than their own. Charity (and culture if I may add) begins at home.

- Agencies often create induction kits for clients to enable them to welcome new employees into the fold and yet the agency's new employees are greeted with a desultory "welcome to the madhouse".

- Agencies observe and announce the Employee Stock Option Plans of their clients and yet, when it comes to their own employees, they studiously look the other way.

- Agencies create and produce ideas on internal communication to help keep their clients' employee attrition rates lower and yet their own internal communication leaves a lot to be desired. Today with everyone jumping the agency ship, we have a huge problem on our hands.

- Agencies very often research the campaigns they produce for their clients, yet how often do agencies research their clients' 'customer satisfaction levels' with the agency? The big software companies are continually monitoring clients satisfaction and service levels across the globe. Do agencies know how their clients feel about them ? I wonder.

- I can almost hear you saying that all these are not earth-shattering revelations. Perhaps, But consider this. Infosys and Titan have announced their succession plans:

Mr. Nandan Nilekani has succeeded Mr. Narayana Murthy and Mr. Bhaskar Bhat has succeeded Xerxes Desai. The same clarity in succession is not evident in large agencies, resulting in heartburn and loss of key senior people.

• Andy Grove said, *"Only the paranoid survive"*. I can observe increasing paranoia amongst my clients. There is tremendous accountability and increasing pressure from the board and the stockholders to perform quarter after quarter. Add to this, the attention (?) from the television channels and the business press. Agencies being closely held face less pressure (perhaps?). Whilst that is arguable, what is not arguable is the fact that clients are really aiming for the skies in terms of growth and bottom lines. Agency growth rates seem flatter and their growth targets less ambitious. A cause for worry?

I remember a signage in the New York office of DDB Needham, which said,

'We resolve to care more about our clients'

I thought I could take the liberty of turning it around slightly to read as follows :

"We resolve to learn more from our clients".

Let's learn. So, that we may live.

PUBLIC RELATIONS

"Branding demands commitment; commitment to continual re-invention; striking chords with people to stir their emotions; and commitment to imagination. It is easy to be cynical about such things, much harder to be successful"

- *Sir Richard Branson, CEO Virgin*

CHAPTER

Picnic with a Tiger

"Wooing the press is an exercise roughly akin to picnicking with a tiger. You might enjoy the meal, but the tiger always eats last" – Maureen Dowd. Most Indian business houses, and corporate executives exhibit similar (if not greater) paranoia in dealing with the press. For all you know, many senior executives may be viewing a press conference as preparing for battle. Why is this?

The non-Controllable World of Press Relations

Actually marketing people are a lot more comfortable with the world of advertising. Advertising (strange as it may seem) is actually far more predictable! Whilst Bill Bernbach said that advertising must surprise the viewer, the average marketer believes that the news headline (about one's own company) goes beyond mere surprise, it actually shocks the people concerned.

Press Reporting – A lot more blunt today

Today's reporting is a lot more blunt than in the days of Mark Twain whose report read *"A woman giving the name of Mrs. James Jones, who is reported to be one of the society leaders of the city, is said to have given what is purported to be a party yesterday to a number of alleged ladies. The hostess claims to be the wife of a reputed attorney"*. Contrast this with a news headline, which appeared in England, classifying Andrew Parker Bowles as *"...the man who cheerfully laid down his wife for his country"*. If that is the situation with celebrities, one can understand the plight of ordinary corporate mortals. And the reality is that journalistic reputations are easier made by negative stories than by positive stories. And that's one reason why most journalists don't mind taking potshots at leaders.

Inaccurate Reporting – the Bane of our times?

Many companies have experienced a situation wherein what they have believed they have said, is significantly different from what they actually see in print the next day. This is probably the most common complaint and is probably indicative of the fact that poor communication is as much a problem here, as in the rest of the world. And an even greater problem is the worrying quality of journalism more so in the context of the Indian sub-continent.

These are real problems and of great concern to the largest of companies. Making them diffident, indignant and nonchalant in turn. Is there a method in this madness? What can organizations do to cope? And to go further, how do we mould public opinion? What changes must we make in our own actions?

A Positive Mental Attitude

> 'The need to be unfettered by past biases and to have a genuine desire to build bridges is acute'

The most important change is attitudinal. Jim Whitaker one of the men who climbed Mount Everest said, *"You never conquer the mountain, you only conquer yourself"*. And what is required today from most clients is a positive attitude towards the media. An attitude, which believes, that media relations can be handled successfully. An attitude that ensures that they (the clients) would be helpful, obliging and honest. The need to be unfettered by past biases and to have a genuine desire to build bridges is acute.

Reputation is Built over the Long Term

Many corporations suffer from an obsession with the current quarter. They are unable to think long-term about their image. If clients have realized the logic of having long-term contracts with advertising agencies, it is because they have benefited from it. I hope PR does not go the market research way of being an assignment-based (read press conference) activity.

Companies need to think long term on media relations. And the first step would be the signing up of PR agencies for three-year terms giving them elbow- room and time to think long term. Ad-hoc work has gone out of advertising. Even public sector companies sign on three-year advertising contracts. Why can't public relations follow suit?

The Need to Prepare

Sadly enough I find many corporate executives firing from the hip at press meets. Adequate preparation, prediction of questions and a sense of humour make all the difference in successful media relations. And one finds that in telephonic interviews the maximum (alleged) misreporting happens. The onus therefore is on executives to leave as little to chance as possible. Typically, this would require sending written responses, asking for time to get one's thoughts in order and almost anything which would help the quality of reporting.

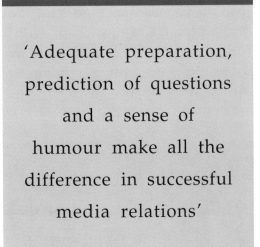

'Adequate preparation, prediction of questions and a sense of humour make all the difference in successful media relations'

The More Time You Spend the Better the Results

Given the tremendous mileage which one can get from positive press coverage, it is disappointing to note that organizations and CEOs are extremely reluctant to spend time with the press. There is a direct relationship between time spent with the press and the results one gets out of such an activity. And I have found that truly visionary CEOs always find time for the press.

Off the Record...

Many of us who talk to the press have a very hazy idea of what 'off the record' means. Media people very often believe that the information may be published if it is not attributed to its source, others interpret it to mean that the information cannot be published at all. There are enough instances of 'off the record' replies turned into horrendous press stories. The logic really seems to be 'Let the speaker beware'.

I could write volumes about the do's and don'ts of successful press relations but I'd like to end on a positive note. Media relations may seem like a minefield. But it's manageable. The trick to having good media relations is to treat it as you would treat life. Sincerely. And without add-ons. And, with empathy for the media person. You would do well to be seen as a person who is genuine and accessible. And with a genuine desire to help. Just try it. And it will be roses all the way.

> 'The trick to having good media relations is to treat it as you would treat life. Sincerely. And without add-ons'

CHAPTER 2

A Photograph is Worth a Thousand Ads

He is a dream client to have if you are a PR agency. He is a nightmare to have as your competitor. I speak of Richard Branson who flew in to India with a bright 'Virgin' red 'Bhangra' outfit, turban et al. The Indian press lapped it up like 'lassi'. We talk about 'photo opportunities' today but Richard Branson has been busy with them for years – he probably invented the term.

For the inaugural press conference of the launch of his airline, Branson came wearing a 'Biggles' style brown leather aviator's helmet. Newspapers, after all are thirsty for pictures. Editors are human beings too and they dutifully splashed his pictures in their respective newspapers. He continued his war games as he launched Virgin Cola in the U.S. by driving a full battle tank down a busy New York city street to demolish a wall of Cola cans. The buccaneer (as some refer to Branson) went a bit further at Heathrow. Dressed as a buccaneer, complete with eye patch, he lowered the Virgin livery onto Concorde, stealing the UK national carrier's thunder. Lord King, British Airways Chairman obviously saw red in more ways than one as Fleet Street clicked merrily away. Who knows, the thought must've passed through their minds that pirates might go out of fashion. Richard Branson is a one man PR army that many of us who yearn to get noticed, can learn from.

The fancy dress is an important part of Branson's make-up. His comments on (fancy dress) are fairly

> 'Richard Branson is a one man PR army that many of us who yearn to get noticed, can learn from'

interesting, "I've worn every costume there is to wear. It makes a back-page photo into a front-page one". And yet the reality is that the corporate world is perhaps a bit too starchy so someone with a `school boy' image and someone who has the makings of a prankster, will be the centre of all attention (of the right kind), with or without the fancy dress. And this enormous media coverage enables him to get by with a much smaller ad budget than his competitors.

Breaking the Rules

Today, management gurus have raked in the bucks by advising companies to keep it simple. Others advise you to remain 'focussed'. The earlier piece of advice 'Stick to your knitting' has yielded to the more focussed 'core competencies'. But Virgin is an example of a completely diversified business group that straddles several industries and caters to a wide variety of consumers offering them a range of services at extremely competitive prices. If you live in the UK, you could buy a record in a Virgin mega store, tune into Virgin radio, take a Virgin holiday in the Caribbean, flying there on a Virgin plane. You can watch films in a Virgin cinema, guzzle a Virgin Cola, borrow from Virgin Finance, ride a Virgin train, stay in a Virgin hotel in Scotland and have your wedding arranged (if you are still single, that is), by Virgin wedding co-ordinators! And yet it is important to remember that holding all these diverse offerings is one `personal' brand – Richard Branson. Yes, the USP is the reassurance and excitement that the Branson name provides. Richard Branson has used this celebrity status to sell a wide range of products.

'The USP is the reassurance and excitement that the Branson name provides'

We continue to see more and more of this trend. Anita

Roddick (Body Shop), Dave Thomas (Wendy's Hamburgers) and Herbert Kelleher (South West Airlines) have all used their celebrity status to sell products, perhaps with less flamboyant success. How does this make sense in today's world of core competencies? Eminent, I would say!

Virgin's list of core competencies might well include

- the ability to identify appropriate growth opportunities.
- speed
- empowering teams and
- managing joint ventures

Over and above all this is the advantage of Branson's personality - to motivate people and push them to their limits.

Stretch your Way to Success

Branson has been a workaholic and always pushed himself to the limit. But that's nothing compared to the stretch that Branson has done to the Virgin brand. The purist might well ask whether or not the brand name is being diluted by multiple extensions. Branson thinks otherwise and believes his brand is infinitely elastic as its integrity is not compromised. The Virgin name works quite well across this diversity. Another name Slipped Disc, was initially considered and as Branson says cheekily, "Slipped disc condoms might not have worked as well". He looks eastwards at Japan and says, "What limits stretching is the cautious approach of brand management and advertising agencies in the Western world. "No one has a problem playing a Yamaha piano, having ridden a Yamaha motorbike that day, or listening to a Mitsubishi stereo in a Mitsubishi car, driving past a Mitsubishi bank", says Branson. Whilst marketing wizards can argue till the cows come home, Branson has the results to speak for his strategy. But there is no arguing against these facts. In a recent survey in the UK, 96% of British consumers have heard of Virgin and 96% named Richard Branson as its founder.

You can call it what you will, product/service/corporate/
individual, but clearly Branson epitomises the statement. "A brand
is a brand is a brand".

And yet...

Everyone hasn't been universally kind to Branson and his
activities (read antics). He has been called a 'hippy capitalist' and
several other epithets, which are a lot less charitable. But Branson
embodies the brand principles of being `unique' and `different';
certainly he is unique.

Can you imagine the Chairman of British Airways climbing onto
an auto at Connaught Place to provide a better photo opportunity?
Can you imagine the Chairman of Nestle daring to ski downhill
stark naked all the way, for a 10 pound bet? Can you imagine the
head of a company answering a question on how to become a
millionaire by saying *"You start off as a billionaire and then open an
airline"*. So it's obviously a management style and strategy that
works for him. And yet, it is perhaps important not to forget that
despite all the show and bluster, there is 'news' in whatever he
does. And you don't need to be a savvy public-relations
professional, to realise that news means coverage. As someone in
the communication business, I always admire people and ads,
which you can't ignore. You may hate Branson or love him, but
you can't ignore him. If you do, you do so at your peril as his
competitors have discovered. Although he is a scratchy public
speaker at best, he communicates excellently with the man in the
street, reason why he is known as 'the people's business man'.
Communication is all about getting people to do the things you
want. As someone said, "Make them laugh, make them cry. But
for God's sake make them do something".

Right now he's making his competitors sweat.

CHAPTER

Photo Opportunity! Are you Missing the Picture?

"When the client moans and sighs,

Make his logo twice the size.

If he still should prove refractory

Show a picture of his factory.

Only in the gravest cases

Should you show the clients' faces".

This limerick, oft-quoted by David Ogilvy, vividly illustrates the sentiments of frustrated advertising professionals. The Public Relations expert however has to play a very different role. If the client's photograph gets published the client is usually happy, the account is significantly safe, and the monthly retainer fee is not subjected to relentless questioning. A word of caution though: herein lies a possible problem. Let me clarify. There is this company in the consumer goods category that I am familiar with. Although I can't bet my bottom dollar on it, I can still say with a fair amount of certainty that the brands are struggling, competing as they do with the giants in the FMCG space. The uncertainty at my end about the company's profitability is because the company is closely held and is under no obligation to declare its profitability. But there is no lack of publicity of the CEO who is blatantly visible in the media. Every now and then, one or the other, blazons his photograph and his ideas on future trends in consumer behaviour and so on. I am a bit confused and I can almost hear you saying, "What's new?" Allow me to put forward the reasons for my confusion. They are largely to do with the mandate to the PR agency. What must it do? Focus on the brands or on personal profiling of the CEO? Do I blame the PR agency alone? No. I think one of the most important and primary tasks in any client-agency relationship is to determine and set objectives.

What do we set out to achieve? *"No wind serves him who addresses his voyage to no certain point"*, says Seneca.

One of the most important and primary tasks in any client-agency relationship is to determine and set objectives.

Having said that, I must say this too in defence of PR agencies. Often they are confronted by clients who are in pursuit of their own private agenda which may be contrary to the overall corporate objectives. They are subtly and yet firmly skewed towards the personal profiling of the client who, sad to say, is interested in increasing his market value instead of thinking about furthering his brand's visibility and value. Is this your experience? Then you have something to think about.

Inform by All means, But Only after You Perform

Today thanks to the increasing vigilance of regulatory bodies, publicly listed companies tend to be extremely careful about making forward-looking statements to media. That's a starting point and laudable. Indeed it is a far cry from the late 80's and the early 90's where companies were anxious to 'inform' the world about themselves before they were ready to even think of 'performance'. I remember the slew of IPOs on Aquaculture, Granite and what have you, which sprung up out of nowhere. One wonders, where these companies are today and what has happened to the money collected from unsuspecting, gullible investors like me. Is your client keen to 'inform' before he/she 'performs'? Then your antennae, as a PR agency, must be up.

The second category is something that we are all too familiar with. This is the category of companies that perhaps do not even use a PR agency. These companies have a good track record, are dependable but their management is low profile and their image is exceedingly low-key. They suffer from a multiplicity of problems.

"Why should I talk about my success, others should".

"I don't want to reveal my strategies".

"I can't be as loud as XYZ".

Haven't we heard this all before? And yet I believe that somewhere, individuals holding senior positions let their own personal preferences, biases and pet theories come before the benefits to the organization. A strong-willed and yet shy executive who refuses to talk to the media is hurting an organization and its stakeholders in the long run. I can understand a CEO refusing to appear in 'Lifestyle' or on Page 3, but it is necessary to get the visibility that a corporation deserves for its hard-earned genuine achievements. The PR Agency's task (assuming that one exists in this case) is clearly defined. To my mind that includes educating the client, on an ongoing basis, on the value of PR and the credibility that it brings to the table.

'Somewhere, individuals holding senior positions let their own personal preferences, biases and pet theories come before the benefits to the organization'

The third category is what one would describe as a 'dream client'. These are clients that perform and then keep informing their publics. The name that comes to mind, without too much prompting, is Infosys. The Company's success, its several achievements have been given to the media and, by and large they have been given the recognition they deserve. Whilst it is perhaps difficult to find too many companies in this league, it is also a fact that several companies have significant achievements as well. The problem however seems to be that at times companies do not realize the significance (in media terms) of all their achievements.

Share as much as you can with your PR Agency. It might surprise you to discover the nuggets that lie hidden in the mounds of data accumulated in the company's databank. No fact is too small to be ignored. Properly packaged, it can make a difference and will make its way to the pages of the daily newspaper.

And What About the Client

It would be remiss of me not to talk about clients. After all, it takes two to tango. I know that many PR Agencies in the country who do terrific jobs, are, to borrow an old expression, likely to end up being, 'unwept, unhonoured, unsung'. Clients, despite protestations to the contrary, view and use PR agencies as suppliers. They surreptitiously and overtly monitor how many media people attend press conferences.

"Why hasn't so-and-so not come", they ask and the PR executive who would like to say, "He didn't come because he thinks you are a bore" just mumbles something about handing over the press release to him in person. They want quantity and not quality and some of them want reports on

> '...dream clients... perform and then keep informing their publics'

the number of column centimeters. I have no problem with accountability but the norms for this must be sensible. Clients spend an hour with a reporter and frantically call the PR Agency telling them that they have spoken out of turn and can they stop the interview.! It is not easy being a PR Agency. Sometimes, only sometimes, one wishes that clients would make the agency's job easier. We could certainly do with some assistance here.

Keep it Simple

Public Relations is not rocket science regardless of how PR Agencies wish to package it. All it requires is a clear strategy and relentless execution. Day after day; in one centre after the other. It is a bit like Glenn McGrath's bowling. He really keeps it simple. He bowls with boring (and for the batsman depressing) regularity on the same spot, 9 times out of 10. The batsman obliges, 9 times out of 10. Consistency is the key to success. In bowling and in Public Relations. And this is the question that PR Agencies need to ask themselves. How consistent are we? A question that is perhaps easier to ask than to answer. If your delivery consistently meets objectives, then we don't have to run around frantically looking for photo opportunities for the CEOs of companies that are our clients!

> 'Public Relations is not rocket science regardless of how PR Agencies wish to package it'

"A house of brands is like a family,
each needs a role and relationship to others"

- Jeffrey Sinclair

CHAPTER

AYE BHAI ZHARA DEKH KE CHALO

Saturday, the 18th of June 2005, started as just another day in Mumbai. It was hot and humid. And that was nothing strange. Sofia Gardens in Cardiff experienced similar weather. It was hot and humid there too, and that was certainly strange. After all Cardiff is in the U.K. But what was stranger still was what happened on that same Saturday in a one-day cricket match between Australia (the top team) and Bangladesh (the team of the lowest order) in a hot and humid cricket stadium in Cardiff, which had a fair sprinkling of Bangladeshis.

The minnows (as they are often derisively referred to) won. That made news in England. The English were gloating as this was beyond their wildest imagination. It made news in Australia. The Aussies were seething as this was beyond their worst nightmare. It made news in Bangladesh. The Bangladeshis were celebrating even as they

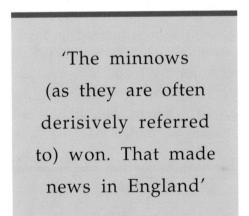

'The minnows (as they are often derisively referred to) won. That made news in England'

kept saying that they were not as bad as the rest of the world said they were. It made news in Mumbai too. Though news of greater significance was being made in that very place, on that very day.

The Ambani brothers who had not seen eye to eye for some time and who have been scrapping(!) from July 27th,2004(to be precise) had finally arrived at a settlement. Actually Kokilaben, their mother ensured that they did. Boy, did that make news! The media went to town on the settlement and continued to keep the Ambanis in the news, as they have been doing for close to a year now. (I have a sneaking suspicion that they will be hard-pushed to fill their pages in the next few months unless we have another stock market scam!).

The saga of the brothers and possibly Reliance as well, has demonstrated several things. And I strongly believe there is a learning for all of us here. The saga of the Australian defeat is at a personal level more interesting to me, because I write the column of 'The Third Umpire', but I shall exercise self-control and stay with the adventures of the brothers and the learning therein.

'Only Vimal' to 'Only Mukesh'

In the mid-eighties Dhirubhai was actually involved in advertising. (It was only later that his aspirations and interests grew!). He is supposed to have approved the tag line **'Only Vimal'** attributable to the late Frank Simoes. After Dhirubhai's demise, if rumours are to be believed, there was 'Only Mukesh'. There was no will, and consequently only ill-will between the two. The brothers fought their battles through a media that was more than anxious to oblige. Mukesh was the leader, the understated elder brother. Anil was the aggrieved, the aggressor. He spoke about corporate governance. He spoke about shareholders' rights. He spoke to whoever cared to listen. And the media listened. And wrote. And Anil has used a strategy that could have so easily have gone wrong successfully.

'Dhirubhai... approved the tag line **'Only Vimal'** attributable to the late Frank Simoes'

Anil wooed the media and how ! If reports are to be

believed he even sent food to a waiting (and hungry) pack of journalists on that eventful Saturday. And yet it is perhaps important to add a word of caution here. Anil owes a lot to the media. And while the media may or may not want their pound of flesh, they will certainly want continued access to him. Media cannot be switched on and off at will. And despite all his new-found responsibilities, Anil will have to find time for those who were his allies during his darkest days.

Anything can be Managed

Reliance is an amazing company in several ways. It has been through crises that would have sent other companies packing. In 1987(if my memory serves me right) Mr. Gurumurthy or SG as he is fondly known, was going hammer and tongs at Reliance.

Every day the Indian Express carried one expose after another on the beleaguered company. It was either absolutely brilliant, investigative journalism or totally biased reporting, depending on whose side you were on. To me working in Mudra, it was at once frightening and illuminating. Frightening because the parent company (notwithstanding the agency's protestations about its independence) was in trouble. And illuminating because of the confidence which Reliance demonstrated. It published huge ads in major newspapers - including the Indian Express - clarifying its position.

Reliance managed that crisis and several others that followed over the years. Despite the fervent hopes of its ardent critics, it survived

> 'Reliance is an amazing company in several ways. It has been through crises that would have sent other companies packing'

and thrived. In fact the attitude of Reliance has always been 'We can handle it'. In a country that is stoical and believes in Vedanta and the statement 'this too shall pass', Reliance has been active in handling major problems successfully. Euphemistically it can be called 'Managing the Environment', but it is quite simply 'Crisis Management'. And what crisis can be bigger than two brothers fighting over control of India's largest private sector company? Now, that this crisis too has been managed, the onus is on the brothers to move forward. And here is something which the brothers who are in a sense starting out with a clean slate, need to consider. They should focus less on managing the environment and more on managing their enterprises. India is changing. Look what has happened to the Nawab of Pataudi.

We might see the emergence of a Ralph Nader like 'protector of the small investor' who may not view some of the questionable activities of companies like Reliance with the same level of tolerance in future. And Anil who has used the words "corporate governance" and "transparency" quite freely in the last year must ensure that his new ventures stand the strictest scrutiny.

Brand or Business

The late Dhirubhai Ambani believed that growth was a way of life. Reliance grew, confounding its critics. The bubble never burst. The brand was secondary. It was a result of growth, profits, per capita appreciation... all attractive to the investor. But not meaning too much to other target groups. Reliance was not admired by peers. (Not that too many people genuinely appreciate someone else's success). They were skeptical. They were gloating when the brothers fought. And the brothers provided grist for the mill.

Now perhaps is the time to build the brand. Time to look beyond the past and into the future. Time to look at softer issues. Time to look past the investor. Time to look inwards. So far, the brand has been successful. It is huge. It is globally competitive. It has taken over companies. But beyond that...now is the time to figure out what the brand stands for, beyond these number-driven achievements. It must soften and broad-base its appeal. Its interest in 'corporate social responsibility' as manifested by activities like 'Harmony', has to be seen as integral to its philosophy rather than interests of family members, thus spending their time fruitfully. The new entities need to work on their brands and Anil has to work on his own brand image.

> 'Now perhaps is the time to build the brand. Time to look beyond the past and into the future. Time to look at softer issues. Time to look past the investor. Time to look inwards'

Different Brothers, Different Positions

The last few years have created different perceptions of the two brothers. Anil was on Page 3, Mukesh was on Page 1. Anil was running the Mumbai marathon, Mukesh was running marathon meetings. Anil was speaking to media. Mukesh was speaking to CII. Anil was sitting in parliament while Mukesh was trying to influence it and get things done. Anil was the MTV youth icon whilst Mukesh was in Forbes. These may be perceptions but perception can be reality. Branding is all about being relevant and different. Mukesh has been relevant while Anil has been different. Anil has to take a long hard look about current perceptions about himself. Brands continually reposition themselves, usually for the better. I, for one, without the benefits of research feel that Anil needs a position that is more corporate, more substantive, more work-driven and more focused on his achievements with the new ventures. The aggressor has to now consolidate and demonstrate his capabilities to a world that is waiting and watching.

And of the Future

I remember Reliance being guided by the statement that "Success is a process, not an event". The event of June 18th is an enormous success for everyone including the astrologer who allegedly pushed the deadline of the settlement! And yet the battle of ownership has become a battle to demonstrate credibility as managers and leaders. These are a few valuable lessons for lesser mortals like us:

- Whether you leave behind Rs 6 or Rs 60,000 crores, leave behind a will!

- Managing the environment can be heady, but few can do it the way the Ambanis have done.

- Media matters. And we have seen evidence of that.

- Business growth is very creditable but what about the brand? Who is looking after it?

- Companies must try to think beyond investors. There are other audiences as well.

- Leaders need to continually review their position.

And yet I must clarify my position. I have always been a great admirer of Reliance and its growth, its down-to-earth ability to take on the world, its understanding of India and its (lack of) systems. I am bullish about the future of the ventures that will be run by the brothers. After all they have Dhirubhai's blood. My prediction is that both brothers will lead their companies on different growth paths.

And what about Australia which has had an eminently forgettable week in England? It will retain the ashes whatever the British media have to say!*

I was subsequently proved wrong as Australia surrendered the Ashes after 16 long years

CHAPTER 5

"Oye Bubbly, Oye Oye Bubbly, Mind those Bloggers Bubbly".

In the latter part of 2005, the female anatomy was in the news, for all the wrong reasons. No prizes for guessing which part. It was the middle finger. Henry Gray whose book 'Anatomy of the Human Body' has been the bible for many medical students for 147 years, (many of whom have religiously gone to bed with it) not surprisingly had not given the middle finger anywhere near the importance that bloggers in the US have. The middle finger, that Indira Nooyi, CFO and President of PepsiCo, likened to America in her speech to Columbia University has suddenly caused hackles to rise and bloggers to rise in arms (or is it fingertips) to the slight to America and Americans by Ms. Nooyi. How can a speech made to the graduating class of a top-flight university create such a storm? How can an analogy however offensively shown create a public relations scare of the highest proportions? The answer my friends, though not blowing in the wind is what the world of technology would describe as blogging. Blogs (or weblogs) have been described as different things. A blog at the simplest level could be an online journal with freshly updated content. At a more sophisticated level it is "Something that will revolutize

> 'A blog at the simplest level could be an online journal with freshly updated content. At a more sophisticated level it is 'something that will revolutize the web''

the web". At a more flippant level a blog is 'something to keep you occupied when you're unemployed'. Obviously if the reaction to Ms. Nooyi's speech is any indication, lots of people whether they care to accept it or not, seem to fit into the last category!

The Dreaded Middle Finger

Here is what Ms. Nooyi said, *"As I grew up and started to study geography, I remember being told that the five fingers can be thought of as the five major continents".*

The index finger is Europe, pointing the way up; the ring finger is Latin America, sensual and romantic (think Salma Hayek or J-Lo); the thumb is Asia, proud and aspiring; the little finger is the Dark Continent, while the middle finger – yes, you guessed it – is the United States of America.

"As the longest of the fingers, it really stands out. The middle finger anchors every function that the hand performs and is the key to all of the fingers working together efficiently and effectively," she says in her speech.

"Remember that the middle finger – the US – always stands out. If you are smart, if you exhibit emotional intelligence as well as academic intelligence, if you ascribe positive intent to all your actions on the international business stage, this can be a great advantage," she concludes.

Well does that really seem all that objectionable? But the reaction from bloggers has been swift and negative. Angry bloggers have called it "A Shame", "Condescending", "Patronizing" implying that she was biting the hand that fed her, the United States of America, the country that had made her rich and famous... her speech was offensive, in poor taste... the infuriated bloggers went on and on. Subsequently, Ms. Nooyi has offered an unconditional apology.

Tone and Manner

The speech to the casual reader seemed innocuous, inane even with a heavy attempt at humour. But it did not seem to be as offensive as the bloggers had made it out to be. In fact, a third of the people who responded did not consider it objectionable. Maybe the 'tone and manner' of the communication was what upset the audience and excited a chain reaction. Rather than going into the propriety or impropriety of her speech, it might be worthwhile to look at the whole event from a communication perspective and see what are the learnings.

a) Perception is reality. If you are perceived to be arrogant, condescending and patronizing then you are that! (And God help you!) It is important to understand perceptions more so when they are different from reality.

b) What you say is perhaps less important than how you say it. More important is who is perhaps saying it. A lady from India? A highly paid immigrant? Telling America what is to be done!

c) Today dangers or PR disasters if you will, can lurk in any corner. In 1985 when Coke launched its new product and failed, a real estate investor from Seattle, Gay Mullins founded the 'Old Cola Drinkers of America' hotline for angry customers. Today Pepsi has realized the damage that bloggers can cause. And bloggers are the newest kids on the block and a potential PR hazard.

d) Speed of response is extremely critical in crises. Pepsi's delay in posting the controversial speech on the site raised the ire of bloggers.

e) Needless defence of her speech by public relations personnel, touting the company line clearly construes that the situation was misread.

f) You don't win blog wars with angry people by reason. And it seems, it does not take much to upset a blogger.

g) What seems like a small ripple can quickly turn to a tidal wave.

And What about India?

A lot of this seems to be far removed from the world we live in despite the fact that Pepsi is losing money here and Ms. Nooyi is originally from Chennai. This a shortsighted way of looking at things. Despite our advancement and being accorded (grudging) admiration from the rest of the world, some parts of corporate India seem to be pretty naïve about technology and its uses in marketing particularly. India has its share of technophobes (some of whom are in fairly senior positions) who rely on secretaries for their email. With a mindset like that, it becomes well nigh impossible to understand a relatively new phenomenon like blogging and what it can do.

Blogging affords a great opportunity for customer intimacy and allows sales people to really get into their customer's business. In fact blogging, at least in certain categories, could be as powerful as 'word-of-mouth'. There are approximately 10 million blogs currently, so it is an emerging medium and opportunity. Very often, we fail to understand the need for and importance of speed. Blogging calls for speed in execution and response. We also believe that any crisis can be managed. Reliance seems to be doing it all the time. Their slogan *'Growth is a way of life'*, just as easily could read *'Crisis is a way of life'*. Perhaps this philosophy seems to be pervading corporate India that

> 'Blogging calls for speed in execution and response'

seems to pride itself on its ability to think on its feet! Never mind its propensity to fall on its face! So very few companies seems to have a crisis management programme in place. After all, lightning never strikes twice. Does it?

And the Future?

Tom Zeller Jr., writing in the New York Times says *"Bloggers are not always the kingmakers that pundits sometimes credit them with being"*. They may not be much of a political force, but if the latest Pepsi fizz is anything to go by, they can be a potent force in the world of marketing and communication. Prof. Cornfield an expert on the subject describes *"the blogosphere is half forensic and half tavern"*. Ms. Nooyi would agree with that, seeing the way her speech has been dissected and the irrational manner by which some bloggers have reacted. Sadly you cannot wish this away. This is the new economy. Welcome to its harsh realities. And we in India must realize this sooner rather than later.

And my personal advice (unasked for and certain to be rejected) to Ms. Nooyi and others like her.

* Get a better speech writer and

* Think twice before accepting a speech invitation from a business school!

> **"The blogosphere is half forensic and half tavern"**
>
> **- Prof. Cornfield**

"The goal in creating
a brand identity is not just surface
consistency but inner coherence"

- *Aubrey Balkind*

CHAPTER

Crisis? It Can't Happen to Us!

What would your reaction (heaven forbid) be if one of your acquaintances were to have a heart attack? You might have one drink less in the club that evening and even go for a walk the following morning. And if you are bold enough you might even force your spouse to join you. Your comments on the incident could range from:

"Man, could he pack a drink"

"God, he loved to eat"

"He was really overweight" - after all he was a kg heavier than you.

Central to all this, is a state of mind that all of us know, have experienced and keep experiencing. It is a misplaced self-confidence embodied in the belief that *'It can't happen to me'*. This belief is not restricted to individuals, but companies as well. Hardly surprising given the fact that companies are run by people with similar dispositions to you and me. They see other companies struggling under the burden of one crisis or the other and yet seem strangely oblivious to their own risks. *'It can't happen to us'* seems to be their attitude.

> 'They see other companies struggling under the burden of one crisis or the other and yet seem strangely oblivious to their own risks'

Here's hoping that your company is not one of them.

It Can Happen to You

Crisis can come in all sizes, shapes, and magnitudes. Most of them catch us napping. Reliance is just coming out of a crisis caused by brothers who took their fight to the media. Other crises may seem less dramatic and less in the public domain but they can still cause damage.

Here Are a Few Examples

- You are a biscuit manufacturer. A consumer finds broken pieces of glass bangles in a packet of biscuits he has bought. He threatens to go to the media.

- You sell branded rice. There are cockroaches in a pack that a cantankerous lady has bought. She feels that gives her an opportunity to come on TV.

- In torrential rain, your new building collapses killing people on site.

- Your senior executive is embroiled in a messy sexual harassment case involving a foreign worker.

- Your company employee is involved in an embezzlement case

- There is a leak of toxic substances from your plant.

- You run a national retail chain. The escalator fails causing a major accident involving children

- There is a fire in your factory.

- The flood in Gujarat damages your stocks and impacts your bottom line.

All of these are events that we would not like to happen. But they have happened. And will continue to happen. The question is, do you have a crisis management program in place? And the worrying thing is that even as you are running like a headless chicken (one hopes you are not) trying to handle the crisis, the media wants you to handle a press conference as well! NGOs are snapping at your heels even as they anxiously scan the environment for media opportunities to air their views and wave their banners. The situation can be daunting. And it is hardly surprising that many of us are found wanting. Whenever one thinks of crisis, the first name that comes to mind is Tylenol. One remembers John F. Kennedy's statement, *"When written in Chinese, the word "crisis" is composed of two characters – one represents change and the other represents opportunity"*. The handling of the Tylenol case by Johnson & Johnson certainly underlines one fact: behind every crisis lies an opportunity to keep your head; and to demonstrate that you care. Although the Tylenol case has been often quoted and talked about, we can still learn from it and it is still worth repeating in brief.

The Mother of all Crises

In 1982, seven people died in Chicago mysteriously within a few days. Authorities determined that each of the people that died had ingested an extra-strength Tylenol capsule laced with cyanide. News spread. The result was panic and chaos. Jerry Della Femina said, *"I don't think they can ever sell another product under that name (Tylenol). There may be an advertising person who thinks he can solve this and if they find him, I want to hire him, because then I want him to turn our water cooler into a wine cooler"*.

He was wrong. Perhaps like most advertising people, he had a hazy view of public relations. Tylenol regained its position as one of the top selling 'Over–The-Counter' drugs in the USA. They did this first by handling the crisis and secondly by handling the comeback of Johnson & Johnson and Tylenol. An effective PR strategy, that was meticulously executed was responsible for the return of both. It started with putting the customer first. All Tylenol products (a staggering 31 million bottles worth US $100 million) were recalled. The company established relations with the Chicago Police, the FBI and the Food and Drug Administration to search for the criminal and announced rewards. The media praised the company for their socially responsible actions in an environment filled with callous corporate entities. A few months later, Tylenol was reintroduced with a new triple – seal tamper resistant packaging and this launch was enthusiastically received by media. And later analysis revealed that the Tylenol story was found in over 125,000 news clippings across the country! It had made even bigger news than J.F. Kennedy's death! Tylenol is testimony to the value of how good public relations can turn a potential disaster around. I wish more Indian companies would look inwards at their own state of (un) preparedness to potential crisis.

Crisis Calls

The UK tabloid, 'The Sun' (which is hardly my cup of tea) certainly made news with its report that it was able to buy information regarding bank accounts and credit card details from a Delhi based person who collected data from call centres. This had all the makings of a potential PR crisis. The industry quickly rallied around in defence, knowing the western media's paranoia about losing jobs to India. Let's not forget that BPOs were in the news in April for siphoning off over Rs.2 crores as people were arrested. This raised security concerns. An industry that makes news can be at the short end of the stick when things go wrong. And the problem with industries like these is that media tars the whole industry with the same brush as the company in the crisis. So a crisis in one company in the industry could have larger-than-life repercussions on the whole industry. Does your industry suffer from similar flaws?

> 'Tylenol is testimony to the value of how public relations can turn a potential disaster around'

At the End of the Day

I don't wish to be the harbinger of bad news, but we just cannot wish crises away. They strike like the Tsunami when we are least prepared for it. Like a tidal wave in broad sunlight! From a company perspective, it is perhaps worthwhile to have a contingency and action plan in place.

> 'An industry that makes news can be at the short end of the stick when things go wrong'

- Identify possible and potential crisis
- Put together a crisis management team
- Designate and allocate responsibilities to your team members
- Train them on how to handle media
- Train them on how not to rush to media!
- And keep subtly hinting that it could happen, without raising a false alarm every time.

Time to recall Rudyard Kipling's famous words,

"If you can keep your head while all about you
Are losing theirs and blaming it on you,
If you can trust yourself when all men doubt you,
But make allowance for their doubting too.
...You'll be a man, my son".

Yes, though no one wants a crisis, it does give us an opportunity to be men. And before you have a personal crisis do yourself a favour: just go for that annual health check-up.

"A brand for a company is like
a reputation for a person.
You earn reputation by trying to do
hard things well"

- *Jeff Bezos*

CHAPTER

Unwept. Unhonoured. Unsung.

"Here Rests in Honored Glory an American Solider known but to God" is the inspiring inscription on the tomb of America's unknown soldier. At the risk of exaggeration one must say that the plight of the poor public relations agency in India is similar. The PR agency's glory, it seems, is known only to God. I always thought that advertising

'Comparatively speaking, folks in advertising seem to be a blessed lot'

agencies are the ones that go unrecognised for their efforts in client service and brand building. But now that I am in the thick of things in the public relations business, I realize that, comparatively speaking, folks in advertising seem to be a blessed lot.

Why Don't You Just Tell Me?

A few years ago, I had a talented lady executive working with us who was extremely competent and committed. I remember her single-handedly organizing a product launch in a city in Kerala. She spent quite a few days away from home base organizing several things including a traditional welcome by elephants! It was a very creditable achievement involving enormous pressure and working at unearthly hours in an unfamiliar place. To my mind she (and if one may add the agency) did a fantastic job. And yet the client didn't have a single word of praise for her or the agency. In defence of the client it might be said that he must have had a few things on his mind, launch et al; singing the praises of the agency was not at top of his mind at that time. All that was required was a brief note later, to the lady complimenting her on the excellence of the project. But there was no such note forthcoming and my former colleague, (as the status soon changed to) was extremely disappointed, to put it mildly. She left not only our agency but, the advertising business as well to pursue other interests where I am sure her abilities and contribution are at least acknowledged, if not appreciated. Sadly, clients who are wonderful at motivating their own teams tend to take their advertising agencies and most certainly their public relations agencies for granted.

> 'Sadly, clients who are wonderful at motivating their own teams tend to take their advertising agencies and most certainly their public relations agencies for granted'

Recognition, the Name of the Game

Today, there is enough recognition for the advertising agency's contribution to brand building. Today more and more companies report their brand's value in the balance sheet. Not because they have to; but because they want to. Today it is common knowledge that a brand's value has nothing to do with the physical assets owned by the company. And if brand Coca-Cola has been valued at $ 67.39 billion then, clearly the advertising agency's role in this is being accepted, even if grudgingly. Categories like soft drinks are dependent and driven by advertising. Advertising agencies can and will give an arm and a leg to handle a soft drinks major. Pitches to handle accounts like these are viewed as major projects bringing input and support from the agency's global network. The media keeps a close watch reporting the agencies that are in the shortlist and predicting who is right up front. When the account is gained, the agency goes to town and the whole world knows. Agencies have also used their portfolios to acquire visibility, awards and more business. The world knows that JWT has been behind Pepsi's visibility in India, O&M behind Cadburys, Lowe behind Surf Excel, Mudra behind Vimal and Rasna and so on. All these brands are dependent on advertising. Rightly so. But there are many technology, business-to-business and corporate brands who do not have the luxury of huge advertising budgets and a global agency network at their beck and call. They depend on public relations agencies to provide them visibility and build their brands. And here lies the difference. Who really knows which is the public relations agency behind some of India's most visible brands? And how often do clients go on record to acknowledge the role of the PR agency as contributing to their brand's success.

Creating Visibility is Boring

Having been involved with both advertising and public relations, I can tell you that advertising is not only a lot more glamorous, but also a lot more fun. TV commercials make it to people's drawing rooms and eventually even to cocktail parties as people discuss not only the sensex but the latest TV advertising as well. And mind you, a lot of advertising that we see on TV today is really very, very interesting. Never a dull moment! Whereas the life of the PR executive can be reasonably dull. One more store gets opened, one more branch office is inaugurated, one more senior executive joins the organisation, and that must be reported which must be reported and another senior executive quits and that must not be reported and so on. It is a matter of relentless execution day after day. Yes, we do have our highs – a major announcement that breaks through the clutter or a cleverly conceived photo opportunity that comes off. And yet rarely if ever do we talk about it outside closed doors and never do our clients publicly acknowledge the travails of their PR agency.

If you Can Make your Clients Visible

The reality is that public relations agencies who struggle to keep their clients in the news and who argue with their clients, who are publicity shy, about opening up, seem to be suffering from the same malaise. It is true that PR agencies have come a long way, and so has the public relations function in companies. It is no longer the travel desk that they are manning. Today the PR agency is competent. It can think beyond mere media relations. It understands brands and the strategy that needs to go into it. And savvy PR agencies even understand the value of internal communications in building the employee brand. It can handle a crisis and not talk about its role in defusing it. And yet, I believe that the time has come for the PR agency not to rise in revolt against the hand of the client that feeds but to place on record what it brings to the table. PR agencies that push their clients to 'inform' when they 'perform' now need to push themselves into the reckoning if not into the limelight. They must share their experiences. They must document their achievements as case studies. They must speak at forums. And the time is now. Otherwise we may have to use Sir Walter Scott's words to write our own epitaph: *"dying,* (we) *shall go down to the vile dust, from whence he sprung, unwept, unhonour'd and unsung"*.

People who have the capability to create history for their clients shouldn't end up consigned to the forgotten realms of history.

INSPIRATIONS

Any book on advertising would be incomplete without a paean of praise to Bill Bernbach. And what better tribute than having a vignette of quotations from the great man himself.

Bill Bernbach Said ...

"You can say the right thing about a product and nobody will listen. You've got to say it in such a way that people will feel it in their gut. Because if they don't feel it, nothing will happen"

"If your advertising goes unnoticed, everything else is academic"

"Nobody counts the number of ads you run; they just remember the impression you make"

"I can put down on a page a picture of a man crying, and it's just a picture of a man crying. Or I can put him down in such a way as to make you want to cry. The difference is artistry – the intangible thing that business distrusts"

"Properly practiced creativity can make one ad do the work of ten"

"Can you really judge an idea from a storyboard? How do you storyboard a smile?"

"Dullness won't sell your product, but neither will irrelevant brilliance"

"An important idea not communicated persuasively is like having no idea at all"

"The real giants have always been poets, men who jumped from facts into the realm of imagination and ideas"

CHAPTER 1

An Open Letter to a Legend

Dear David,

I have never met you, although I believe I know you well.

You transformed my life.

I was a struggling pen-pusher in a bank counting cash and maintaining ledgers of other people's wealth. I was chafing at the reins of the orderliness and boredom of retail banking, when I read your 'Confessions' like a million others before me. I decided that I *had* to be in advertising. I chucked my bank job, went to management school, soaked myself in books on advertising and ended up in advertising. I have to thank you for helping me graduate from being a pen-pusher to becoming an executive who pushed clients to spend money on advertising and brand building. All my life, I have followed your writing, your private papers and public fulminations, admired your value systems and the agency network that bears your name.

I admired your determination to make it into advertising at the young age of 38 after being a cook, a salesman and a farmer (among other things) and becoming the world's most famous copywriter. All of it

> 'I have to thank you for helping me graduate from being a pen-pusher to becoming an executive who pushed clients to spend money on advertising and brand building'

made me take heart and believe that "It doesn't matter if you are a late bloomer, as long as you make it to the flower show". And boy did you make it!

I remember (who doesn't) the much quoted and much written about headline for Rolls-Royce *'At 60 miles an hour the loudest noise in this new Rolls-Royce comes from the electric clock'*. I remember too, your '...Man in the Hathaway Shirt' , creating an aura of mystery and romance for a product way back in 1952. Today, we may have books on brand personality, but you were out there alone – a pioneer leading the way for others less talented to follow and applaud.

I admire the discipline you bought into your own work and that of your agency. A discipline, which led you to follow the old Chicago philosophy as practised by Claude Hopkins. A sentiment shared by Bill Bernbach who said, *"Our job is to sell our client's merchandise – not ourselves"*. Today, amidst all the talk on creativity, we all know that "It isn't creative, if it doesn't sell". And you, arguably, more than anyone else, drilled this concept into our heads. You advocated and practiced consistency in a fast-changing advertising world which can (in its desire to be creative) advocate change (at times) for the sake of change itself. Campaigns like Hathaway, Schweppes and Dove ran for several years underscoring the value of creating a campaign for a brand's long-term personality.

> **'I value your Russian dolls principle of finding people who are better than you'**

I value your Russian dolls principle of finding people who are better than you. A principle more violated than practiced. I wish more managers would find people who complemented their skills rather than hiring clones. The advertising strategists are better off getting people who can execute their ideas and vice-versa.

I admire your philosophy that hard work never killed anybody and always recall your damning description of a copywriter, when I see a clock watcher. *"You know that every day at exactly five o' clock, BLANK gets up from his desk, puts on his hat and coat and goes home? Think of the extraordinary*

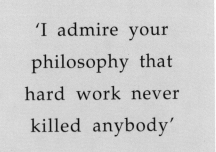

'I admire your philosophy that hard work never killed anybody'

self-discipline that takes". Yes, the discipline of hard work. I recall, also your inimitable answer to a question at the ADGRO at Delhi in 1982. *"I can't hear, I don't understand and I don't agree"*.

It's always easy to believe that a person of your stature had all the answers, all the time. And yet, you kept an open mind. Your original belief that *"People don't buy from a clown"* modified itself to *"You can't save souls in an empty church"* reflecting the need to reward the reader a la Bernbach. You recognised genius even if it was the competition by saying "I couldn't write the Volkswagen campaign if I lived to be 100".

It's easy to wax eloquent about a legend. You were a legend in your own life time unlike several people in our business who specialise in 3 martini lunches and are legends in their own lunchtimes. How does one describe a legend like you?

You had an expression for it – "Trumpeter Swans" – men who combine personal genius with inspiring leadership.

David, you may not be around but your legendary genius and leadership principles will remain forever.

Your unabashed fan

Sridhar

"Brands are the rock stars of commerce,
and create many fans,
both at home and abroad"

- *Simon Anholt,* (*Brand New Justice*)

CHAPTER

Frank. A Flashback in Fashion

"Be orderly in your normal life so you can be violent and original in your work" is the advice of a famous copywriter to budding writers, Frank Simoes who was as original a copywriter as one is likely to come into contact with, died on August 25th 2002. He was 68 years old. He was a writer whom the current generation of advertising professionals may not readily know. And that's their loss really. Frank certainly didn't lead a normal or boring life. 'The boy from Byculla' left home at 17 to work as a deck-hand on a Japanese ship. His career as a sailor ended a year later with the princely sum of two pounds fifty pence in his pocket and his entire worldly possessions in a backpack. And Frank's adventures continued as he drifted from a 'Hey-You' in the kitchen, a waiter, a rather reluctant porter, to a 'dedicated lay-about at dubious establishments' in Europe. The same Frank Simoes wrote some of the earliest and finest fashion advertising created in India and founded his own advertising agency in 1967. And that was not all. Frank made it to the Hall of Fame, CAG (Creative Artists' Guild), recognition at the Ad Club and wrote a book on his native state titled, 'Glad seasons in Goa'.

You came a long way Frank, without the giant sized ego that people with half your ability have.

"Talk to the reader don't shout. He can hear you. Especially if you talk sense".

I haven't talked to Frank but I've seen his work and been influenced by it like most people who were in advertising in the seventies and eighties. The person who waxed lyrical about Frank was a guy called Abijit Almeida, a friend of mine who was 6'3" tall and a mere 100 kg. He belonged to Goa himself (where he has now settled) and used to work in Frank's agency which handled the Vimal account. Frank's greatest claim to fame was his campaign for Vimal with the line *'Only Vimal'*. I remember my induction programme at Mudra. I heard a lot about Frank and his work then. Legend has it that Dhirubhai was briefing the agency about his brand. He used to do this in the seventies. (It was only later that his brief changed and he began to worry about who the next Finance Minister would be). He was telling the agency how "Only Vimal used the most modern technology". "Only Vimal used merino wool". "Only Vimal had the most designs" The tagline 'Only Vimal' was a simple step for Frank but a giant leap for the brand. The fact that the brand still uses the same tagline is as much a tribute to the longevity of the campaign as it is to the wisdom of Reliance Industries Ltd. Brand building is all about the long-term and about consistency. But it needs a classy tag line, a memorable punch line, which is the essence of the brand, for it to stand the test of time. And Frank was a writer of classy lines.

They do say that it takes a man to understand a woman. Particularly if she is your consumer. This was Frank's line for Vimal sarees, another line that endured (and endeared him to us) for 20 years. 'A woman expresses herself in many languages. Vimal is one of them'. Frank Simoes and his agency used to work for Vimal till 1979 after which Mudra started to do the advertising for Vimal. But Frank's affair with fashion continued. His path-breaking campaign for Raymonds with the line, 'A guide to the Well Dressed Male' was another classic. His work for Liberty shirts made people sit up and read. The campaign showed a sensuous woman's hands straying all over a man's shirt, caressing the fabric, feeling the buttons and making males aspire to buy the brand. As Frank had to say himself, "It's a challenge to get into people's minds. They are wrapped in a cocoon of ego, worries, opinions and biases. Least concerned with advertising appeals, they filter out most of what they see and hear. You can only get through by startling them with an unexpected stimulus that makes them sit up and listen". The work he did for the Taj hotels also made people sit up and read. We have a simple question that enables us to evaluate any advertising campaign. Is it the best in the category? Clearly Frank's campaigns were the best in the fashion and hospitality industries.

As Bill Bernbach said, *"If your advertising goes unnoticed, everything else is academic"*.

Whatever brand Frank portrayed came out smart, attractive and aspirational. His was creativity which though hardly clever clearly affected and rewarded the reader at the same time. Frank went back to Goa where he built a lovely beach house. He, unlike some of his advertising contemporaries and successors was a private person. He left behind a host of fans, friends and people like me who admired the man, his work and his attitude to life. He in his own modest way attributed much of his success to a lack of formal education. Dear MBA reader, are you still with me?

He shared a love for the good life, which the people of Goa are famous for. Feni, fun and fashion. That's just half the story of Frank. He was first of all a writer. And no ordinary one at that. Here is what a writer had to say about writing in a different context, "And remember, once it (an ad) is printed, you can't change a thing. You want to be able to read this ad in years to come and be proud". Today, Frank is no more. And yet, he and all of us would be very proud of the work he has done for over 3 decades. Farewell Frank.

> 'Whatever brand Frank portrayed came out smart, attractive and aspirational. His was creativity which though hardly clever clearly affected and rewarded the reader at the same time'

"Products are created in the factory.
Brands are created in the mind"

- Walter Landor, advertising great

CHAPTER 3

From Madras to Madison Avenue

How do you write about a legend, you have had the privilege of working with? I, for once, am at a loss for words and run the risk of becoming emotional. I am not alone in this as thousands of people who came into contact with Mr. R.K. Swamy, personally and professionally over the last several decades, must be feeling the loss of this great leader and wonderful human being.

I first came into contact with the agency he founded a decade ago, R.K. Swamy Advertising Associates, in 1983. I used to wend my way through J.C. Road (one of the more crowded parts of Bangalore, in those years) to Silver Jubilee Park on my trusted Rajdoot motorcycle to the agency. I was exposed to his largesse on the day I got my first salary. As the agency was celebrating its tenth year, I too got a bonus of a month's salary, though I had been with the agency for a mere 4 weeks. I was to spend 4 more of my formative years in R.K. Swamy Advertising Associates (as it was then called) and I used to meet Mr. Swamy, not as often as I would have liked, but certainly on important issues. His door was always open. His professional ability was legendary, often recognized, frequently written about and greatly experienced by people who had the privilege of working with him. And yet there was a personal side to him that left an even larger impression on people who knew him. Advertising has been traditionally full of high-flying, smooth-talking, gin-guzzling executives. Mr. Swamy

'His professional ability was legendary, often recognized, frequently written about and greatly experienced by people who had the privilege of working with him'

was an exception. Despite his enormous success, he was a simple man with no pretenses. Although I am sure he could have gone anywhere for a meal, he took all of us at R.K. Swamy Bangalore to Sapna, a functional restaurant on Residency Road, where he ate his 'Vada Sambhar' with great relish.

He always valued his employees and empathized with them. I remember the agency organizing a big event for Ind-Suzuki Motorcycles Ltd, (as TVS Motor Company used to be called in those days). It was a high-profile event in which the then President of India, Sri R. Venkataraman was present. The entire Bangalore office of R.K. Swamy worked day and night, in the pouring rain to make the event a big success. Mr. R.K. Swamy was a guest and he later told my boss, Mr. N.S. Rajagopalan, a director of the company, "I might have been sitting as a guest, but my heart was with you and your team". Yes, Mr. Swamy believed in his people and empowered them.

Mr. Swamy, despite his humble beginnings, had a grand vision for his agency. The advertising industry in this country used to be Mumbai-centric. It was perhaps even more so three decades ago. Mr. Swamy's greatest contribution, to my mind at least, was to put Madras on the advertising map of India. In 1973, when he started R.K. Swamy Advertising, HTA (JWT) felt the pinch as one client after the other chose to go with Mr. Swamy's start-up. He had the vision to tie up with BBDO, (one of the finest and most creative agencies in the world) nearly two decades ago. Oh yes, Mr. Swamy knew Madison Avenue was the place to go for a network, for technology and training. And one would feel proud to be an Indian and to be part of an Indian agency when one observed how all of the dignitaries from the global network treated him with great respect, veneration even. Yes, Madison Avenue too knew his worth. He may not have been as high - profile as David Ogilvy, Bill Bernbach or Rosser Reeves but he was our own Indian legend who dutifully took his place in several Advertising Halls of Fame in this scountry.

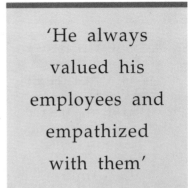

'He always valued his employees and empathized with them'

I left R.K. Swamy/BBDO in 1987 to join Mudra. I used to meet Mr. Swamy on and off. I attended several of his lectures as they were always prepared very carefully. No 'off the cuff' speeches for him. He became an expert on whatever subject he chose to. I remember an eminent banker of yesteryear commenting about a presentation Mr. Swamy made on the 'Euro Dollar'. The 'Euro Dollar'! I wonder how many of other dream merchants can do this. I have heard him make erudite presentations at management associations where he has held better-qualified captains of Industry spellbound. Preparation and hard work were essentials in Mr. Swamy's book. Qualities that helped propel the man from Kumbakonam to podiums across the length and breadth of this country.

When I went back to the agency 10 years later, Mr. Swamy though Chairman, was not directly involved in the functioning of the agency. And yet, he would take a keen interesting in everything that came within his purview. He had written down my list of new business prospects in a small notepad and would ask me the progress every time I met him. His enthusiasm was boundless and his desire to succeed phenomenal. He transferred the same zeal and enthusiasm to raising funds for religious and charitable causes after he retired. Restoration of temples was his passion. There was an extremely helpful side to his nature. The doors of his house

> 'His enthusiasm
> was boundless
> and his desire
> to succeed
> phenomenal'

were always open and I know of an enormous number of people whom he helped without ever mentioning it, in a day and age where a 1001 rupee donation promptly finds its way into the local newspaper.

I know, he hadn't been in the best of health for some time now. And yet, he accepted the AAAI Premnarayan award and delivered a 3711-word address, standing ramrod stiff to a spellbound audience in 1998. I quote from his speech, "In conclusion, let me say that the advertising industry has arrived at a point of great relevance to the customers we serve, namely our clients. Therefore, borrowing a phrase, I say to those who are in the business today, *"People, it is an exciting time to be alive"*.

Sir, you are no longer alive but Indian advertising will always remember your contribution and find your shoes impossible to fill.

CHAPTER

In Praise of a Living Legend

Advertising has its fair share of legends. And, we in India have been fortunate to have been blessed with two men who have become legends in their own lifetime. I refer to the late Mr. R.K. Swamy and Mr. S.R. Ayer. I had the privilege of working for R.K. Swamy and knowing Mr. Ayer professionally. I was richer professionally because of these people as I am sure were several others whose careers benefited because of these two fine 'gentlemen with brains' as David Ogilvy would have described them.

I have written a tribute to the late Mr Swamy in the previous chapter. Here, I would like to speak about Mr. S.R.(Mani) Ayer who headed an organization successfully and then smoothly handed it over to someone who is leading it to even greater heights. I will always think of Mr. Ayer as a man who started ordinarily and reached commanding heights through his inbuilt sense of professionalism, his absolute dedication to the industry and his total passion for this wonderful (and yet maligned)

'...reached commanding heights through his inbuilt sense of professionalism, his absolute dedication to the industry and his total passion for this wonderful (yet maligned) profession of advertising'

profession of advertising. An eminently well-read gentleman, with a phenomenal memory and an amazing capacity for putting people at ease.

So You want to Get into Advertising?

I met Mani Ayer way back in 1982. I was a management graduate enamoured with David Ogilvy's 'Confessions' and his Magic Lantern. My more distinguished namesake R. Sridhar, who was the branch manager of O&M Bangalore at that time, had asked me to meet Mr. Ayer, who was speaking at the Ad Convention at Madras. I went in with great trepidation to his room at the Connemara. As my luck would have it, someone was replacing a leaky cistern, the telephone was ringing, an art director was waiting anxiously with some layouts and Mr. Ayer was quizzing me on why I wanted to go into advertising. I ended up behaving like an unemployed youth desperate to get a job, any job, so enamoured was I with OBM (as the agency used to be referred to). Mr. Ayer (I later discovered) had found me diffident. The rest as they say is history. For OBM!

During the last 20 years, the agency has grown from strength to strength. In no small measure due to the young Matunga lad who took over as Managing Director at the age of 38 and who was recognized by David Ogilvy as "the most outstanding individual" in the Ogilvy network. I continued to meet him at one airport of the other. He was always courteous and nice to someone who in age, wisdom and designation was several notches below him. He also rescued me at the Ad Club convention at Madras of which he was the chairman when I ruffled a speaker's feathers with my well-intentioned (and ill-directed) humour. I admire what he has done for MICA. People are known less for what they take than for what they give. He has given his time, skills and guidance to the institute. A leader must sell his industry and ideas to the next generation and the Indian advertising industry, as a whole will be richer for Mr. Ayer's efforts.

Nice People don't have to Finish last

I think there's an important lesson in management. You don't need to be a cigar chomping, expletive-hurling toughie to be successful. You can be equally successful by being an individual with "a cigarette in one hand, ashtray in the other" (as someone described Mr. Ayer), who knows his clients business like your own. Or you can build an institution that embodies the values you stand for which are ethics and transparency. And the sad reality is that these large shoes are going to be very difficult to fill for us ordinary mortals.

So how does one sum up the achievements of this talented gentleman? Let me quote what Mr. T.S. Nagarajan (formerly of Brooke Bond had to say about Mani Ayer). *"In a world where hyperbole is king and larger-than-life images are sought after, he remains the quintessential 'Madrasi' – and I mean it as a great compliment to a tribe cerebral, highly-motivated, insightful and industrious, perfectly at home with either Caviar or Cadamba Sadam"*. Yes, we have been fortunate to have this very real-world giant in our midst. And as Bill Bernbach said, *"The real giants have always been poets, men who jumped from facts into the realm of imagination and ideas"*.

> 'We have been fortunate to have this very real-world giant in our midst'

"Brand is the DNA of our
communication"

THE FUTURE

"A brand is more than a word. It is the beginning of a lifetime dialogue"

- *Martin Lindstrom*

CHAPTER

Tough Times Don't Last But Thick Skins Do

We have been pampered by good times recently and yet, tough times may be just around the corner.

"We live in tough times"

"Business is bad"

"Are we heading towards stagflation?"

"Things will get worse before they get better".

Sounds familiar? Those were the sound bytes that one heard from Corporate India not so long ago, when corporate India's 'movers and shakers' seemed more like mopers and sobbers. We don't have a clue how to solve corporate India's problems, but being a consultant I will offer some unasked advice on how to accept this situation or even lie back and enjoy it. The key as always will have to be innovation. Come on corporate India, think differently. Think like this:

- Take a Bangalore Metropolitan Transport Corporation,(BMTC) bus to work leaving your car behind. Not only will you save petrol but you will also have the ride of your life which will enable you to forget your current travails. You would also have spent an hour commuting rather than going early to work and scowling at your secretary. Also this will improve your marketing skills, as you will know how your consumers actually live (or is the right word exist).

- Organise an internal training programme for your staff. Call some of your jobless senior management colleagues to teach. At least, give your employees something to laugh about.

- Go and speak at other companies' training programmes. Companies don't have money to pay qualified trainers and will welcome you.

- Invite similar jobless senior executives to speak at your company. Give them your company's T-shirts as mementos. They will become your brand ambassadors in early morning walks, so that your company will be top-of-mind to milkmen, vegetable vendors and newspaper delivery boys.

- Meet new business prospects for lunch at the club. Clubs are the cheapest and the best, particularly those in which you are not a member.

- Recheck your frequent flyer mileage points and spend time calculating how much money your company could have saved if you had not travelled so much.

- Call your suppliers and threaten to reduce their rates. Do unto others what your clients did to you.

- Leave office early every day. You will save on electricity bills.

- Take your most pessimistic revenue budget and divide it by two. You will feel good when you exceed it.

- Go for a vacation. Your office (and furniture) will still be there when you return.

- Don't read the financial and business pages. Look at the cartoon strips instead.

- Don't worry unduly about people sitting on the bench otherwise you could be on the psychiatrist's couch.

- Do not attend parties. This way you will save both your liver and your ears. You won't drink nor will you hear further stories of corporate gloom, which may actually induce you to drink more.

- Talk to other industries, which are doing worse than yours. You will experience the 'feel good' factor which management gurus espouse.

- Bond with your family. Take them to a movie hall and experience what home theatre means in an empty hall with no air conditioning.

- Take your children swimming. Maybe you'll meet a bored housewife at the pool.

- Try to improve your golf handicap. You will realise that it's easier to improve your business.

- Go to a Rotary meeting and hear a guest speaker. You will realise how the most serious things can sound comical.

- Watch CNBC India and listen to people who bought Zee Telefilms at Rs.1600. You will be counting your blessings.

- Keep telling yourself that every day, every way, you are getting better as the economy is getting worse.

- Keep cool even when it is 38^0C in the shade.

And finally, pray like mad.

Famous forecasting faux pas

Forecasting is difficult, particularly of the future. Here are a few forecasts made in the past.

- In 1926, Lee Dee Forest, the man who invented the cathode ray tube, said: "While theoretically television may be feasible, commercially and financially, I consider it an impossibility, a development on which we need waste little time dreaming".

- Take a shot at who might have said this: "I think there is a world market for about five computers". Yes, it was Thomas J. Watson, Chairman of the Board of IBM, in 1943.

- Wrote Business Week in 1968: "With over 15 types of foreign cars already on sale here, the Japanese auto industry isn't likely to carve out a big share of the market for itself".

- Said a recording company executive, turning down the Beatles in 1962: "We don't think they will do anything in this market. Guitar groups are on the way out".

- And in 1945, Admiral Leaby said this about the atomic bomb: "This is the biggest fool thing we've ever done – the bomb will never go off – and I speak as an expert on explosives".

CHAPTER

Future Tense?

A survey conducted by a British newspaper way back in 1999 revealed an interesting insight. Over 60% of the respondents were clueless as to where they would be or what they would be doing on the eve of the new millenium. I am sure corporations would have a much better fix on what they plan to do during the next millenium, even if they are stressed about what it may have in store for them. Yes, predicting the future can be hazardous as the enclosed box suggests; but in the same breath, one must concede that there is also a sense of anticipation about the impending changes and the furious pace at which this change is likely to take place. As Jack Welch says, *"Anytime there is change, there is opportunity"*. Change and opportunity seem to be the two sides of the brand new millenium coin.

Here are a few predictions about the future (people in communication don't seem to learn from other peoples mistakes, do they?!)

The 'MTV' generation will reign and we are not referring to fans of the channel alone here, although they might well be viewers of TV. Prof. P.N. Thirunarayana of the Indian Institute of Management, Bangalore, describes this generation succinctly.

M-multiple processing, **T**-time compressed and **V**-value seeking. True, the consumer will get younger, do several things at the same time and aggressively seek value. Just take a look around you and you will find the factory outlets of young brands like Levi's and Nike buzzing with this generation. Companies that understand this generation and cater to their fleeting attention will succeed.

"Dinks will be Joined by Dints"

Some of our tribe are familiar with the concept of this demographic entity - Double Income, No Kids which is an opportunity area for several products and services. This will be supplemented by a new entity, which will bring more and more families into its fold - The Double Income No Time entity. This will be a force to reckon with too. People from this segment do not mind paying a higher service fee, if the service provider will call on them to execute the documents, say, for a car loan. After all, this generation knows that a microwave meal takes all of 90 seconds to get ready, nail polish dries in 30 seconds, cash from an ATM can be withdrawn in 60 seconds and a photograph takes just an hour to print. Tomorrow's customers will want faster, better service. United Airlines for example, has systems in place to enable a customer to check her frequent flier miles at 11.30 pm. on Sunday or order a special diet airline meal at the click of a button. The frontrunners of tomorrow will understand the needs of this generation in a hurry and satisfy them, for profit.

> 'The frontrunners of tomorrow will understand the needs of this generation in a hurry and satisfy them, for profit'

Here at Bangalore, Citibank's experience with Suvidha, one believes, is already showing signs of becoming a runaway success! 'Anytime banking' once the 'concept of tomorrow', has become an accepted reality through the length and breadth of India.

'Quick' or 'Dead' only time will tell

"In the future, there will be only two sorts of companies - those that are quick and those that are dead" said an expert on brands

and branding. Successful companies will beat 'the time to market' clock to win. 'Brand building' the way we knew it took time. Procter and Gamble, Levers, Nestle all have successful examples of brands built over a period of time, some taking even decades to be established. No longer. Amazon.com was launched in 1995 and quickly became the leading web commerce site and arguably, the best-known web brand, in the space of just 2 years. America Online, Netscape, the palm pilot, PDA (personal data assistant) to name just a few, have crunched this hitherto long brand-building process. Yes, brands particularly technology brands, are being built much better and much quicker. Brands will be built at a furious pace and make the past seem leisurely.

Brand - a Marketing Concept or a Financial Concept?

The brand has always been a marketing concept but it is fast becoming a financial concept. Financial analysts have calculated that the Marlboro cigarette brand alone represents about 40% of the entire valuation of the Philip Morris company. Amazon.com in the first six months of 1998, had revenues of $204 million and lost $30 million. But the market valuation of Amazon.com was about $5 billion! Even though there was a slump in technology stocks in the US, the entire publicly-quoted American newspaper industry at one point in time, was worth less than America Online(AOL), an internet portal! Companies like Dell Computers, Intel, Microsoft, Sony, Hewlett Packard, IBM have all created financial value for their shareholders through their

> 'The brand is now and will be even more in the future, a tangible financial asset rather than a vague marketing concept'

brands. We are already seeing evidence of this in India in the software sector. Yes, the brand is now and will be even more in the future, a tangible financial asset rather than a vague marketing concept. And promoters might well worry equally about 'exit' strategies as they will about 'entry' strategies.

Buy low. Sell more

It's easy to talk of companies that brand successfully and sell aggressively. What is also likely to happen is that companies will buy better and in the process make more money. Interestingly, Wal-Mart and Toys 'R' Us make as much money buying merchandise and toys at aggressively negotiated rates as by selling them. In the new millenium, companies will have to find ways of cutting costs without compromising on quality. Efficiencies, virtual manufacturing, economies of scale, global sourcing, lean, mean operations, will all become greater necessities in the near future.

Strategy the Key

As someone said *"A strategy is a carefully devised plan to murder the competition"*. A unique strategy that sets apart your company and brand will become even more crucial to success in the ensuing millennium.

Amazon.com pioneered e-tail. e-tail will change the way business is being conducted. Successful companies will be those who can make shopping a pleasant experience for consumers. Someone who has shopped with Amazon.com might well believe that there was actually a caring, considerate human being at the other end and not a computer. Amazon.com seems to have the best of both worlds - the concern and helpful advice of a small independent bookstore with the size and clout of a large chain. That's strategy for you. Strategy has been behind the success of Starbucks, Dell Computers and Body Shop to name just a few. One will see more such successes in the future. Without a doubt, a killing strategy will separate the winners from the losers.

Youth Won't be a Disadvantage

Historically, we have been led to believe that corporate leadership will happen in the age group of 45-55. Just look at today's whiz kids who are making and losing millions no sooner have they shed their diapers. Youth power will prevail . Risks will be taken and fortunes will be made and lost by people who are younger. People who come to the party with ideas as hot as their terminals, uncluttered by the past and unfazed with what the future might hold for them. The nerds will win.

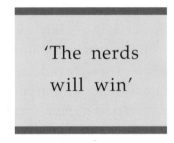

'The nerds will win'

How Good is your Latest Web-site?

Clients and agencies have historically looked to press and TV to build their image. "Have you seen our new ad on TV" has done the party rounds. Future conversations, impressions and image will depend on one's web site. How sophisticated it is. How easy it is to download and how frequently it is updated. The principles of direct response will rule the roost in the next millennium.

The Agency of the New Millenium

Historically, agencies have been looking up to clients for business, revenue and leadership. Today, a client, Procter and Gamble, has in the twilight of the century led the way to the future by instituting an agency compensation system linked to performance and sales. Accountability, remuneration based on needs and not mass media, incetivising performance will become a way of life. Agencies have to come to terms with the new realities of the market place. 'Guaranteed results' is what agencies will have to gear themselves for. Value addition will be the key. Agencies will have to continually renew themselves and bend over backwards to earn their monthly retainer as the commission concept dies a natural death. Ideas will be at a premium and an agency will be only as good as its latest idea.

And Yet...

Amidst all this frenetic change and trauma, the basis for success will endure! Bill Bernbach is simply the most admired advertising man ever and the Volkswagen campaign created in 1959 was rated first in the century's top 100 ads by Advertising Age, recently. Yes, 'think small' is a recognition of the power of an idea. Ideas that are surprisingly simple will cause customers to smile and more importantly buy.

> 'Ideas will be at a premium and an agency will be only as good as its latest idea'

What the new millennium needs is leadership. Most certainly in advertising. As advertising goes through severe soul-searching, it will need giants. As Bill Bernbach said, *"The real giants have always been poets, men who jumped from facts into the realm of imagination and ideas"*. It's difficult to predict whether the new millennium will throw up some giants. But it's easy to say that we need them more than ever.

> 'Ideas that are surprisingly simple will cause customers to smile and more importantly buy'

Bibliography

Banking on Advertising
- Dylan, Bob, *www.brainyquote.com/quotes/authors*

One Land, a Billion Minds
- Rigby, Sir Hugh, *Ogilvy on Advertising, 1985*
- Ogilvy, David, *Confessions of an Advertising Man*
- Peters, Tom, *Brand YOU, Excel A California, 1999*

Do You know Your Customer?
- 'The Independent', *TV commercial by Lowe*

Can You Read My Lips?
- Peters, Tom, *A Passion for Excellence*

The Consumer is King. Sez who?
- McKenna, Regis, *www.geocities.com/Wall Street*

Every Little Bit Counts
- Saatchi & Saatchi, *Advertisement 'Labour isn't working.'*
- Richard Branson-Dearlove, Des,
  The Richard Branson Way, 1999

A Question of Brands
- Hamel, Gary, *Online Journal Archive, 1999*
- Ries, Al and Trout, Jack, www.quickmba.com/
  marketingtrout/positioning
- General Electric – Advertisement
- Rilke, Rainer Maria, *The Quotations Page*

Imagine a Life Without Brands!
- Ries, Al and Laura, *22 Immutable Laws of Branding*
- Schultz, Howard, *The Future of Brands,*
  Interbrand Group Macmillan Press, 2000

The Relevance of Being Different
- Fortune Magazine, 1977

Be First or Be Different
- Kaun Banega Crorepati, 2004
- Krishnamurthy, A.G., *at a Mudra gathering in 1989*
- Shakespeare, *Julius Caesar*

New Venture? Start Up Right!
- Johnson, Floathe, *Technobrands, Chuck Pettis,*
  American Management Association 1995
- D' Alessandro, David, *Brand Warfare,*
  co-author Michel Owens, McGraw-Hill, 2001

Jumpstart Your Venture — Shakespeare, *Romeo & Juliet*
Brand it Right — Wodehouse, P.G.

A Very Good Paper — Schultz, Howard, *The Future of Brands,*
But a Very Bad Habit — Abbott, David, *Steve Ulin, Triangle Business Journal, 2001*

'Baggy green'-a Brand with — Blatter, Sepp, President of FIFA,
a Difference   *The Future of Brands, Macmillzan Press, 2000*

How Cool is your Brand — Crisp, Quentin, *en.thinkexist.com*
    — Kestia, Janet, *hinduonnet.com/businessline, 2001*
    — D'Innocenzo, Lisa *http://www.strategymag.com*
    — Yankelovich Report
    — J. Walker Smith and Ann Clurman,
      Harper Business, New York, 1997

Yeh Dil Mange — Reinhardt, Keith, *www.quotationspage.com*
"More Consistency" — Churchill, Winston, *www.brainyquote.com*
    — Berry, Norman, *MagnaIndia.com*
    — Welch, Jack, *www.businessweek.com*

Do an Image Number! — Ollins, Wally, *The Identity Expert-British*
      Library Cataloguing-in-Publication Data, 1989

Are You a Brand Champion? — Mackay, Graham, *www.sabmiller.com*
    — Hamel, Gary, *Online Journal Archives, 1999*
    — Karakas, Rita, *The Future of Brands, Macmillan Press, 2000*
    — Ind, Nicholas, *Living the Brand, Kogan Page,*
      Publication, 2001

Why Aren't You a Brand Yet? — Burns, Robert, *To a Louse, Poems and Songs,*
      The Harvard Classics, 1909–14
    — Peters, Tom, *Brand YOU, Excel A California, 1999*
    — Puttnam, Lord, *The Future of Brands Interbrand Group*
      Macmillan Press 2000
    — Bernbach, Bill, *Bill Bernbach said, DDB Needham*
      Worldwide Publication
    — Hartman, Jason , *The 7 Laws of Personal Branding,*
      Magnetism, 2002

Technology Today but Brands Forever

- Bell, Tim, *Advertising: An essential input for economic growth. Adgro '82*
- Ballmer, Steve, *http://www.microsoft.com*
- Handy, Charles, *Thought Leaders, Edited by Joel Kurtzman, Booz & Hamilton*
- Gibson, Rowan *www.omg.co.nz*

Can Indian Industry Learn from Software?

- Darwin, Charles, *The Origin of the Species, Signet Publications, Penguin Group, USA, 2003*

And what Software needs to Learn about Branding

- *GTE, Advertisement*
- Pettis, Chuck, *Technobrands, AMACOM, Library of Congress Cataloging-in-Publication Data, 1995*

How to Make Your Brand 'Buzz"

- Douty, Steve, *Hi –Tech, Hi -Touch Branding, by Paul Temporal and KC Lee, John Wiley and Sons, 2001*
- Ogilvy, David, *Confessions of an Advertising Man*
- Isaacson, Mike, *Sierra-On-Line*
- Jurvetson, Steve, *Fresh News.com 2004*

Good Brief or Good Grief?

- Lewellyn, Michael S., *Truth, Lies and Advertising by Jon Steel, John Wiley and sons, 1998*
- Hamel, Gary, *www.summitcircuit.com*
- DDB Needham New York, *signage*
- Grove, Andy, *Only the Paranoid Survive, Random House Inc., 1999*

Can you Recognize a Great Ad?

- Ogilvy, David, *Ogilvy on Advertising, Multimedia Publications, UK., 1983*
- Hopkins, Claude, *Scientific Advertising, www.geocities.com/Madison Avenue*
- Bernbach, Bill, *Bill Bernbach Said, DDB Needham Worldwide Publication*

Are you Waiting for Opportunity to Knock?

- Faulkner, William, *William Faulkner on the Web*

The power of TV Advertising - Hopkins, Claude, *Scientific Advertising,*
www.geocities.com/Madison Avenue
- Bernbach, Bill, *Bill Bernbach Said,*
DDB Needham Worldwide Publication
- Belasco, David, *The David Belasco Page, www.angelfire.com*

Humorous Ads? Are You Joking? - Caples, John, *Tested Advertising Methods, Prentice Hall, 1997*

Present Persuasively or Perish - Mehrabian, Albert, *Biographical Sketch of*
Albert Mehrabian, www.kaaj.com/psyc

Radio is Hot. Are you Tuning In? - McLuhan, Marshall, *marshallmcluhan.com*
- Stein, Gertrude, *www.tenderbuttons.com*

Is your Ad Agency - Keynes, John Maynard, *JMK Theories*
Truly your Partner? - Ogilvy, David, Confessions of an Advertising Man
- Twain, Mark, *www.allspirit.co.uk/kipling.html*
- Lincoln, Abraham, *The Gettysburg Address,* 1863
- Armstrong, Neil, *www.allstar.fiu.edu*
- Churchill, Winston, *www.brainyquote.com*
- Shakespeare, *Julius Caesar*

Picnic With a Tiger - Dowd, Maureen., *http://en.thinkexist.com/quotes*
- Twain, Mark, *www.allspirit.co.uk/kipling*
- Whitaker, Jim, *http://www.everesthistory.com*
- Scott, Sir Walter, *www.bartleby.com*

A Photograph is Worth
a Thousand Ads

- Dearlove, Des, *The Richard Branson Way, 1999*

Photo Opportunity!
Are you Missing the Picture?

- Ogilvy, David, *Ogilvy on Advertising Multimedia Publications, UK., 1983*
- Seneca, Lucius Annaeus, *Brainy Quote*

"Oye Bubbly, Oye Oye Bubbly,
mind those Bloggers Bubbly"

- Nooyi, Indra, *powerlineblog.com/archives*
- Zeller Jr, Tom,. http://*topics.nytimes.com*

Crisis? It can't Happen to Us!

- Femina, Jerry Della, *www.brainyquote.com*
- Kennedy, John F, *www.whitehouse.gov/history*
- Kipling Rudyard, *If, www.brainyquote.com*

An Open Letter to a Legend

- Bernbach, Bill, *Bill Bernbach Said, DDB Needham Worldwide Publication*

Frank. A Flashback in Fashion

- Bernbach, Bill, *Bill Bernbach Said, DDB Needham Worldwide Publication*

In Praise of a Living Legend

- Bernbach, Bill, *Bill Bernbach Said, DDB Needham Worldwide Publication*

Tough Times don't last
but Thick Skins do

- Welch, Jack, *www.businessweek.com*

Index